S0-AUU-669

CRIMINALS, MILITIAS, AND INSURGENTS: ORGANIZED CRIME IN IRAQ

Phil Williams

June 2009

The views expressed in this report are those of the author and do not necessarily reflect the official policy or position of the Department of the Army, the Department of Defense, or the U.S. Government. Authors of Strategic Studies Institute (SSI) publications enjoy full academic freedom, provided they do not disclose classified information, jeopardize operations security, or misrepresent official U.S. policy. Such academic freedom empowers them to offer new and sometimes controversial perspectives in the interest of furthering debate on key issues. This report is cleared for public release; distribution is unlimited.

*****

This publication is subject to Title 17, United States Code, Sections 101 and 105. It is in the public domain and may not be copyrighted.

NO Longer
Property
LIBRARY, MONTEREY INSTITUTE
OF INTERNATIONAL STUDIES MIIS
460 PIERCE STREET
MONTEREY, CA 93940

AUG 2 7 2009

HV
6453
.I72
W55
2009

*****

In the course of researching and writing this manuscript, the author has had help from a number of people. In particular, Dr. Steven Metz was a source of constant help, encouragement, and advice. Working in the Strategic Studies Institute (SSI) under the director, Professor Douglas Lovelace, has been a delightful and highly congenial experience, and I am grateful for his unfailing support and encouragement. Several other colleagues were very helpful in the preparation of this monograph. Dr. Alex Crowther was particularly generous with his time and provided invaluable insights into kidnapping in Iraq, while Dr. W. Andrew Terrill and Dr. Sharifa Zuhur answered many questions about political developments in Iraq and the roles played by a wide variety of actors. Mr. Nathan Freier, Dr. Max Manwaring, Dr. Douglas Johnson, Dr. Robin Dorff, Dr. Stephen Blank, Dr. Dallas Owens, Dr. Antulio Echevarria, Colonel Trey Braun, and Colonel Louis Jordan were unfailingly stimulating and encouraging.

The author is also grateful to several people outside SSI, especially Dr. Paul Kan of the Department of National Security and Strategy at the U.S. Army War College, and Dr. Lawrence Cline, both of whom read the manuscript and offered many incisive comments and suggestions. Mr. Marc Hess provided invaluable comments on the law enforcement efforts in Iraq and the difficulties of combining law enforcement and military intelligence. He was also of great assistance in framing the oil smuggling issue. In addition, Dr. William Rosenau and Mr. Austin Long at the RAND Corporation provided helpful comments and advice as well as constant encouragement. The author was helped by several former students from the Graduate School of Public and International Affairs at the University of Pittsburgh who provided invaluable insights. Mr. Daniel Malik of the Department of Treasury offered candid and constructive comments on insurgency and terrorist finances. During a presentation on organized crime in Iraq at the Matthew B. Ridgway Center, University of Pittsburgh, Professors Donald Goldstein, Dennis Gormley and Michael Brenner offered constructive comments. In addition, Mr. James Cockayne and Dr. Adam Lupel of the International Peace Institute offered helpful suggestions on an earlier iteration of the analysis.

*****

ii

Comments pertaining to this report are invited and should be forwarded to: Director, Strategic Studies Institute, U.S. Army War College, 122 Forbes Ave, Carlisle, PA 17013-5244.

*****

All Strategic Studies Institute (SSI) publications are available on the SSI homepage for electronic dissemination. Hard copies of this report also may be ordered from our homepage. SSI's homepage address is: *www.StrategicStudiesInstitute.army.mil.*

*****

The Strategic Studies Institute publishes a monthly e-mail newsletter to update the national security community on the research of our analysts, recent and forthcoming publications, and upcoming conferences sponsored by the Institute. Each newsletter also provides a strategic commentary by one of our research analysts. If you are interested in receiving this newsletter, please subscribe on our homepage at *www.StrategicStudiesInstitute.army. mil/newsletter/.*

ISBN 1-58487-397-3

CONTENTS

FOREWORD

Organized crime, by and large, has been a neglected dimension of the conflict in Iraq. Yet, its importance is difficult to overestimate. As Dr. Phil Williams shows in this monograph, both criminal enterprises and activities had a debilitating impact and made the attainment of U.S. objectives much more difficult. Organized crime inhibited reconstruction and development and became a major obstacle to state-building; the insurgency was strengthened and sustained by criminal activities; sectarian conflict was funded by criminal activities and motivated by the desire to control criminal markets; and more traditional criminal enterprises created pervasive insecurity through kidnapping and extortion. Organized crime also acted as an economic and political spoiler in an oil industry expected to be the dynamo for growth and reconstruction in post Ba'athist Iraq.

In this monograph, Dr. Williams identifies the roots of organized crime in post-Ba'athist Iraq in an authoritarian and corrupt state dominated by Saddam Hussein and subject to international sanctions. He also explains the rise of organized crime after the U.S. invasion in terms of two distinct waves: the first wave followed the collapse of the state and was accompanied by the breakdown of social control mechanisms and the development of anomie; the second wave was driven by anarchy, insecurity, political ambition, and the imperatives of resource generation for militias, insurgents, and other groups.

This monograph looks in detail at major criminal activities, including the theft, diversion, and smuggling of oil, the kidnapping of both Iraqis and foreigners, extortion, car theft, and the theft and smuggling of antiquities. The author also considers the critical role played by corruption in facilitating and strengthening organized crime. He shows how al-Qaeda in Iraq, Jaish-al-Mahdi, and the Sunni tribes used criminal activities to fund their campaigns of political violence. Dr. Williams also identifies necessary responses to organized crime and corruption in Iraq, including efforts to reduce criminal opportunities, change incentive structures, and more directly target criminal organizations and activities. His analysis also emphasizes the vulnerability of conflict and post-conflict situations to organized crime and the requirement for a holistic or comprehensive strategy in which security, development, and the rule of law complement one another.

DOUGLAS C. LOVELACE, JR.
Director
Strategic Studies Institute

SUMMARY

Although organized crime has been the neglected dimension of the conflict in Iraq, both criminal enterprises and criminal activities have had a profoundly debilitating impact. Organized crime inhibited reconstruction and development and became a major obstacle to state-building; the insurgency was strengthened and sustained by criminal activities; sectarian conflict was funded by criminal activities and motivated by the desire to control criminal markets; and more traditional criminal enterprises created pervasive insecurity through kidnapping and extortion. Organized crime also acted as an economic and political spoiler in an oil industry expected to be the dynamo for growth and reconstruction in post Ba'athist Iraq.

The rise of organized crime in Iraq was a strategic surprise for decisionmakers and military planners. Although organized crime developed in particularly concentrated and corrosive ways in Iraq, it had parallels elsewhere — including the Balkans (especially Albania), as well as Russia, Mexico, and Nigeria. Warnings about the rise of organized crime came from several sources, including the United Nations Office of Drugs and Crime (UNODC).

Organized crime in Iraq, as elsewhere, can be understood in two distinct forms: (1) as entities or criminal enterprises which treat crime in Clausewitzian terms as a continuation of business by other means; and (2) as a set of illicit activities appropriated and utilized by various entities for specific purposes. Terrorist organizations, insurgents, ethnic factions, sectarian groups, and militias all use organized crime activities as a funding mechanism. Not surprisingly, therefore, organized crime in Iraq challenges existing concepts and categorizations, casts doubt on strategies that focused narrowly on the military dimension of a complex problem, and demands new measures of effectiveness. If the conflict in Iraq is a hybrid or mosaic form of warfare, organized crime in Iraq has an analogous form, adding another dimension to the anti-coalition violence.

Objectives.

Chapter 1 serves as the introduction to an analysis which seeks to explain the rise of organized crime, pervasive criminality, and widespread corruption in contemporary Iraq. It contends that organized crime did not suddenly arise from the chaos of invasion and occupation but had deep roots in an authoritarian and corrupt state subject to international sanctions. The analysis explores how criminal activities were used not only by traditional for-profit groups, but also by insurgents, militias, sectarian groups, political parties, and tribes seeking to enhance their resource bases and prosecute their campaigns of violence more effectively. The monograph identifies key actors exploiting the criminal opportunity space in Iraq and explores the intersections and overlap between criminal organizations and more political or sectarian actors. Finally, it identifies necessary responses to organized crime and corruption in Iraq. These include efforts to reduce criminal opportunities, change incentive structures, and more directly target criminal organizations and activities.

The Rise of Organized Crime in Iraq.

Chapter 2 examines the rise of organized crime in Iraq, emphasizing that the actions of the international community in the 1990s unintentionally widened and intensified the scope of organized crime and the illicit economy. By 2003 all the conditions for an upsurge of organized crime were present; the toppling of the regime provided the catalyst. The upsurge itself had two distinct if overlapping waves. The first wave followed the collapse of the state and was accompanied by the breakdown of social control mechanisms and the emergence of social instability. The U.S. decision to react passively in the face of widespread looting was a major mistake, creating a climate of citizen insecurity and criminal impunity. The second wave of organized crime was driven more by the forces of anarchy, insecurity, political ambition, and the imperatives of resource generation for militias, insurgents, and other groups.

Major Criminal Activities.

Chapter 3 focuses on the diversion, theft, and smuggling of oil, probably the most lucrative source of illicit income for tribes, insurgents, and militias, as well as many criminal groups and corrupt officials. The legacy of oil smuggling during the sanctions era combined with growing demand, limited supply, and the desire to exploit arbitrage opportunities, thus intensifying and perpetuating the criminalization of the oil industry. This process was facilitated by the lack of standardized measures, the absence of meters or gauges on pumps and tankers, and the inadequacy of oversight.

Three different kinds of illicit activity—the theft and smuggling of crude oil, some of which involved oil bunkering; the theft, fraudulent diversion, smuggling, and black market sales of imported refined fuels; and theft of locally produced gasoline from the Baiji refinery—became almost a national pastime in Iraq, while funding much of the violence.

Chapter 4 examines another major criminal activity in Iraq—kidnapping. This chapter distinguishes between economic or for-profit kidnapping and political kidnapping, while acknowledging that the distinction is sometimes blurred. Activities which initially appear to be politically inspired, for example, sometimes turn out to be primarily concerned with profit. The participants in the kidnapping business are identified, as are its changing patterns over time. An assessment is also made of the profits obtained through kidnapping—profits which were significantly enhanced by the willingness of France, Italy, Germany, and several other countries to pay large ransoms. Although the kidnapping of foreigners led to some spectacular ransom payments, it was found that the kidnapping of Iraqis, because of its sheer volume, might have been more lucrative.

In Chapter 5, the focus shifts to extortion and related criminal activities which also helped to fund much of the violence in Iraq. Extortion was highly profitable partly because of the scale of reconstruction and partly because of the loss of security on Iraqi roads. Other crimes include bank robberies, various forms of commodity smuggling across Iraq's highly permeable borders, drug trafficking (which is a modest but growing problem), the theft and smuggling of antiquities, car theft and smuggling, and the trade in black market weapons, as well as human smuggling and trafficking in women.

In Chapter 6, attention is given to business and government corruption, which not only undermined efforts to reestablish effective governance, but also contributed to a general feeling of impunity on the part of would-be perpetrators. Activities heretofore under centralized authoritarian control suddenly became diffused and democratic. In addition, the U.S. presence brought with it a massive injection of cash for reconstruction, much of which was administered in an ad hoc manner with insufficient oversight, thereby providing opportunities for corporate malfeasance on the U.S. side, along with skimming and personal profiteering on the Iraqi side.

Corruption was not only a condition characterizing government and bureaucracies, but also an instrument used by criminal organizations to advance their illicit business interests and protect the illicit markets in which they operated. Corruption in Iraq was also buttressed by violence, which effectively neutralized the mechanisms and institutions put in place by the United States to fight it.

The Players.

Chapter 7 looks more closely at the entities involved in organized crime, considering some of the ways in which they have interacted with one another. It identifies four major kinds of groups involved in organized crime in Iraq: traditional criminal enterprises; tribal-based criminal organizations; foreign jihadi groups; and militias which include splinter or rogue factions. The wide variety of criminal organizations active in Iraq make analysis more complex and generalizations risky.

Traditional criminal enterprises vary in size and scope. Some are highly specialized while others have a broad portfolio of activities. An important component of organized crime in Iraq was traceable to prisoners released by Saddam Hussein. Many of these criminals were prone to violence, with their presence contributing significantly to the post-invasion lawlessness. In some cases, they were organized by former regime elements.

Many of Iraq's tribes have a long tradition of smuggling, an activity that ballooned after 2003. Some of the tribes were heavily involved in oil smuggling in Basra, while those along the border with Syria smuggled livestock and various other commodities.

Foreign fighters and jihadis groups, especially al-Qaeda in Iraq (AQI), exploited various criminal activities to augment their financial base. Kidnapping, as we have seen, was very lucrative, surpassed only by the profits from the theft, diversion, smuggling, and black market sales of oil. Car theft was another important source of funding for AQI, having become particularly important in Mosul when AQI and its affiliates concentrated there after setbacks in Al-Anbar and Baghdad. Extortion and various kinds of fraud are also core funding activities.

Shiite militias, especially Jaish-Al-Mahdi (JAM), have been among the most powerful and important groups engaged in organized crime in Iraq—although how much has been carried out under the direct control of the organization and how much by rogue factions is uncertain. Four criminal activities provided Mahdi Army members with important revenue streams: extortion and protection; black market sales of petroleum; seizures of cars and houses inextricably linked with, if not done completely under the guise of, sectarian cleansing; and involvement in oil smuggling in Basra. The Iraqi army offensives (supported by U.S. forces) in Basra and Sadr City in the first half of 2008 had a major role in reducing the power of the organization, including its criminal reach and illicit activities.

Control over smuggling activities became a major factor in the defection of the Sunni tribes from AQI, which had sought to take over their traditional smuggling and black market activities. In Anbar Province, in particular, tensions over illicit activities and the attendant profits created opportunities for the United States. The U.S. military, as the "strongest tribe," became adjudicator and enforcer in criminal disputes dressed up as political differences, siding with one set of violent armed groups engaged in criminal activities against other groups judged more dangerous. The tribes were losing the turf wars to AQI until the U.S. military came to the rescue. The result was the Anbar Awakening and the defeat of AQI in the province. Nevertheless, AQI's criminal activities continue to finance its resistance in and around Mosul.

Conclusions and Recommendations.

Chapter 8, Conclusions, has four purposes: (1) to offer reflections on the nature of organized crime in Iraq; (2) to assess the impact of organized crime on the efforts to reestablish security and stability; (3) to suggest initiatives that could be taken in Iraq to combat organized crime more effectively; and (4) to elucidate the broader considerations and lessons for future U.S. military intervention.

It suggests that organized crime in Iraq is a complex system exhibiting emergent behavior, characterized by high levels of adaptability and resilience, and driven by a mix of need, greed, and creed. Organized crime is also a means of "primitive capital accumulation" and is closely linked to alternative (that is, nonstate) forms of governance, whether these provide security when the state fails to do so or provides services when the state marginalizes or neglects certain populations. Indeed, organized crime is both a safety valve and safety net amid massive economic and social dislocation. Yet, it is also highly predatory, and in Iraq has both sustained and precipitated conflict. In the final analysis, criminal activities and corruption have had profoundly debilitating effects, not only on U.S. efforts to restore political and military stability in Iraq but also on economic reconstruction.

Unfortunately, the very conditions that allowed the blossoming of organized crime in post-Hussein Iraq make it difficult to counter. Nevertheless, it is possible to outline a broad program that seeks to reduce the criminalization of Iraqi political and economic life, in tandem with the rebuilding of the state, the re-creation of infrastructure, the revitalization of the Iraqi economy, and the generation of legitimate employment opportunities. Unless combating organized crime is integrated into this broader program for Iraq, it stands little chance of success. Conversely, unless the attempt to rebuild Iraq incorporates an effective strategy to combat organized crime, the prospects for stability will remain poor.

The monograph highlights the need for a fusion of military and law enforcement intelligence as the basis for a three-pronged strategy seeking (1) to constrict the opportunity space for organized crime; (2) to change the incentive structure for criminal, corrupt, or violent behavior; and (3) to target the most dangerous organizations and networks linked to crime and corruption.

More broadly, Iraq, like the Balkans and Afghanistan, reveals the vulnerability of conflict and post-conflict areas to organized crime, and the need for a holistic strategy in which security, development, and the rule of law complement one another. Such an approach is not a guarantee of success, but the absence of a holistic strategy is a guarantee of failure.

CHAPTER 1

INTRODUCTION

Organized Crime in Iraq.

Organized crime for most of the 20th century was a law enforcement problem evident in relatively few countries such as the United States, Italy, and Japan. During the 1990s, this changed. Organized crime, especially transnational organized crime, emerged as a worrisome, wide-ranging security issue when more traditional security challenges appeared to have diminished. After September 11, 2001, however, organized crime all but disappeared from the national security agenda, maintaining traction and demanding attention only when it appeared to be linked to terrorism. Consequently, when the United States invaded Iraq in March 2003, organized crime was the last thing policymakers, intelligence analysts, or even military planners were thinking about. However, both criminal organizations and organized crime activities came to have debilitating effects on U.S. efforts to combat the insurgency and establish stability. These effects both delayed and complicated economic reconstruction. Indeed, organized crime proved to be the unrecognized joker in the pack, or to use Steven Stedman's term, a "spoiler."[1] Though Stedman focused narrowly on such spoilers in the negotiations to end conflict, his concept has much broader applicability: spoilers have an impact well beyond hindering or derailing peace negotiations; they can also inhibit reconstruction and development and become major obstacles to state-building. This is certainly the case in Iraq. The insurgency was strengthened and sustained

1

by criminal activities; sectarian conflict was funded by criminal activities and motivated by the desire to control criminal markets; and more traditional criminal enterprises created pervasive insecurity through kidnapping and extortion. Organized crime also acted as an economic and political spoiler in the oil industry which was expected to be the dynamo for growth and reconstruction in Iraq. To some degree, the oil sector is now finally fulfilling its promise, albeit several years later than anticipated and only after significant theft, diversion, and black market activity robbed the government of substantial revenues.

Unfortunately, organized crime in Iraq is still given far too little attention. The U.S. Department of Justice has undertaken several initiatives in Iraq, including the creation of a Law and Order Task Force to "train, mentor, and assist Iraqi police and judges," plus a Major Crimes Task Force (MCTF) which it describes as "a unique joint Iraqi-U.S. organization, formed in 2006 in response to a rash of high-profile murders, assassinations, and acts of sectarian violence" to provide "on-the-job training, support, and mentoring to Iraqi law enforcement and task force members."[2] In spite of these initiatives, the United States has regarded law enforcement as primarily an Iraqi responsibility. More significantly, it has treated organized crime as a stand-alone problem rather than recognizing its intersection with other challenges and problems. In fact, reducing the criminalization of Iraqi political and economic life is inextricably linked with rebuilding the state, reestablishing infrastructure, and revitalizing Iraq's economy. Indeed, unless strategies to combat organized crime are integrated into the broader rebuilding program for Iraq, they stand little chance of success. Conversely, unless the attempt to rebuild Iraq incorporates more effective strategies to combat organized crime, the prospects for long-term stability will remain tenuous. Organized crime has been the neglected dimension of the Iraq conflict, and unless efforts to contain and reduce it are included in a comprehensive approach that goes well beyond the current counterinsurgency model, then it will continue to provide a resource base for insurgents as well as sectarian militias. This situation could become particularly challenging after the withdrawal of U.S. forces, undermining many of the security and political gains made in 2007 and 2008.

Organized Crime as a Strategic Surprise.

When the United States invaded Iraq in March 2003, it did not appreciate either the pervasive criminality in that society and economy or the stark divisions existing within the country — divisions that were based on sectarian identity, class politics, tribalism, and the tension between the center of power in Baghdad and outlying local and regional power and authority structures.[3] Nor did it understand the potential for pernicious interactions between these political structures and organized crime. Yet, the salience of organized crime in post-Saddam Hussein's Iraq should not really be a surprise. During the 1990s, organized crime, as facilitated and driven by globalization, emerged as a far-reaching phenomenon. It became a particularly thorny challenge for developing states and states in transition from authoritarian rule and a command economy to liberal democracy and a free market. Organized crime flourished in countries with weak state structures, questionable levels of legitimacy, and chaotic, dislocated, or dysfunctional economies. Such crime also became an integral feature of post-conflict situations in countries as diverse as Bosnia and Haiti. Although Iraq does not fit neatly into the post-conflict category, it has become home to a particularly concentrated and virulent strain of criminality that has deeply pervaded a variety of other countries ranging from Mexico to Guinea-Bissau.

Many aspects of organized crime in Iraq are far from unique. In Mexico, for example, the intensifying struggle between drug trafficking organizations and the Mexican state is characterized by high levels of violence that are beginning to approximate those in Iraq. In some instances, the killing of policemen in Mexico is simply a settling of accounts with law enforcement officers involved in the drug business. Increasingly, though, the trafficking organizations target policemen and military personnel committed to fighting the drug business. In the same way, insurgents and criminals in Iraq threaten or kill those trying to fight corruption in the ministries. And even beheadings are not limited to Iraq.

Mexican drug trafficking organizations have also made extensive use of beheadings as a weapon of intimidation in their struggle against one another and the forces of the state. On one occasion, five severed heads were thrown into a disco; on another, the severed heads of policemen were prominently displayed outside a police station as a warning to others. In yet another incident in August 2008, 12 headless bodies were found on the outskirts of Merida in Yucatan, a city which had hitherto been largely spared drug-related violence. Many of these bloody episodes can be understood in terms of what Sebastian Rotella describes as "the semiotics of murder" in which the message is as important as the killing.[4] Such grisly displays have a powerful psychological impact, and it is not surprising that in both Iraq and Mexico videos of the murders have been displayed on the Internet.

While such displays became a trademark of AQI under the leadership of Zarqawi, the beheading phenomenon in Mexico also reached the Internet with decapitation videos posted on You-Tube.[5] Multiple law enforcement agencies across Mexico have also been infiltrated by trafficking organizations; in Iraq, as discussed more fully below, the infiltration has been predominantly by sectarian militias. In other words, the manifestations of organized crime in Iraq and Mexico have many things in common even though in Iraq the connections to insurgency and sectarian violence create additional complications without an obvious parallel in Mexico.

The centrality of oil and oil smuggling in Iraq might appear distinctive, but even this is not without analogues elsewhere. The tapping of oil pipelines, the theft of oil, and its subsequent transportation in small boats out to sea where it is transferred to oil tankers—a process known as illegal oil bunkering—characterizes both the oil-rich province of Basra and Nigeria's Niger Delta.[6] In both cases, the smuggling is bound up with militia violence and facilitated by corruption at high levels. In both cases, smuggling is in part a response to the government's monopoly over oil extraction and sales. The effect in both cases is to deprive the government of revenues. Although much is made of the battle among rival political and criminal groups for control over oil smuggling in Basra, even this had an analogue (discussed more fully in Chapter 3) in the Ukrainian port city of Odessa in the mid-1990s. More generally, the oil and gasoline industry in Russia and other parts of the former Soviet Union were also heavily criminalized during the 1990s, with criminal organizations vying for control and engaging in contract killings against their rivals.[7] In Iraq the conflict over oil is of a larger scale—but so too is the prize.

Another parallel with events in Russia is the growth of extortion. During the 1990s extortion of shopkeepers and small businesses became pervasive in Moscow and other large cities. Payoffs had to be made to organized crime simply for the business to operate. Protection rackets became big business in Russia because law enforcement was weak while the regulatory apparatus for business was absent.[8] In Iraq too, deficient law enforcement was a major factor. Even though protection rackets have been driven more obviously by militias rather than traditional criminal gangs, the dynamics are very similar. The militias are both predatory and protective, while in Russia some extortionists developed a vested interest in the commercial success of the businesses they were targeting and actually acted as protectors.[9] Other groups, of course, remained merely parasitic, while dressing up the demands as payments for services rendered. In Baghdad and elsewhere in Iraq, protection payments often take the form of ostensibly legitimate and innocuous payments for market stalls or kiosks. The result, however, is that profits are diminished, entrepreneurial initiative is stifled, and the legitimate capital accumulation required for economic regeneration is undermined.

Post-Saddam Hussein's Iraq has also witnessed the emergence of a kidnapping industry. Once again this is not unique. Other countries facing challenges from insurgencies and terrorist or criminal organizations also have to contend with abductions. This is certainly the case with the Philippines, where kidnapping has been concentrated in Mindanao and Metro Manila; in Colombia, where both FARC and the ELN have made extensive use of kidnapping as a fund-raising device;

and in Mexico, where the capital, Mexico City, has become particularly dangerous. According to some assessments, by 2004 Mexico City had become the kidnapping capital of the world with targets including not only unwary foreigners, but many middle class Mexicans.[10] Baghdad subsequently took over this dubious distinction, with kidnappings reaching a peak in 2005 and 2006 and continuing (albeit at a lower level) in spite of the improved security situation. Once again, however, Iraq is hardly distinctive. In all the threatened countries, the impact on public security has been serious. In Iraq an added twist is that families which had invested their savings in businesses intended to meet demands for commodities and consumer goods in post-Saddam Hussein's Iraq became a major target of kidnapping gangs; their entrepreneurial energy was dissipated and their resource base depleted by ransom payments.[11]

Perhaps an even more striking parallel—yet one rarely mentioned—is that between Iraq and Albania. In 1997 the Albanian state imploded after the collapse of massive pyramid schemes in which many people lost their savings. In effect, this was the culmination of a period of dismal and increasingly corrupt governance. According to Daniel Vaughan-Whitehead, the failure of the Albanian state had its roots in:

> fragile economic growth characterized by the collapse of industrial activity, the absence of substituting activities from an emerging and weak service sector, and a banking system still unable to assume its role as a financial intermediary; . . . the failure of the mass privatization program; . . . the growth in unemployment and the fall in real wages and living standards which combined to condemn a growing proportion of the people to total destitution; finally, the fragility of public authority and institutions.[12]

In the case of Iraq, the collapse was the result of the U.S. invasion and the decapitation of the regime—although significantly not the defeat of the total country in the same way that Germany and Japan were defeated in World War II.[13] The regime collapse had more far-reaching consequences than anticipated because of an underlying brittleness in state structures which had not been evident from the outside. In both cases, however, the result was an orgy of looting which in Albania included the looting of the national armory and in Iraq encompassed the sacking of ministries and the National Museum, and the theft and diffusion of weapons and ammunition from depots and caches spread through the country.

Nor was this the only parallel. The cultures of both Iraq and Albania were based on tribal or clan laws and traditions—including blood feuds and vendettas—rather than the rule of law as understood in western societies. Such affiliations came to the fore in the aftermath of state collapse and, in both cases, complicated and intensified the difficulties of reestablishing the power of a centralized state.

Obviously, there were differences, and the analogy is far from perfect. Nevertheless, it is interesting that organized crime, which was already flourishing in Albania prior to 1997, consolidated its position after the crisis, allowing Albania to become a safe haven not only for Albanian criminals but also for criminal organizations from Italy and elsewhere. In May 2000, for example, it was reported that more than 500 Mafiosi of different nationalities were in Albania.[14] In Iraq after the fall of Saddam Hussein, there was an even more dramatic upsurge of organized crime than in Albania—although the high levels of violence and instability probably inhibited the influx of foreign criminals.

There are even some parallels that pre-date the U.S. military intervention and the fall of Saddam Hussein. During the 1990s, Hussein's son, Uday, and Marco Milosevic, son of the then Serbian leader Slobodan Milosevic, were both heavily involved in cigarette smuggling—although independently of one another. In both cases, approval and protection of their criminal activities was provided at the very highest levels of government. More generally in Iraq, smuggling—which was a time-honored tradition—reached new heights prior to the downfall of the regime as part of Hussein's efforts to circumvent sanctions. It was to become even more prominent in post-Hussein Iraq, partly reflecting the new availability of goods but also the differential prices of commodities in contiguous countries. Once again, this situation is not unique. Smuggling across the border to and from Iraq's neighbors responds to the same dynamics as smuggling elsewhere. In the early 1990s, for example, increased taxes in Canada created large price differentials with the United States. Almost inevitably, this was followed by large-scale smuggling of cigarettes into Canada—often through Indian reservations such as the Akwesasne reservation which extends from New York State into Quebec and Ontario provinces.

None of this is intended to ignore or downplay the unique features of Iraqi culture, the role of tribal allegiances, the religious divide between Sunni and Shiite, or the particular historical experience and geographic location of the country. The argument is simply that organized crime in Iraq resembles organized crime in other countries—up to a point. Organized crime in Iraq is far from *sui generis*, but its concentrated forms are probably unmatched anywhere and possibly unprecedented in depth and extent. In effect, Iraq has been transformed into a magnified Sicily—with oil.

Indeed, organized crime in Iraq combines aspects of organized crime in Nigeria with Prohibition Chicago, gang warfare in Los Angeles with organized crime in the Balkans and Russia, and the power of Mexican drug trafficking organizations with religious zeal and nationalist passion. In short, organized crime in Iraq is a true witches' brew, a powerful concoction with internal dynamics that remain little understood. Iraq also suffers from an insurgency that uneasily combines foreign terrorists, Iraqi nationalists, and former regime elements, with a sectarian conflict that is sometimes overshadowed by intra-sectarian clashes. It is an internal conflict with external meddling, a battleground between the United States and al-Qaeda, and a proxy conflict for the on-going cold war between the United States and Iran. At stake are the norms and rules for the society, issues of identity, and control over resources — all of which are a prize of the conflict and a way of sustaining the struggle. Criminal activities help fuel these battles, while criminal organizations exploit the opportunities provided by an environment characterized by conflict, disorder, and weak government.

Accordingly, this analysis explores the organized crime dimension of the conflict in Iraq, a dimension given scant attention even though it weaves through many other facets of the conflict. The importance of understanding organized crime in the country was highlighted in July 2003 by Mark Edmond Clark of the Strategy Group. As he noted, "Combating organized crime in Iraq will be an issue that will demand further consideration as the humanitarian and reconstruction efforts get underway."[15] He added that "the Balkans could possibly serve as a model for understanding what is now taking place in Iraq."[16] In August 2003 a delegation from the United Nations Office of Drugs and

Crime (UNODC) provided an even more detailed and emphatic statement on the central role of organized crime in Iraq, noting that it was already contributing to instability and complicating reconstruction.[17] The report focused on oil smuggling, trafficking in firearms, human trafficking, theft and trafficking of artifacts, kidnapping and extortion, and car-jacking, while emphasizing that the large-scale theft of copper from electricity pylons and power lines would have a serious effect on the electricity infrastructure.[18] It added that the process of copper smuggling had developed remarkably quickly, and had reached "industrial scale" proportions.[19] The report also noted that "the conditions for the expansion of organized crime include the absence of the rule of law, the disintegration of state institutions, and the promotion of various forms of smuggling under the previous regime. Such factors have taken place against the backdrop of deterioration in socio-economic conditions in the past decade."[20] In sum, the UNODC report revealed that conditions in Iraq were ripe for a tsunami of organized crime. Although the report was both prescient and compelling, it had little impact on high-level decisionmaking.

In spite of this deficit of attention at high levels, some U.S. military units were quick to recognize the nature of the challenge they were confronting. A July 2004 report from Pamela Hess, United Press International's (UPI) Pentagon correspondent, observed that Marine commanders were already acknowledging that it was difficult to

> overemphasize the importance of organized crime in the insurgency. . . . The perpetrators are motivated by self-interest and greed. They not only plan and carry out violence but pay others to do the same. One commander compared the intransigence of Iraqi organized crime

networks to that of the mafia in Sicily before World War II. It has the same stranglehold on whole local economies and populations, and is protected by family and tribal loyalties.[21]

Although this report was picked up by a few blogs in the United States, it received little or no attention from the mainstream news media. For the most part, the intensifying challenge posed by organized crime was still largely ignored, both at the official level and in the public debate.

There were a few other exceptions, especially among Iraq specialists. Toby Dodge, for example, consistently and vigorously asserted that criminal activities were a major cause of public insecurity following the invasion and needed to be countered in a serious and systematic way. In his view, lawlessness and the ready availability of weapons combined with the absence of effective policing to provide a highly permissive environment for criminal organizations which terrorized "what remains of the middle class, car-jacking, house-breaking, and kidnapping, largely with impunity. Groups like these also regularly rob and kidnap foreign workers. In many cases, these gangs are better armed and organized than the Iraqi police trying to stop them."[22] Dodge also concluded that the continued capacity of these groups "to operate is the most visible sign of state weakness."[23] Such observations, however, were largely disregarded as the focus switched to the growing violence and the improvised explosive device (IED) phenomenon.

Once again, there were important exceptions. Steven Metz, in particular, characterized what was going on in Iraq as a complex insurgency within which reinforcing streams of activity were embedded. He observed that the insurgency in Iraq resembled other contemporary insurgencies in the widespread

12

use of criminal activities as a funding mechanism.[24] John Robb made a similar point in a different way, referring to the development in Iraq of what he termed a "bazaar of violence . . . composed of many entrepreneurial groups—each with its own bond . . ., sources of funding, and motivations."[25] Finally, on October 28, 2007, the importance of organized crime was acknowledged at a high level when General David Petraeus highlighted the importance of nonsectarian crimes such as kidnapping, corruption in the oil industry, and extortion, noting that in certain areas of Baghdad, there is "almost a mafia-like presence."[26] Although General Petraeus stated that all this had become more visible because of the improvements in the security situation, it is important to emphasize that organized crime in Iraq is not something separate from the insurgency, the sectarian conflicts, or the activities of AQI; rather, it is interwoven with these other organizations and activities, exacerbating the fault lines in the society and creating negative but very powerful synergistic effects.[27]

This becomes particularly evident when it is acknowledged that organized crime in Iraq, as elsewhere, can be understood in two distinct ways. First, it can be understood as entities or criminal enterprises which see crime as a continuation of business by other means. Organized crime can also be understood as a set of activities which can be appropriated or utilized by a variety of different entities for their own narrow purposes.[28] Terrorist organizations, insurgents, ethnic factions, sectarian groups, and militias can all use organized crime activities as a funding mechanism to support their political and military activities.

There have even been a few cases of states—typically pariahs such as North Korea, Serbia under Milosevic, and Saddam Hussein's Iraq—using criminal activities to offset their isolation in the international community and to counter sanctions directed against them by that community. The particular crimes depend on the state carrying them out. North Korea, for example, executed a broad portfolio of criminal activities,[29] while Hussein's Iraq focused primarily on oil smuggling to reduce the impact of sanctions and provide a revenue stream which funded both the construction of new palaces and a renewed weapons program.

Similarly, for nonstate entities, specific criminal activities depend in part on the range of opportunities in the environment. This in turn helps to explain why some groups specialize while others develop a broad portfolio of criminal activities.

In post-war Iraq it is possible to discern both criminal enterprises interested primarily in profit and other entities using organized criminal activities as a way of furthering and funding their political agendas. Indeed, both criminal enterprises and criminal activities appropriated by other violent nonstate actors have become an integral part of the situation in the country. Post-Hussein Iraq provided an almost unprecedented opportunity space for organized crime, the exploitation of which contributed significantly to the difficulties faced by the United States in its efforts to create stability, reestablish a legitimate, effective state, and reconstruct Iraq's infrastructure and economy.

Once again, there are parallels, this time with the situation in Bosnia-Herzegovina, where the central state envisaged in the 1995 Dayton Accords has still not fully materialized. One of the reasons is that in Bosnia the nationalist parties working with organized crime groups have controlled most of the contraband trade, thereby depriving the state of much-needed customs revenues.[30] Similarly in Iraq, organized crime activities, corrupt officials, and smuggling networks significantly hindered the reestablishment of a viable and effective central government and delayed the regeneration of the Iraqi oil industry, an industry expected to provide the momentum for reconstruction in post-Hussein Iraq.[31] In addition, organized crime not only contributed significantly to the pervasive climate of fear in the country but also provided funding to the multitude of violent groups engaged in combat with one another and with American and Iraqi government forces. At the same time, crime and corruption within the governing political elite and key ministries undermined both legitimacy and effectiveness.

Furthermore, the emergent police force, intended to uphold the rule of law, was infiltrated by militias and riddled with sectarianism and corruption. Consequently, it has been part of the problem rather than part of the solution. For many ordinary Iraqis, the very force that was designed to protect them preyed on them instead, engaging in sectarian killings, extortion, robberies, and kidnapping. In addition, insurgent tribes and AQI targeted occupation forces, reconstruction efforts, and emerging forms of governance, while funding their campaigns of violence partly through criminal activities. In the early years of the insurgency, in particular, the Ba'athist former regime elements (FREs) who wanted to regain power used their access to the illicit economy to finance this effort.

Although the component parts of the challenge in Iraq are old and familiar, the overall picture in the aftermath of the U.S. invasion in 2003 was new and different. In fact, the rise of organized crime in Iraq challenges existing concepts and categorizations, casts doubts on strategies that focus narrowly on the military dimension of a complex problem, and demands new measures of effectiveness or metrics of success. Much as the conflict in Iraq can be understood only as a hybrid form of warfare, so too must organized crime in Iraq be understood. Furthermore, criminality has added to the hybrid quality of the anti-coalition violence.[32] In the final analysis, however, the failure to foresee the emergence of organized crime and subsequently to understand the relationship between organized crime and much of the violence in Iraq, are sufficiently serious that they constitute what can only be described as strategic surprise.

Purpose and Scope of the Analysis.

Against the background of organized crime, violence, and insurgency, this analysis attempts to fill what has been an important gap in our understanding of developments in Iraq since March 2003. Specifically, it seeks to:

- explain the rise of organized crime, pervasive criminality, and widespread corruption in contemporary Iraq. Organized crime did not suddenly arise from the chaos of invasion and occupation; rather, it had deep roots in an authoritarian and corrupt state subject to international sanctions;

- explore the dimensions of organized crime and specifically criminal activities which are used not only by traditional for-profit groups but also by insurgents, militias, sectarian groups, political parties, and tribes to enhance their resource base and thereby prosecute their ends more effectively;

- identify the major actors exploiting criminal opportunity in Iraq and to explore the ways in which criminal organizations and political or sectarian actors merge or overlap with each other. The actors include many members of the political and administrative elites who have used their positions in the state apparatus to advance personal or private agendas rather than to serve the public good; and,
- suggest a range of possible and necessary responses to organized crime and corruption in Iraq. These responses run the gamut from new priorities in governance and reconstruction efforts to a new emphasis on law enforcement and the establishment of greater transparency. They include environmental modification to reduce criminal opportunities, changes in incentive structures, and the direct targeting of criminal organizations and activities.

Although these tasks appear relatively straight-forward, there are inevitable gaps in both knowledge and understanding as well as inherent obstacles to the kind of analysis being undertaken here. Any deep examination of a conflict zone has to confront major challenges and problems. In Iraq, the complexity and dynamism of the situation, combined with the gaps in intelligence and the lack of open-source reporting, make conclusive judgments problematic. Some of the social connections that provide a basis for trust networks are not clearly discernible to the outsider even though they facilitate illicit transactions. Similarly, much of the extortion that occurs, by its very nature, goes unreported or is reported only in very general terms. Another challenge is to identify those responsible for criminal activities which are often obscured by denial

17

and deception efforts. The problem, however, is not only one of information but also of analysis. In this connection, an important challenge is to determine the extent to which particular organizations in Iraq are monolithic and centralized or so highly factionalized that some members act without central authority. Notwithstanding these problems, difficulties, and challenges, piecing together large parts of the puzzle is possible.

Accordingly, in Chapter 2 we shall examine the rise of organized crime in Iraq. It shows how the reign of Saddam Hussein combined with international sanctions to create all the conditions for an upsurge of organized crime. The upsurge itself can be understood in terms of two distinct if overlapping waves which are also elucidated. In Chapter 3, the focus is on oil theft and oil smuggling, which are probably the most lucrative sources of illicit income. Chapter 4 analyzes the practice of kidnapping, which also became pervasive yet was rarely accorded a level of attention commensurate with its significance unless it involved foreigners. In Chapter 5, the focus moves to extortion and a range of other criminal activities which, although less important than oil smuggling and kidnapping, cannot be ignored. In Chapter 6, the subject of corruption in Iraq comes to the fore. This malady has not only undermined efforts to reestablish effective governance but also contributed to a climate of prosecutorial impotence and facilitated many criminal activities. Chapter 7 looks at the entities involved in organized crime and considers some of the ways in which they have interacted with one another. Finally, Chapter 8 develops a set of recommendations regarding responses to organized crime in Iraq as well as a set of lessons distilled from the Iraq experience which might be relevant to other conflicts and post-conflict situations.

ENDNOTES - CHAPTER 1

1. Stephen J. Stedman, "Spoiler Problems in Peace Processes," *International Security*, Vol. 22, No. 2, Fall 1997, pp. 5-53.

2. *Fact Sheet: Department of Justice Initiatives in Iraq*, February 13, 2008, available at *www.usdoj.gov/opa/pr/2008/February/iraq-factsheet021308.pdf*. I am grateful to Mark Hess for a helpful and informative discussion of the work of the task force.

3. Eric Herring and Glen Rangwala, *Iraq in Fragments*, New York: Cornell University Press, 2006.

4. Sebastian Rotella, *Twilight on the Line: Underworlds and Politics at the U.S.-Mexico Border*, New York: Norton, 1998.

5. See Ioan Grillo, "Behind Mexico's wave of Beheadings," *Time*, September 8, 2008, available at *www.time.com/time/world/article/0,85991839576,00.html*.

6. The process itself, known as bunkering, is predominantly a legitimate activity, but one that has an illegal counterpart. In Nigeria, the government has a complete monopoly over oil export, so any export not authorized by the government is illegal. See, for example, *Transnational Organized Crime in the West African Region*, New York: United Nations Office of Drugs and Crime, April 2005.

7. For an excellent analysis of the role of violence in Russian organized crime, see Vadim Volkov, *Entrepreneurs of Violence: The Use of Force in the Making of Russian Capitalism*, Ithaca, NY: Cornell University Press, 2002.

8. Federico Varese, *The Russian Mafia: Private Protection in a New Market Economy*, New York: Oxford University Press, 2005.

9. *Ibid.*

10. See, for example, "Welcome to Mexico City, The New Kidnap Capital of the World," *The Independent on Sunday*, September 5, 2004.

11. Matthew Fisher, "Iraqis Suffer Most from Kidnapping: It's a Scourge that Kills Entrepreneurs' Dreams," *The Gazette*, Montreal, Quebec, Canada, July 25, 2004, p. D4.

12. Daniel Vaughan-Whitehead, *Albania in Crisis: The Predictable Fall of the Shining Star*, Northampton, MA: Edward Elgar Publishing Inc., 1999.

13. For this point, I am grateful to John Keeler, Dean of the Graduate School of Public and International Affairs, University of Pittsburgh, Pittsburgh, PA.

14. Report by Z. F., "Italians Come First, Followed by Greeks and Russians," *Tirana Republika*, May 25, 2000, p. 5.

15. Mark Edmond Clark, *Understanding Balkan Organized Crime: A Key to Success in Iraq?* July 2003, Columbia International Affairs Online (CIAO).

16. *Ibid.*

17. United Nations Office of Drugs and Crime (UNODC), *Addressing Organized Crime and Drug Trafficking in Iraq: Report of the UNODC Fact Finding Mission*, August 5-18, 2003, Vienna, Austria, August 25, 2003.

18. *Ibid.*

19. *Ibid.*, p. 7.

20. *Ibid.*, p. iii.

21. Pamela Hess. Her report has been reproduced on the blog "Zen and the Art of Counterinsurgency," available at *powerblogs. com/pipermail/inteldump/2004-July/000106.html*.

22. Toby Dodge, *Chapter One: Order and Violence in Post-Saddam Iraq*, Adelphi Papers, Vol. 45, No. 372, p. 15.

23. *Ibid.*

24. This is reflected in the concept of complex conflict developed by Steven Metz. See *Rethinking Insurgency*, Carlisle, PA: Strategic Studies Institute, U.S. Army War College, June 2007.

25. John Robb, *Brave New War*, New York, Wiley, 2007, p. 15.

26. "Petraeus: Al-Qaida Presence in Baghdad Has Been 'Significantly Reduced'," *Associated Press*, October 28, 2007.

27. On negative synergies, see Thomas Homer-Dixon, *The Upside of Down*, Washington, DC: Island Press, 2006, p. 106.

28. For a fuller analysis of this distinction, see Phil Williams, "Terrorist Financing and Organized Crime: Nexus, Appropriation or Transformation?" in Thomas Biersteke and Susan Eckert, eds., *Countering the Financing of Terrorism*, London, United Kingdom: Routledge, 2008, pp. 126-149.

29. David E. Kaplan, "The Wiseguy Regime: North Korea Has Embarked on a Global Crime Spree," *U.S. News and World Report*, February 7, 1999, available at *www.usnews.com/usnews/news/articles/990215/archive_000266.htm*. See also Sheena Chestnut, "Illicit Activity and Proliferation: North Korean Smuggling Networks, *International Security*, Vol. 32, No. 1, Summer 2007, pp. 80-111.

30. U.S. General Accounting Office, *Bosnia: Crime and Corruption Threaten Successful Implementation of the Dayton Peace Agreement*, Testimony Before the Committee in International Relations, House of Representatives, July 19, 2000.

31. With the increase in oil prices, Iraq's oil industry in 2008 began to generate large revenues, but these subsequently contracted as a result of the global recession and declining oil prices.

32. The author is grateful to Dr. Paul Kan for this observation.

CHAPTER 2

THE RISE OF ORGANIZED CRIME IN IRAQ

The Roots of Organized Crime in Iraq.

The rise of crime in Iraq was a result of several separate but intersecting factors, some of which are part of a broader pattern and some of which are unique. Organized crime had its roots in authoritarian and corrupt political structures, but increased in response to the sanctions imposed on Iraq following the 1990 invasion of Kuwait. The U.S. invasion in March 2003 and the subsequent collapse of Iraq's political structures marked a turning point after which organized crime expanded into a formidable problem for the United States and the nascent Iraqi government.

Although organized crime is usually discussed in relation to weak states, it can also flourish — albeit within strictly defined limits — in strong, authoritarian, or "fierce states" in which there is little oversight or control.[1] Robert Klitgaard's argument that corruption flourishes where there is monopoly plus discretion minus accountability applies equally well to organized crime.[2] This notion accords with what has been termed the elite exploitation model of organized crime. Developed by Peter Lupsha and Stanley Pimentel, the central proposition is that the political elites control and manipulate criminal organizations for their own purposes.[3] Good examples of this can be found in Mexico under successive Institutional Revolutionary Party (PRI) governments and in the Former Soviet Union where the Communist Party typically used black market organizations to ensure a consistent and abundant supply of commodities for members that were not available to ordinary citizens.

It is only a small step from the elite exploitation model to what might be termed the criminal state model, in which the regime does not simply exploit independent criminal organizations but develops centralized control over many criminal activities and mobilizes state resources in carrying them out. This is not a case of organized crime taking over the state but of the state taking over organized crime. Perhaps the most obvious example is North Korea, which has been heavily involved in methamphetamine production, trafficking in endangered species, diamond smuggling, counterfeiting, money laundering, and other criminal activities.[4] In many cases, North Korean diplomats posted abroad engaged in such activities, while in North Korea itself currency counterfeiting and other activities were under the control of Bureau 39, the agency responsible for obtaining hard currency.[5] The other obvious example is Milosevic-era Serbia, where members of the cabinet were given control over critical economic sectors, often exploiting them for personal gain.

Iraq under Saddam Hussein was, in some ways, very similar. According to one observer, the process of criminalization really began with the nationalization of the oil industry in 1972 and the subsequent development of a party "slush fund" by leading members of the Ba'ath Party, a fund which reportedly amounted to $17.4 billion by 1990.[6] This development marked the beginning of a slippery slope. Gradually, if inevitably, "Iraqi officials began to use the powers of the state for personal benefit through criminal activities of one kind or another."[7] In certain respects, therefore, Iraq in the 1990s resembled an extended mafia family with Saddam Hussein as the "Godfather" presiding over extensive criminal entrepreneurship by party members and particular tribes or groups. The consent, connivance, or collusion of the regime was critical. Some activities, especially the smuggling of oil to circumvent sanctions, were probably directly overseen by Saddam Hussein and his family as they exploited the resources of the Iraqi state including the state-run banks. In effect, Iraq under Hussein combined both the elite exploitation model and the criminal state model of organized crime.

Although authoritarian states provide fertile ground for the growth and operations of organized crime, they also seek to circumscribe criminal activities within defined limits. Yet sometimes this dominance begins to erode as criminal organizations develop more resources, acquire greater power, and exercise increased autonomy. This happened in Iraq. Initially, criminal organizations which could be of use to the regime were allowed to operate within clearly demarcated limits; the activities of these groups were significantly constrained by a regime in which social control mechanisms, although uneven in implementation, were often draconian. As the regime's control declined, albeit in subtle rather than overt ways, it was compelled to turn for help to some of the more traditional centers of power in Iraq.

This process of co-option became increasingly evident in the late 1990s. As Robert Looney has noted, in 1998 "heavily armed and equipped Sunni tribal units were positioned in and around Baghdad to control the restive urban population, a role formerly belonging to the Ba'ath party militia."[8] During the next few years, these tribal units became more autonomous and less dependent on the support and goodwill of the state.

Indeed, it was not long before "clan based groups" not only "controlled the highways around Baghdad," but "increasingly turned to criminal activities—looting, smuggling, and hijacking throughout most of al Anbar province."[9] Not surprisingly, this led to clashes with state agencies such as the police, judges, party officials, and Iraqi military. Yet these clashes do not seem to have had much impact in stemming either a growing criminal economy or the increased power and independence of criminal organizations. "Tribal groups were . . . increasingly involved in criminal-type activities, especially in the western border regions . . . . Illicit criminal networks were initially based on the cross-border smuggling of animals, tea, alcohol, and electronics. Later these activities began encompassing the drug trade."[10] It was perhaps a sign of the brittleness of the regime—a brittleness that was not readily apparent outside Iraq—that "tribal based organized criminal activities increased toward the end of Ba'athist rule with many party members becoming involved due to declining opportunities to acquire official resources. By early 2002, the entire route along the Euphrates River in Al Anbar had essentially developed into a sanctuary for illicit traffickers and criminal entrepreneurs."[11] Rather like paramilitaries in Colombia, tribes which had been utilized and empowered by the Iraqi state escaped the control of the state.

Part of the reason that Saddam Hussein needed to cooperate with other criminal entities in Iraq was outside pressure following the 1991 military defeat. The regime sought to resist and circumvent international economic sanctions which, during the 1990s, became one of the favorite enforcement tools of the international community, partly because such tools were more effective than diplomacy but less drastic than military force. Unfortunately, sanctions are an imperfect mechanism for coercion. They often have unintended and unfortunate consequences, hurting the weaker and more vulnerable segments of society in the target state while leaving the regime and elites unaffected. Often the target state or regime is able to respond to sanctions with circumvention methods that are both ingenious and highly innovative. It is not surprising, then, that international sanctions typically lead to an increase of both smuggling and corruption.[12] Iraq was no exception. The task of evading, undermining, and circumventing sanctions was greatly facilitated by the power and resources of the Iraqi state, combined with the willingness of a variety of groups within society to be co-opted by the state. While post-regime Iraq would almost certainly have had an organized crime problem even without sanctions and their circumvention, it is unlikely that the phenomenon would have been as powerful and widespread. In effect, sanctions contributed significantly to the criminalization of Iraq.

The most blatant aspects of criminality and corruption were associated with the United Nations' (UN) Oil for Food (OFF) program. The main impetus for this program was the desire of the international community to mitigate the impact of sanctions on the most vulnerable sectors of Iraq's population, such as children suffering from malnutrition and inadequate health care. In the event, the program was successful in mitigating some of the suffering. Malnutrition rates dropped from 32 percent in 1996 to just over 20 percent in 1999, while overall gross domestic product (GDP) increased from $10.6 billion to $33 billion.[13] At the same time, the program was unexpectedly but skillfully exploited by Saddam Hussein to provide additional funding for the regime. When this was

27

revealed, it was followed by a storm of criticism, much of it justified. Lax supervision and oversight at the UN, the susceptibility of some UN officials themselves to corruption, and the greed of several corporations allowed Saddam Hussein to exploit the OFF program for his own purposes. The program became so compromised that senior UN officials, along with companies in Australia, Russia, the United States, and several other countries, were deeply implicated in the resulting scandal. Ironically, Hussein had initially resisted this program. According to Central Intelligence Agency (CIA) official Charles Deulfer, "It was only when the effects on the Iraqi country and the population were so devastating that it became regime threatening, that Hussein decided to accept the Oil-for-Food Program as embodied in the December 1996 decision."[14] Not only did this alleviate what was emerging as a major crisis of legitimacy for the regime, it also provided "collateral benefits" that Hussein and his entourage "had not anticipated."[15] The most important of these benefits was the "ability to generate illicit revenue streams of hard currency."[16] Yet, the abuse of the OFF Program provided far less revenue than the often overlooked oil smuggling schemes resulting from "protocols" with Iraq's neighbors.

This is not to deny the significance of the OFF program. The program provided major political opportunities for Saddam Hussein. Particularly important in this respect was "a clandestine oil allocation voucher program" involving "the granting of oil certificates to certain individuals or organizations" in return for efforts to undermine the resolve of the international community to maintain sanctions.[17] The vouchers, negotiable instruments which could be sold or traded at a profit, were also used to encourage people or organizations to be helpful to the regime in more specific ways. Certain vouchers were categorized as "special allocations" or "gifts." These were given to Benon Sevan, the UN official in charge of the OFF program as well as Russian, Yugoslav, Ukrainian, and French politicians and businessmen.[18] Duelfer noted that "frequent buyers of these large allocations included companies in the UAE [United Arab Emirates] as well as Elf Total, Royal Dutch Shell, and others."[19] The voucher system was not itself illegal as it was approved by the UN, but the beneficiaries were not always open and aboveboard. Consequently, the system devolved to an exercise in corruption and influence-buying by Saddam Hussein (who personally approved all recipients of the vouchers). But the vouchers were ultimately less important to the regime than the OFF revenue streams, which provided substantial sources of income in spite of sanctions.

These revenue streams were generated in four main ways. First, the regime imposed surcharges of 10 to 35 cents per barrel on approved oil sales, a scheme that, according to the Volcker Report, earned at least $228.8 million.[20] Second and more lucrative, kickbacks on humanitarian supply contracts brought in at least $1.5 billion.[21] Under the OFF program,

> proceeds from authorized OFF Iraqi oil sales were deposited in a designated UN account to be used for humanitarian purposes, such as purchasing food and medical supplies for the Iraqi people. To circumvent the restrictions on purchases and generate additional illicit revenue, the Iraqi government ordered each of its ministries to institute a 10 percent kickback scheme. Vendors selling goods to the Iraqi government were required to inflate the contractual purchase price typically by 10 percent and kick back the excess charge to the Iraqi government.[22]

Third, oil "cash sales" or private-sector exports, according to the Duelfer Report, yielded approximately $990 million.[23] These were "exports, primarily petroleum, to private-sector buyers" that were not UN approved.[24]

Fourth, and most important of Saddam Hussein's illicit revenue streams, were the trade protocols with Jordan, Syria, Turkey, and Egypt, which preceded and then paralleled the OFF Program. The status of these protocols was ambiguous. They were illicit in the sense that Security Council Resolution 661 passed in August 1990 restricted all UN member states from importing any goods, including oil and its derivatives, originating from Iraq; at the same time, the protocols were agreements between sovereign states and, therefore, had some degree of legitimacy.

According to the Volcker report, $10.99 billion of the $12.8 billion generated in illicit revenue between 1990 and 2003 came from activities associated with these protocols (this figure apparently includes the almost $1 billion identified by the Duelfer Report as "cash sales").[25] The proceeds of the oil sales were split between a trade account and a cash account in the protocol country. While 60 to 75 percent of the proceeds was placed in the trade account and used "to purchase goods from vendors and businesses in the particular protocol-partner country," the other 25 to 40 percent "was transferred to bank accounts in Jordan and Lebanon — usually through bank accounts set up in the names of front companies or individuals, to further disguise the scheme and the movement of the funds. Eventually, the cash account funds generated under all of the protocols were deposited in bank accounts controlled by the Central Bank of Iraq, Rasheed Bank, or Rafidian Bank."[26] The money was later withdrawn in cash and sent back to Iraq where it was deposited at the Central Bank of Iraq. A network of front companies, each using multiple accounts, was set up to move the money.

These flows were strategically significant: between 1996 and 1998 Iraq was able to establish "a growing underground network of trade intermediaries, front companies, and international suppliers willing to trade oil or hard currency for conventional weapons, WMD [weapons of mass destruction] precursors, and dual-use technology."[27] The more important result for the long term, however, was the development in Iraq of a set of sophisticated skills in criminality combined with methods of smuggling and repatriating funds that survived the downfall of the regime and its replacement first by the Coalition Provincial Authority (CPA) and then by the reconstituted Iraqi government. This should not have been surprising. Peter Andreas, in a compelling and incisive analysis, has demonstrated that sanctions almost invariably have a criminalizing impact on the targeted country as well as its neighbors.[28] As he shows, the criminalizing consequences of sanctions occur at several distinct but overlapping levels.

First, while sanctions are in effect, the target state typically goes "into the business of organized crime to generate revenue, supplies, and strengthen its hold on power, fostering an alliance with clandestine transnational economic actors for mutual gain. This alliance may, in turn, persist beyond the sanctions period."[29] Iraq clearly exemplifies this tendency. Although in many respects the regime was already primed for criminal activity, it was during the imposition of sanctions that corruption and state-controlled

31

smuggling really expanded, with Hussein using "the implements of the State — the central bank, commercial enterprises, and his diplomatic and intelligence assets — to help skirt international restrictions."[30] Smuggling became one of the central activities of the state and one in which "all levels of the government were complicit."[31] It also proved to be a remarkably resilient activity. Moreover, just as "profiteering, black market trafficking, and sanctions-busting became the principal activity of the Iraqi elite,"[32] so profiteering, corruption, and crime subsequently became major activities for many members of the post-Hussein elite.

The second development contributing to criminalization was the creation of regional linkages in smuggling and other criminal activities. In this connection, Andreas notes that "an elaborate regional clandestine trading network developed in the 1990s to evade sanctions, largely involving the smuggling of oil by truck to neighboring Turkey and Jordan, by ship to Iran, and by pipeline through Syria."[33] This process was facilitated by a long tradition of smuggling in the region. As the Duelfer report acknowledges, Iraq exploited "long-established business relationships with its neighbors, cross-state tribal connections, and use of ancient smuggling routes."[34] These smuggling routes crossed land borders with such Iraqi neighbors as Turkey, Syria, Jordan, Saudi Arabia, Kuwait, and Iran. In addition, Iraq used its own access to the Gulf from Basra as well as the Jordanian port of Aqaba.[35] Specific examples included:

- Smuggling across the Habur gate on Iraq's northern border with Turkey where the heavy volume of traffic "hindered the adequate monitoring of cargo."[36] UN monitors had the capacity to inspect only one in every 200 trucks crossing into Iraq.[37]

- Smuggling goods by truck from Dubai via Saudi Arabia.[38] There was also smuggling of "foodstuffs, luxury goods, and especially cement and asphalt" along the highway between Khorramshahr in Iran and Al-Basra, Iraq's most important southern city.[39]
- Smuggling oil out of Iraq and other commodities in and out using "a pool of private dhows, barges, and tankers."[40]
- Smuggling oil using "routes through the northern Arabian Gulf," as facilitated by the Iranian Revolutionary Guard Navy "in return for a fee."[41] It was estimated in 2000 that Iran was taking about 25 percent of the profit from smuggled Iraqi oil, a margin made possible because Hussein charged well below the market price of oil "to earn revenue that was not tracked by the UN."[42]
- Smuggling military and dual-use goods by air.

In sum, the smuggling enterprise was comprehensive, characterized by diversity of routes and exploitation of the "entire spectrum" of smuggling methods.[43] Typical schemes included "disguising illicit shipments as legitimate cargo; hiding illicit goods in legitimate shipments; avoiding customs inspections; and, for high-priority, low-volume shipments, using Iraqi diplomatic couriers."[44]

Although sanction-busting smuggling was built on existing connections, it clearly took these to new levels. In effect, Saddam Hussein established a clandestine transnational network based on trust relationships and mutual profitability. Moreover, these cross-border connections and social capital, once established, were relatively easy to maintain in changed circumstances.

The networks not only continued to operate after the removal of sanctions but also adapted in ways which ensured continued profitability. Mutual interest ensured that smuggling continued to flourish after Hussein. Although it was the trade with Jordan which provided his major lifeline during the 1990s, other countries were also important. The smuggling of oil to Turkey, for example, was driven in part by price differentials between Iraq and Turkey. These in turn were the result of taxation levels which led to remarkably high oil and gasoline prices in Turkey. It is not surprising, then, that even after the collapse of the Hussein regime and the removal of sanctions, smuggling oil and oil derivatives into Turkey was sustained at very high levels.

A third effect of sanctions and their circumvention is the criminalization of the economy and society. For Iraq, the consequences outlasted Saddam Hussein. In spite of the drastic change in the composition of government after the collapse of the regime, illicit activities in Iraq were marked by strong continuity. Part of the reason is that although Hussein used the state apparatus to direct both the oil smuggling and the money flows, the elite also developed collusive relationships with smugglers and facilitators, who continued their business activities after the Ba'athists had lost power. Moreover, as Andreas notes, the imposition of sanctions typically gives such activities as smuggling a legitimacy they do not always enjoy.[45] The circumvention of sanctions also elevates the status of organized crime groups within the society, enabling them to move from the periphery to the very core of economic life. In short, sanctions and embargoes not only promote smuggling but also empower smugglers and other organized crime groups. Once criminal activities have become accepted as the norm, "reestablishing societal acceptance of legal norms can be one of the most challenging tasks after the sanctions are lifted, as old habits can be difficult to break."[46] Similarly, as power structures associated with criminal activities are consolidated, they become difficult to weaken, let alone remove, and they only rarely revert to their pre-sanction norms. They are far more likely to remain entrenched in the illegal economy, which does not simply disappear once sanctions are removed. All this became evident in Iraq after the 2003 invasion. Indeed, oil smuggling after the fall of Saddam Hussein resembled the smuggling and associated corruption that were an integral part of the final decade of the Ba'athist regime.

The same was true of the informal and illicit economies more generally. As Andreas notes, sanctions typically lead to the expansion of the underground economy while simultaneously pushing the legitimate economy into crisis.[47] Furthermore, for those involved in the underground economy, the incentives to continue with their lucrative business activities in the post-sanctions economy are enormous—if only to maintain their existing revenue flows. In many cases, such incentives are strongly reinforced by the devastated condition of the aboveground economy.[48] In Iraq, as in Serbia, sanctions hurt the middle class while allowing the regime and its cronies to flourish. These problems became particularly salient after the U.S. invasion. The shadow economy, which accounted for about 35 percent of gross national product (GNP) at the end of the Hussein regime, subsequently grew to an estimated 65 percent.[49]

In sum, although it is likely that Iraq—like many other authoritarian states which eventually collapsed—

would have developed significant organized crime problems even in the absence of sanctions, their imposition by the international community in the 1990s both widened and intensified the scope of organized crime and the illicit economy in Iraq. This was to have major implications for the occupation.

The First Wave of Organized Crime in Post-Hussein Iraq.

As we have seen, when the United States invaded Iraq in March 2003, organized crime was already primed for growth. Systemic and structural preconditions for a massive expansion of organized crime and the illicit economy were present, and needed only the collapse of the regime as a catalyst. Several U.S. strategic mistakes then compounded the problem.

As the United States moved to occupy Iraq, there was little understanding of the criminality that had permeated Iraqi society during sanctions, the latent power of criminal organizations, the resources (including competencies, social capital, established smuggling routes, and transnational connections) these organizations had accumulated, or of the opportunities the United States was inadvertently providing to them. Nor was the United States sensitive to the profound divisions under the surface of Iraqi society, divisions which had been held in check by Saddam Hussein but were soon to have full rein. While many commentators have rightly criticized the lack of planning for the aftermath of the military campaign, even better planning would probably have omitted measures to constrain and respond to criminal organizations and the appropriation of organized crime methods by political actors. Thus the United States inadvertently created a highly permissive environment for organized crime and the incentive structure for the new freedom to be exploited. With the experience of a long apprenticeship under Saddam Hussein, criminal organizations had developed significant capabilities and expertise in smuggling and other criminal activities. The fall of Hussein marked their graduation and provided the occasion for an extended coming-out party.

Unfortunately, the collapse of Saddam Hussein's authoritarian state not only removed constraints and expanded the power of organized crime but also enabled organized crime to develop in ways that complicated the challenges facing the successor state. In one sense, this was not unusual or particularly surprising. Weak, failed, or collapsed states typically provide highly permissive environments for organized crime—especially if collapse is sudden and dramatic. The introduction of U.S. military power caused the state to collapse in Iraq—although in retrospect considerable evidence of state erosion existed prior to the invasion. The collapse of the state was accompanied by the breakdown of social control mechanisms; this provided an ideal environment for organized crime. In effect, the U.S. decapitation strategy in Iraq worked almost too effectively and too rapidly. The problem was that U.S. occupation forces were expected to fill the vacuum; but military forces typically focus on the maintenance of order at the macro level rather than the enforcement of law at the micro level. Consequently, emergent behavior—in this case criminality—at the micro level was unconstrained and had far-reaching consequences at the macro level.

If this was the same kind of upsurge of organized crime as had occurred in Russia, Ukraine, Georgia, Central Asia, and elsewhere after the collapse of the

Soviet Union, Iraq also resembled the former Yugoslavia in terms of the disparate ethnic and religious groups that had hitherto been tightly contained within a single authoritarian framework. And just as the various ethnic groups in the Balkans had used organized crime activities and links with criminal organizations to fund their separatist ambitions, so too did the various factions and groups within Iraq. Indeed, the lack of centralized authority after the collapse of the regime created a highly permissive environment—for the forces of retribution and revenge, for sectarian division and rivalry, and for the growth of organized crime. The incubation period had ended and the period of rapid—and in many respects unconstrained—growth of organized crime had begun. In the absence of a strong state, criminal organizations were able to operate with impunity, taking advantage of the power vacuum to extend their activities and strengthen their influence. One of the most immediate manifestations of this was the upsurge of copper theft and smuggling. Under the Ba'athist regime, this activity—which is lucrative because of the lack of indigenous copper deposits in the Middle East—"was limited by harsh penalties and by a complex system of patronage that ensured that local tribal groups provided protection to the infrastructure in the areas of their influence and control."[50] With the removal of these penalties and obstacles, the theft and smuggling of copper increased, causing great harm to the power grid and complicating the task of reconstruction. Iraq after the fall of Hussein became a huge space of opportunities for organized crime—and these opportunities were fully exploited.

In the immediate aftermath of the toppling of the regime, Iraq was also characterized by anomie. The concept of anomie, developed in the work of Emile

Durkheim and subsequently Robert Merton, has been surfaced most recently by Nikos Passas.[51] Anomie involves a degeneration of rules and norms and the emergence of forms of behavior unconstrained by standard notions of what is acceptable. For Durkheim, this typically resulted from a crisis or transition in society in which legal restraints are removed and the norms and inhibitions which had hitherto guided behavior are discarded.[52] Merton, in contrast, saw anomie as a result of a gap between aspirations in society and the availability of means to fulfill them. Passas, in some respects closer to Merton, focuses on the lack of opportunities to fulfill expectations. As defined by Passas, anomie is a withdrawal of allegiance from conventional norms and a weakening of these norms as guides to behavior.[53] For both Passas and Merton, the lack of congruity between expectations and the availability of the means to meet them typically results in social deviance or criminality.[54] In other words, the decline of behavioral norms and standards feeds into the spread of crime—both organized and disorganized.

Iraq reflects both Durkheim's notion of crisis and sudden change and the emphasis by Merton and Passas on the gap between expectations and opportunities. In Iraq, brutal authoritarianism, a series of wars, and deprivation had resulted in an erosion of social norms. Because of the fear created by the regime, this erosion was held in check and was not readily apparent. With the U.S. invasion and the toppling of the regime, however, what had been a long-term decline of social norms became a full-scale collapse. It was not simply that penalties for deviant or criminal behavior were suddenly removed; in Iraq something much more fundamental was at work. The aftermath of the collapse of the regime was characterized by the rejection of morality and decency by significant portions of the population; by a marked absence of respect for fellow citizens, who became simply targets to be exploited for financial gain; and by a readiness to engage in forms of behavior that are normally regarded as reprehensible. In short, Iraq witnessed the rise of anomie in a way that was comprehensive and brutal.

Anomie in Iraq went through two stages. The first was spontaneous and disorganized. According to a thoughtful piece published in *Oxford Analytica*,

> Following regime change on April 9, [2003,] law and order experienced a short-lived but complete collapse, resulting in a massive redistribution of almost any commodity, fixture, or fitting. As well as highly organized looting of banks and museums by regime security forces, this period of looting normalized criminal activity for a considerable period of time, creating huge markets for looted items.[55]

This disaster was followed, however, by a more restricted and controlled anomie which lacked the breadth of that immediately following regime change but in some ways was deeper and more serious. The second phase was characterized by an increased incidence of violence and sexual crimes and the consolidation of criminal organizations.[56] During both stages, the problem was almost certainly exacerbated by the former convicts who had been released under an amnesty by Saddam Hussein in October 2002. Estimates of the number of convicts released range from 30,000 to 100,000.[57] Regardless of the exact number, however, the former prisoners almost certainly added to the pervasive violence and intensified the insecurity of Iraq's population.

Such developments helped to ensure that post-conflict reconstruction in Iraq took place against a background of revenge and vendettas, a cycle of violence which, in turn, created a dynamic which proved difficult to overcome. The lack of accepted norms also resulted in a behavioral sink in which almost all forms of action became acceptable, short-term gain became prized over long-term mutuality, greed became unbounded, need was enormous, and creed sometimes defined the targets of violence. This behavioral sink encompassed politicians and bureaucrats, officials in the oil industry, political parties, sectarian factions, tribes, and many ordinary citizens. It was manifested in extensive corruption throughout government and security forces at all levels, in the debasement of almost anything and anyone to the level of mere commodities to be exploited for financial gain; and in collusive relationships among criminals, insurgents, officials, and businessmen.

None of this should be surprising. Iraq had suffered enormously since Saddam Hussein first came to power. He led them through three wars, and the regime's ruthless control of the country inhibited the development of civil society, the rule of law, and the attainment of personal and financial security. As one commentary notes, "Saddam's regime destroyed morality and legality, and in the 1990s the middle classes were shattered by sanctions. Furthermore, most of the population is very young and has grown up brutalized and traumatized by dictatorship and war, with little concept of the wider social good outside family, tribe, or sectarian community."[58] Not surprisingly, therefore, anomie as intensified by the persistence of major economic problems proved enduring in Iraq.

In fact, the massive dislocation of Iraq's economy caused by successive wars and sanctions became a systemic or structural problem that interacted with and compounded the difficulties created by political fragmentation and the anomie discussed above. Although the state of affairs improved briefly in the latter half of the 1990s as a result of the OFF program and expanding oil sales, progress was not sustained. The overall trend from the Iran-Iraq war onwards was down. It bears emphasis that prior to U.S. intervention, the Iraqi economy had "suffered 20 years of neglect and degradation of the country's infrastructure, environment, and social services."[59] In addition, the country's economy had

> . . . been degraded by the effects of a highly centralized and corrupt authoritarian government, sanctions, and by a command economy where prices played little role in resource allocation, and where the state (and in particular the ruling regime) dominated industry, agriculture, finance, and trade. In short, the country's rich potential for economic prosperity, including water, human capital, and the world's second largest oil reserves, were squandered by the past regime, which directed public resources and efforts at the military and its own preservation and enrichment.[60]

These events were reflected in the stark decline of per capita income from over U.S.$3,600 in the early 1980s to approximately U.S.$770-1,020 by 2001.[61]

Although many Iraqi citizens had developed their own coping mechanisms, these were also disrupted by the invasion. Indeed, the economic dislocation following the invasion contributed to high levels of unemployment. Estimates, according to the Iraq Study Group Report, "range widely from from 20 to 60 percent."[62] When underemployment is also taken into account, the situation resembled that of the former Soviet states during the transition period in the early 1990s when an economy which had enjoyed full employment—if often notional and unproductive—experienced rapid dislocation and high levels of unemployment. As in Russia in the 1990s, so too in Iraq a decade later high levels of unemployment ensured that involvement in criminal activity became an important safety net. Where the collapse of the state is accompanied by the breakdown of licit market structures and operations, illicit profit-making activities have enormous appeal even for those who are not part of existing criminal organizations. When legal markets do not function and are unable to meet peoples' needs, illegal markets flourish as alternatives. If people cannot find employment and economic opportunities in the legal economy, and cannot emigrate, then involvement in criminal activity is—by default—the only option. Thus,

> after the fall of the old regime, new forms of criminality emerged as the systems of power, control, and resource distribution collapsed. Tribal groups alienated from the previous regime . . . used the opportunity to obtain economic resources through illicit activities, including smuggling. New criminal networks . . . emerged to take advantage of the absence of state authority.[63]

Very useful to understanding this situation are distinctions made by Jonathan Goodhand. In his work on Afghanistan and other conflict and post-conflict scenarios, Goodhand distinguishes among the informal or coping economy, the criminal economy, and the conflict or insurgent economy.[64] He argues that in times of economic duress people develop a set of activities in what he terms the coping economy. During the period when sanctions were imposed on Iraq, this outlet became critical. At the same time, because of the sanctions-busting activity of the regime and its criminal allies, a large-scale criminal economy also developed. And because the coping mechanisms are little more than an inadequate safety net, the criminal economy began to look even more attractive. In this sense, the informal economy is a very natural gateway into the more lucrative criminal economy. The third economy is an insurgent or conflict economy in which groups with a political agenda use criminal activities as a means of fund-raising, and in which those who cannot find employment are easily recruited for activities such as the deploying of improvised explosive devices (IEDs).

There was very little the United States could do in the short term about these systemic and structural factors. They existed prior to the invasion and were not only deeply entrenched but also productive of powerful but negative synergies. Their impact was compounded by several coalition strategic blunders in the early days and months of the occupation. In effect, these blunders inadvertently encouraged or pressured people to move from the informal to the criminal economy and also led to much overlap between the well-established criminal economy and a burgeoning conflict economy.

The first mistake was allowing the looting spree to take place. Although there was hope that looting would serve as some kind of catharsis, it actually made things worse in several ways. The looting of ministries in Baghdad, for example, provided both a physical and symbolic confirmation of the collapse of state structures and institutions that greatly complicated the reestablishment of governance in Iraq. As George Packer observed, "The gutted buildings, the lost equipment, the destroyed records, the damaged infrastructure, would continue to haunt almost every aspect of the reconstruction."[65] Even more important was the psychological impact of a lawless environment with high levels of impunity for the perpetrators. In an environment characterized by enormous uncertainty, a lack of clear rules and norms, and the absence of constraints imposed by a strong central government, an apparent indifference to the looting gave the wrong kind of signal. Not only did it embolden criminals, but it also undermined faith in the occupation forces. The sense of disappointment, frustration, and insecurity in Basra was captured by Human Rights Watch (HRW) which interviewed local people, including merchants and doctors, who were dismayed and frightened by the looting and appalled by the inaction of the British troops.[66] The same kind of sentiment was also evident in Baghdad. Moreover, the failure to impose order at the outset made it much more difficult to impose later on.

Indeed, the early situation did not improve very much. Six weeks after the fall of Basra, according to HRW, people in the city felt "very insecure, due partly to the week of frenzied looting that immediately followed the British occupation, and continuing as a result of the lower intensity but steady crime wave (including daily killings, looting of private property, and car-jackings) now engulfing Basra."[67] Moreover, the "fear of violent crimes" was accompanied by "growing concerns about the failure of the coalition forces to provide . . . greater security."[68] Few other places offered the graphic firsthand reports obtained by HRW in Basra. Nevertheless, these sentiments were echoed in other cities in Iraq. Part of the problem was too few soldiers on the ground; the other was that those who were there were neither trained nor prepared for a role in which they were to provide law enforcement and protection for the population. U.S. forces had been designed to win the war, not to enforce the peace.

The second strategic blunder has received more attention than the first. On May 24, 2003, Ambassador Paul Bremer, the new head of the CPA in Iraq, signed a directive disbanding the Iraqi Army.[69] While there were some reasons for doing this, they were far outweighed by the negatives. At one level, this was an opportunity squandered: with a vacuum of power and authority in Iraq, the Army could have been used to maintain order. At another level, it was a fatal error: in a period of economic dislocation and unemployment, the addition of 400,000 specialists in violence to the mix was hugely detrimental. With few other opportunities available, these soldiers had one marketable skill — the application of violence. The impact was very similar to the disbanding of the KGB in Russia after the collapse of the Soviet Union: an army of "entrepreneurs of violence" was unleashed.[70] In Russia, these specialists of violence swelled the ranks of organized crime; in Iraq some of them joined or formed criminal organizations, while others became part of the opposition to the Coalition.

These blunders exacerbated rather than alleviated the structural conditions underlying the growth of organized crime. Not only did the CPA fail to understand the mix of opportunities on the one side and incentives and pressures for involvement in organized crime on the other, but its own combination of action and inaction enlarged the opportunities and increased the incentives and pressures — the very opposite of what was needed.

The situation was made even worse by structural divisions in Iraq that not only led to the emergence of violence but also encouraged several different actors to appropriate the methods of organized crime to fund their political programs and visions. These divisions were brought into bold relief by the power vacuum that followed the collapse of the regime. And although the United States tried to reestablish state structures and state authority, this proved a much more formidable and protracted task than anticipated. In part, this was because of the preexisting divisions in Iraq. These divisions had hitherto been suppressed but came to the fore in an anarchical environment in which the state could no longer provide security. Furthermore, as nonstate actors moved in to fill this vacuum, their need and desire for resources encouraged them to appropriate organized crime methods. In effect, this led to a second wave of organized crime which would overlap and intersect with the first wave but was distinct from it.

The Second Wave: Organized Crime and Conflict.

The structural divisions in Iraq had largely been hidden by the dictatorship of Saddam Hussein. With the fall of the regime, however, they complicated and undermined U.S. efforts at state-building. As Eric Herring and Glen Rangwala argue, Iraq was fragmented "along many axes."[71] As well as the obvious divisions separating Shiite, Sunni, and Kurdish groups, tensions arose between central and local government, between the neo-patrimonial state and the traditional patrimonialism of the Sunni tribes, between those who had benefited from Hussein's regime and those who had not, and between those who had secular visions of the future Iraqi state and those who wanted a theocracy.[72] In addition, Iraq suffered from a large gulf between the state and society, a gulf which became increasingly evident.[73] Without Saddam Hussein, internal divisions crystallized and widened. Although U.S. efforts to balance the long-term requirement of rebuilding the Iraqi state with the more immediate imperatives of establishing security and stability were sometimes successful in ameliorating tensions, at other times, wittingly or unwittingly, they made them worse.[74] One of the difficulties in Iraq was that individual interests took precedence over any notion of the collective interest.[75] And much as the United States tried to rise above the battle and represent the collectivity, this was not how it appeared to other actors. In effect, the U.S. military simply became what one observer called "the strongest tribe."[76]

The U.S. failure to reestablish law and order and create a sense of security had serious consequences going well beyond the initial looting and the activities of predatory criminal organizations. In an environment characterized by division and mistrust and the lack of a legitimate state, the pursuit of group security and self-interest became so compelling that it eliminated any vestigial concept of collective interest or identity. At the same time, the generation of resources by any means possible, including coercion, violence, and other forms of organized criminality, became critical to security and advancement. Just as anomie was important in the initial wave of post-Hussein organized crime, anarchy was important in generating the second wave and especially in the emergence of an insurgent or conflict economy.

The term anarchy in this context refers not to disorder or chaos but to the lack of a central dominant state authority. Where the population is divided by ethnic, tribal, or religious identities, such a situation can readily take on the characteristics of international anarchy in which a lack of trust and feelings of insecurity drive actors towards military action.[77] Moreover, the greater the insecurity, the more likely it is that factional groups within the society will take up arms either to protect their communities against hostile groups or to attack their rivals. As Michael Brown pointed out when analyzing ethnic conflicts during the 1990s, the security dilemma became a domestic phenomenon as well as an international one.[78] In Iraq this was worsened by the widespread availability of weapons. Although many people in Iraq already possessed weapons, large unguarded arms caches were distributed through the country and available for looting, allowing almost any group to arm itself. With U.S. military forces in Iraq lacking the manpower to maintain order, the dynamics of insecurity took on an even sharper edge.[79] The absence of a leviathan, therefore, resulted in a truly Hobbesian environment in which life for many citizens became solitary, nasty, brutish, and short.

This environment created an ideal opportunity not only for criminal enterprises but also for more politically oriented and violent nonstate actors. These entities engaged in behavior which was at times predatory, at times protective, and most often both.[80] It reflected two overlapping dynamics: the need and desire for proxies when the state does not fill its necessary functions, and the exploitation of the freedom provided by an absent or weak central authority. Where security is not provided by the state, the most ruthless members of the society, typically acting in both small and large groups, exploit the opportunity to engage in violent forms of capital accumulation with a high degree of impunity. This is particularly the case where some of the institutions of the state are still up for grabs and where there are natural resources that are nominally under state control. A variant of the "resource curse" certainly developed in Iraq, where control and exploitation of both the licit and illicit markets in oil and oil derivatives became a major bone of contention.[81]

At the same time, groups come into existence not only to exploit opportunities but also to meet needs. Ironically, the militias originated or (where they already existed) expanded largely because of the inability of the CPA and subsequently the Iraqi government to provide security to Iraq's Shiite majority. The militias' response to pervasive insecurity resulting from the state's lack of a monopoly on violence for several years made the restoration of centralized coercive power well nigh impossible. Both Sunni and Shiite armed groups engaged in sectarian cleansing. In effect, they provided a degree of protection and security for some segments of the population while intimidating or terrorizing other groups. And even those whom they protected often had to pay heavily for the service.

The result of this dynamic was the rise in Baghdad and other major cities of organizations that both exploited and aggravated the lack of governance and in turn contributed to the perpetuation of high levels of lawlessness and massive disorder. These organizations used criminal activities to generate funding to prosecute their causes, whether narrowly sectarian, jihadist, tribal, or nationalist. These self-funding mechanisms supported both the asymmetric conflict against U.S. military forces and the internecine warfare of Iraqi groups, factions, and tribes. The difficulty for the United States was how to break out of the vicious cycle in which the lack of law, order, security, and social control generated both opportunities and incentives for the development and consolidation of alternative power centers which had a vested interest in ensuring that law and order were never established by either coalition forces or the new Iraqi government.

In short, the internal dynamic created by the anarchy of a collapsed state in which factionalism, organized crime, sectarian conflict, and tribal antipathies fed on one another proved remarkably powerful. For the United States, responding to the organized crime outgrowth of the power vacuum of Iraq was impossible so long as the internecine violence and the attacks on U.S. forces continued. Yet, responding to these attacks would continue to have limited effectiveness so long as the resource generation opportunities were not stifled. Moreover, organized crime intersected with both sectarian conflict and hostility to American forces, compounding challenges to stability and governance. The intersections—insurgency, organized crime, and sectarian conflict—empowered resilient, highly networked adversaries, and confronted the United States with a situation far more complex than traditional insurgencies. Dilemmas and tradeoffs were inescapable, while even sound decisions generated adverse unintended consequences and cascading effects throughout Iraq.

One of these dilemmas revolved around security versus development. Because of the rise of violent armed groups in Iraq, the United States had little choice other than to give priority to security over reconstruction and development. The difficulty was that this approach perpetuated a situation in which violence became—among other things—an alternative source of employment. Widespread unemployment not only made organized crime attractive, but it also meant that even modest "financial incentives for participating in insurgent or sectarian violence" became "more appealing to military age males."[82] Some senior U.S. officers even suggested that the insurgency had relatively little to do with ideology and far more to

51

MIIS

do with economics.[83] Being part of the insurgency — if only on a part-time basis — paid far better than being a policeman or soldier. Evidence suggests that the close link between lack of employment and the growth of the insurgency was clearly understood by the military very early but was dismissed by the CPA, especially Ambassador Bremer. One former British official in Iraq recounts a meeting in which military suggestions that the economic problem was feeding into the security problem were summarily dismissed by Bremer.[84]

A closely related consideration is that the collapsed state led to a hiatus in the provision of services. Although the United States and nongovernmental organizations (NGOs) tried to fill this gap in the chaos after the toppling of the Ba'athist regime, they encountered major problems. Even after the CPA handed over authority to the Iraqis, the level of services remained inadequate. The centralized distribution of subsidized food and fuel continued, but services such as electricity, water, sewage, and garbage disposal were nonexistent or intermittent. The situation was not helped by the decline in administrative skills which had taken place under Saddam Hussein, by the absence of many of the most competent and skilled Iraqis who fled Iraq because of the dire security situation, or by the pervasive corruption which ran though successive governments. The result was that other service providers, often with a different agenda, arose to fill the vacuum left by the state. In particular, some of the militias which had arisen to fill the security gap also became important in filling the service gap. This was particularly true of the Mahdi Army, whose base of support was in slum areas in Baghdad, Basra, and other cities. The difficulty was that service provision is not politically neutral. The legitimacy of the post-Hussein Iraqi state was already in question because it appeared to be the creation of the occupying forces and was peopled by Iraqis who often lacked deep or wide popular support. In these circumstances, alternative service providers were— and are—a particular challenge to the state. As one analyst observes,

> groups reap three main benefits from providing public goods through their social welfare arms. First, the creation of a social welfare infrastructure highlights the failure of the state to fulfill its side of the social contract, thereby challenging the legitimacy of the state. Second, nonstate social welfare organizations offer the population an alternative entity in which to place their loyalty. Third, a group that gains the loyalty of the populace commands a steady stream of resources with which it can wage battle against the regime.[85]

In effect, the activities of alternative service providers exacerbated political fragmentation. They also added another impulse for nonstate groups to engage in criminal activities as a funding mechanism to provide the resources necessary to maintain their social welfare activities and structures.

In sum, with the second wave of organized crime in which violent nonstate actors were prominent, the criminal economy and the insurgent or conflict economy became increasingly interconnected. Some groups operated primarily in one economy rather than the other, but many began to straddle both. Cooperation occurred between criminal organizations on the one side and terrorist and insurgent organizations on the other; some groups pursued both political and financial agendas; and some individuals and groups were transformed by events or opportunities, in effect moving from one identity to another. Moreover, different actors overlapped and intersected in complex ways. If criminal activities in Iraq were as diverse as their perpetrators, three in particular stand out: the theft, diversion, and smuggling of oil; kidnapping; and extortion. Although these were the main moneymakers, they were accompanied by a series of supplementary activities, which are examined in the next three chapters.

ENDNOTES - CHAPTER 2

1. The notion of the "fierce" state is discussed in Nazih N. Ayubi, *Overstating the Arab State: Politics and Society in the Middle East*, New York: I. B. Tauris, 1996, especially chap. 12. For an excellent analysis of Iraq under Saddam which fits the notion of the fierce state, see Kanan Makiya, *Republic of Fear*, Berkeley: University of California Press, 1998.

2. Robert Klitgaard, "Three Levels of Fighting Corruption," Address at the Carter Center Conference on Transparency for Growth in the Americas, May 4, 1999, available at *www.cartercenter. org/news/documents/doc1193.html*.

3. See Stanley Pimentel, "Mexico's Legacy of Corruption," Roy Godson, ed., *Menace to Society: Political-Criminal Collaboration Around the World*, New Brunswick, NJ: Transaction, 2003, pp. 175-197. Peter Lupsha's concept of the elite exploitative model is discussed on pp. 180-181.

4. David E. Kaplan, "The Wiseguy Regime: North Korea Has Embarked on a Global Crime Spree," *U.S. News and World Report*, February 7, 1999, available at *www.usnews.com/usnews/news/ articles/990215/archive_000266.htm*.

5. *Ibid.*

6. Bilal A. Wahab, "How Iraqi Oil Smuggling Greases Violence," *Middle East Quarterly*, Vol. 13, No. 4, Fall 2006.

7. *Ibid.* See Kanan Makiya as quoted by Wahab.

8. See Robert Looney, "Beyond the Iraq Study Group: The Elusive Goal of Sustained Growth," *Strategic Insights*, Vol. VI, Issue 2, March 2007, available at *www.ccc.nps.navy.mil/si/2007/Mar/looneyMar07.asp*. It should be acknowledged, however, that there was inevitable overlap between the party militia and the tribes.

9. *Ibid.*

10. *Ibid.*

11. *Ibid.*

12. See Peter Andreas, "Criminalizing Consequences of Sanctions: Embargo Busting and Its Legacy," *International Studies Quarterly*, Vol. 49, No. 2, June 2005, pp. 335–360.

13. Charles Duelfer, *Regime Finance and Procurement, Comprehensive Reports of the Special Advisor to the DCI on Iraq's WMD*, Vol. 1, September 2004, p.22, available at *www.foia.cia.gov/duelfer/Iraqs_WMD_Vol1.pdf*.

14. Statement of Charles A. Duelfer, Special Advisor to the Director of Central Intelligence on Iraq's Weapons of Mass Destruction, Central Intelligence Agency, *The Oil-For-Food Program: Tracking the Funds*, Hearing Before the Committee on International Relations, House of Representatives, 108th Cong., 2nd Sess., November 17, 2004, Serial No. 108-157, Washington, DC: U.S. Government Printing Office, 2005, p. 8.

15. *Ibid.*

16. *Ibid.*

17. Duelfer, *Regime Finance and Procurement*, p. 28.

18. *Ibid.*

19. *Ibid.*, pp. 30-31.

20. Independent Inquiry Committee into the United Nations Oil-for Food Program, October 27, 2005, available at *www.iic.offp.org*.

21. *Ibid.*, p. 249.

22. Testimony of Lee Jeffrey Ross, Jr., Senior Advisor Executive Office for Terrorist Financing and Financial Crimes, U.S. Department of the Treasury, before the House Subcommittee on National Security, Emerging Threats, and International Relations, April 21, 2004, available at *www.treas.gov/press/releases/js1446.htm*.

23. Duelfer, *Regime Finance and Procurement*, p. 4.

24. *Ibid.*, p. 24.

25. Independent Inquiry Committee into the United Nations Oil-for-Food Programme, *The Management of United Nations Oil-for-Food Programme*, Vol. 1, September 7, 2005, p. 36. This is summarized very clearly in Christopher M. Blanchard and Kenneth Katzman, *Iraq: Oil-For-Food Program, Illicit Trade, and Investigations*, Washington, DC: Congressional Research Service, January 9, 2006, p. 15.

26. Testimony of Juan Carlos Zarate, Assistant Secretary Terrorist Financing and Financial Crimes, U.S. Department of the Treasury Before the Senate Permanent Subcommittee on Investigations of the Committee on Governmental Affairs, November 15, 2004, js-2100, available at *www.ustreas.gov/press/releases/js2100.htm*.

27. Duelfer, *Regime Finance and Procurement*, p. 10.

28. Andreas, p. 335.

29. *Ibid.*

30. Testimony of Juan Carlos Zarate, Assistant Secretary, Terrorist Financing and Financial Crimes, U.S. Department of the Treasury, in *How Saddam Hussein Abused the United Nations Oil-For-Food Program*, Hearing Before the Permanent Subcommittee on Investigations of the Committee on Governmental Affairs, United States Senate, 108th Cong., 2nd Sess., November 15, 2004, Washington, DC: U.S. Government Printing Office, 2005, p. 57.

31. Kanan Makiya, "All Levels of the Iraqi Government Were Complicit," *Middle East Quarterly*, Spring 2005, pp. 81-87.

32. *Ibid.*

33. Andreas, p. 354.

34. See "Use of Illicit Smuggling and Transportation Networks" in *Comprehensive Reports of the Special Advisor to the DCI on Iraq's WMD*, Vol. 1, September 2004, p. 137.

35. *Ibid.*, p. 139.

36. *Ibid.* It should be acknowledged, however, that in this instance, a significant portion of the proceeds almost certainly went to Kurdish parties and factions.

37. *Ibid.*

38. *Ibid.*

39. *Ibid.*

40. *Ibid.*

41. *Ibid.*, p. 142. The report also noted that smugglers remained subject to interdiction by Iranian authorities further south.

42. *Ibid.*

43. *Ibid.*, p. 137.

44. *Ibid.*

45. Andreas, p. 336.

46. *Ibid.*, p. 337.

47. *Ibid.*, p. 336.

48. *Ibid.*, p. 337.

49. Looney.

50. United Nations Office of Drugs and Crime, *Addressing Organized Crime and Drug Trafficking in Iraq: Report of the UNODC Fact Finding Mission 5-18 August 2003*, Vienna, Austria: August 25, 2003, p. 7.

51. For an excellent summary of the evolution of the concept of anomie, see *The Durkheim and Merton Page* at Middlesex University, London, United Kingdom, available at *www.mdx. ac.uk/WWW/STUDY/yDurMer.htm*. For a more recent and very incisive analysis, see Nikos Passas, "Global Anomie, Dysnomie, and Economic Crime: Hidden Consequences of Neoliberalism and Globalization in Russia and Around the World," in *Social Justice*, Vol. 27, No. 2, 2000, pp. 16-44.

52. *Ibid.*

53. Passas, p. 20.

54. *Ibid.*, p. 19.

55. "Iraq: Serious Crime Thrives on Instability," *Oxford Analytica*, March 17, 2004.

56. *Ibid.*

57. United Nations Office of Drugs and Crime, p. 5, puts the figure at 30,000; while L. Paul Bremer, *My Year in Iraq*, New York: Simon and Schuster, 2006, p. 260, puts the figure at "almost 100,000" after having described it as "tens of thousands" on p. 75.

58. "US/UK/IRAQ: Corruption Hurts Effort to Rebuild State," *Oxford Analytica*, April 21, 2006.

59. *UN/World Bank Joint Iraq Needs Assessment*, October 2003, p. vi, available at *siteresources.worldbank.org/IRFFI/Resources/Joint+Needs+Assessment.pdf*.

60. *Ibid.*

61. *Ibid.*, p. vi.

62. *Iraq Study Group Report*, p. 23.

63. United Nations Office of Drugs and Crime, p. 5.

64. Jonathan Goodhand uses the terms coping, shadow, and combat economies. See "Frontiers and Wars: The Opium Economy in Afghanistan," *Journal of Agrarian Economy*, Vol. 5, No. 2, April 2005, pp. 191-216. See also David S. Ramirez, Student Thesis, *Gaining Control of Iraq's Shadow Economy*, Monterey, CA: Naval Postgraduate School September 2007, pp. 20, 61-69.

65. George Packer, *The Assassins' Gate*, New York: Farrar Strauss and Giroux, 2005, p. 139.

66. Human Rights Watch, *Basra: Crime and Insecurity Under British Occupation*, Iraq, Vol. 15, No. 6, June 2003, available at *hrw. org/reports/2003/iraq0603/Iraq0603.pdf*.

67. *Ibid.*, p. 3.

68. *Ibid.*

69. Bremer, pp. 53-59, 223-224, 235-236.

70. Vadim Volkov, *Entrepreneurs of Violence: The Use of Force in the Making of Russian Capitalism*, Ithaca, NY: Cornell University Press, 2002.

71. Eric Herring and Glen Rangwala, *Iraq in Fragments*, Ithaca, New York: Cornell University Press, 2006, p. 2.

72. *Ibid.*, pp. 127-129, 136-137, for a fuller discussion of traditional patrimonial society and the neo-patrimonial state.

73. *Ibid.*, pp. 55-66.

74. *Ibid.*, p. 207.

75. The importance of this point has been established by

William Reno, *Warlord Politics and African States*, Boulder, CO: Lynne Rienner, 1999.

76. Bing West, *The Strongest Tribe*, New York: Random House, 2008.

77. Neo-realists see international anarchy as the key to understanding international relations. See, in particular, Kenneth Waltz, *Theory of International Politics*, New York: McGraw-Hill, 1979.

78. Michael E. Brown, ed., *Ethnic Conflict and International Security*, Princeton, NJ: Princeton University Press, 1993. See also Oren Barak, "Dilemmas of Security in Iraq," *Security Dialogue*, Vol. 38, No. 4, pp. 455-475.

79. On this failure, see *Operation Iraqi Freedom: DOD Should Apply Lessons Learned Concerning the Need for Security Over Conventional Munitions Storage Sites to Future Operations Planning*, Washington, DC: U.S. Government Accountability Office, March 22, 2007.

80. William Reno, "Protectors and Predators: Why Is There a Difference among West African Militias?" Louise Andersen, Bjorn Moller, and Finn Stepputat, eds., *Fragile States and Insecure People?: Violence, Security, and Statehood in the Twenty-First Century*, New York: Palgrave Macmillan, 2007, pp. 99-122.

81. For a good discussion of the "resource curse," see Nicholas Shaxson, "Oil, Corruption and the Resource Curse," *International Affairs*, Vol. 83, No. 6, 2007, pp. 1123-1140.

82. Department of Defense, Report to Congress, *Measuring Security and Stability in Iraq*, November 2006, p. 13.

83. Richard A. Oppel, Jr., "Iraq's Insurgency Runs on Stolen Oil Profits," *New York Times*, March 16, 2008.

84. Rory Stewart, *The Prince of the Marshes*, Orlando, FL: Harvest, 2006, p. 114.

85. Alexus G. Grynkewich, "Welfare as Warfare: How Violent

Nonstate Groups Use Social Services to Attack the State," *Studies in Conflict & Terrorism*, Vol. 31, 2008, pp. 350–370.

CHAPTER 3

THE THEFT, DIVERSION, AND SMUGGLING OF OIL

STRUCTURAL FACTORS

The previous chapter described not only the deep roots of organized crime in Iraq but also two distinct waves of organized crime since 2003. Yet there has been one particular factor in criminality from the 1990s onwards that merits special attention: the importance of oil. Under Saddam Hussein, some oil was sold outside the United Nations (UN) sanctions; since 2003 the theft, diversion, and smuggling of oil has become a major moneymaker for criminal organizations intent on acquiring wealth for its own sake, and for insurgents, terrorists, and militias intent on funding their campaigns of violence. It has also become a source of conflict. The connection between conflict and natural resources became evident in many conflicts in Africa during the 1990s. In Iraq, much of the conflict among competing factions as well as organized criminal activities and corruption are related to oil. Indeed, the "resource curse" hangs over Iraq in the same way that diamonds helped fuel the conflict in Sierra Leone, that coltan (widely used in cell phones) worsened the conflict in Congo, and that coca and cocaine intensified and perpetuated the conflicts between government, insurgents, and paramilitary forces in Colombia.

In Iraq, oil extraction and sale are a central government monopoly, in theory and law to be controlled by government organizations. The current organizational structure was established in 1987.[1] Formally a pyramid with the Minister for Oil at the apex, the oil sector is in practice managed by several distinct state-owned and state-run companies with considerable independence from one another and a high degree of autonomy. According to Amy Jaffe, "For all practical purposes, North Oil Company and South Oil Company are run as autonomous companies with their own management structures increasingly responding to regional leadership."[2] The North Oil Company has eight fields in and around Kirkuk, whereas South Oil Company's main fields include Rumaila.[3] Contract and refurbishing issues are the responsibility of the State Company for Oil Projects, while State Oil Marketing Company (SOMO) oversees exports of crude and imports of refined products.[4] The infrastructure itself encompasses oil fields, separation plants, three major refineries to turn crude oil into fuel products, 7,000 kilometers of pipeline, the Al-Basra Oil Terminal (ABOT), which is the country's major port for oil and other goods, and export pipelines to Turkey and Syria.[5] Although the infrastructure is impressive in scope, it suffers from years of neglected upkeep. The pipelines and the refineries are vulnerable to theft and sabotage, while refinery personnel, company employees, and ministry officials are susceptible not only to infiltration and intimidation by insurgents or criminals, but also to the blandishments of corruption and bribery. Collusion between insiders and outsiders is almost commonplace.

Part of the problem is organizational fragmentation. Management is distributed among several companies, and little or no effort is made to coordinate, let alone integrate, activities. As the Inspector General of the Oil Ministry notes in the *Second Transparency Report*, the oil sector as a whole suffers from lack of overall management, while control and oversight activities are ineffectual or nonexistent.[6] This provides enormous opportunities for corrupt and criminal activities. Transportation of oil and its derivatives from one area to another, for example, is not subject to adequate coordination, let alone close supervision. Consequently, significant discrepancies between the volume of oil dispatched and the volume delivered are common-place. Political involvement in many transactions makes them even murkier. Indeed, the government monopoly over oil combined with a lack of transparency and an absence of accountability mechanisms have created multiple opportunities for theft, diversion, and smuggling, all of which are facilitated by generalized corruption.[7]

Given the impact of neglect, war, and terrorist attacks since 2003, Iraq's failure to restore earlier production levels of both crude and refined products or even to meet its modest output targets was inevitable. The shortfalls have been quite significant. In addition, although by September 2008 the government had a draft hydrocarbon law, as of early 2009, it had not succeeded in passing legislation which would provide a predictable, equitable, and stable legal framework for investors.[8]

Another serious problem in Iraq's oil sector is the role of organized crime. This is in part a legacy of the oil smuggling during the sanctions era, and in part the result of contextual and structural factors which facilitated the further criminalization of the oil industry after Saddam Hussein had been toppled. Critical to this process were the vested interests of those who had become involved in smuggling oil out of Iraq during the sanctions. Those who had established lucrative smuggling routes and methods did not want to relinquish them simply because of the fall of the regime and the American occupation. Activities which had once been controlled by authoritarian leadership degenerated into a free-for-all involving insiders and outsiders, officials and criminals, tribes and militias, former regime elements, and new players. There is nothing mysterious about this. In a society where economic opportunities were limited, the oil business was the exception. As one close observer noted,

> You really have to think about the oil as just being dollars buried under the ground or buried in a pipeline or coming out of a refinery. . . . It's like printed money. Imagine if in the middle of the night that you could just grab some metal tool and poke it into a pipeline where there is no security, drain out oil, put it into a truck, drive it somewhere, and become a millionaire in one day.[9]

Such incentives were increased by the gap between growing demand for refined oil products on one side and limited supply on the other. Demand was fed by an increasing number of cars as well as the need for fuel for electric generators which were essential, given the virtual collapse of the national power grid and the difficulties and setbacks encountered by the restoration effort. Supply was limited by a decaying and decrepit infrastructure, terrorist and insurgent attacks on the pipelines and depots, and limited refinery capacity. At the same time, the price of fuel oil and gasoline at the pumps was heavily subsidized. As a result, gasoline in Iraq was much cheaper than in neighboring countries. As one report notes, "These subsidies burden the state budget and require selling imported fuel at a loss. They also create arbitrage opportunities which foster smuggling and black market activity."[10] This was true both domestically and regionally, leading to theft and diversion for both the domestic black market in fuel and the smuggling of fuel from Iraq to its neighbors. The *Second Transparency Report* notes that the largest price discrepancies existed between Iraq, Syria, Jordan, and Turkey (which has some of the highest gasoline prices in the world because of the taxes imposed), in some cases more than 50-fold.[11] These price differentials—and the high profit margins accompanying them—created what Nikos Passas broadly terms "criminogenic asymmetries," which provide both incentives and opportunities for criminal activities.[12] Buying low at the official price or diverting and stealing gasoline and other fuels, and then selling high at black market prices in Iraq or at world prices overseas, became a very attractive proposition.

If diversion, theft, and smuggling of oil were driven by growing demand, limited supply, and the desire to exploit arbitrage opportunities, these activities were facilitated by the lack of standardized measures, the absence of meters or gauges on pumps and tankers, and the lack of oversight on those involved in the supply chain. According to one analysis, three different kinds of meters are used to measure oil flows: positive displacement meters, which measure "the rate at which compartments of known volume are filled with the liquid or gas"; turbine meters, which are pipes with spinners that "measure the volume that passes through"; and ultrasonic meters, which use "sound frequencies to measure flow rates."[13] Although American companies—most notably Kellog, Brown and Root (KBR) and Parsons—were contracted to provide meters, this process proved a lot more protracted and difficult than was expected, with the corporate performances leaving much to be desired. Consequently, opportunities for the theft and smuggling of oil remained. One oil expert described it as being like a supermarket without a cashier: "There is no metering . . . at the well heads. . . . There is no metering at any of the major pipeline junctions."[14] Even in instances when meters were installed, they have not always been calibrated, and the reliability of measurements has been low. In these circumstances, documentation has been the only potential constraint on criminal activities, and with widespread corruption, false documentation has become the norm rather than the exception.

The absence of meters meant excessive reliance on the honesty and integrity of officials and workers in the oil industry. Yet, in many instances these qualities have been lacking — with environmental anomie being a prime cause. The degeneration of ethical norms and standards in Iraqi society became especially evident in the oil industry. In a period of enormous uncertainty about the future and given the prevailing culture of lawlessness, many of those in the oil sector became interested primarily in personal and private gain. Notions of collective responsibility were abandoned, and actions for the public good were rare. For some individuals and groups, the goal became getting rich; for others, the goal was simply getting by. For yet others, the proceeds from corruption and crime in the oil sector provided the funds for campaigns of violence against the United States and the Iraqi government as well as against rival factions. Skimming money was also used as a funding mechanism for political parties which nominally accepted the new system and were willing to work within it, albeit corruptly, rather than through resort to violence.[15] This was particularly important in the South.

In all instances, however, the dynamics of corruption played a large part. Where corruption is widespread, there is often a bandwagon effect as those who are not already corrupt try to ensure they also obtain a piece of the pie. It was once noted, in the Russian context, that when an institution is pervaded by corruption, those who do not participate are regarded with suspicion and distrust by those who are involved.[16] The insidious consequences of this psychological irony are difficult to overestimate. Corruption has a highly dynamic quality that is all too often ignored, but which helps to account not only for its perpetuation but also for its expansion. This characteristic can apply at both the individual and group levels and can be understood in part as a manifestation of the anomie phenomenon described above. Moreover, when the future is highly uncertain, short-term gain—by whatever means—becomes an overwhelming imperative. The system also becomes self-perpetuating, provoking persistent complaints about an "oil smuggling mafia" which skims profits and determines the allocation of administrative posts in the ministry.[17]

Whether these complaints reflect genuine ethical concern or resentment at being excluded is uncertain. Whatever the case, corruption is closely linked to coercion designed to protect corruption networks and activities. One former oil minister, echoing the mafia allusion above, has claimed that "oil and fuel smuggling networks have grown into a dangerous mafia, threatening the lives of those in charge of fighting corruption."[18] As a result, the oil ministry itself has been embedded in a miasma of fear and intimidation. The extent of the problem was perhaps best illustrated in August 2007 when Deputy Oil Minister Abdul Jabbar al-Wagga and four of his staff were kidnapped by Shiite rivals of the Oil Minister and held for 2 weeks.[19]

In addition to these internal problems, the oil sector suffered from the vulnerability of its infrastructure to attack by terrorists or insurgents and to theft by groups which found it relatively easy to tap into the pipelines. Sometimes it was difficult to distinguish one from the other. On some occasions, attacks on oil pipelines were attributed to regime disruption by terrorists or insurgents when in fact they were the work simply of criminals seeking to ensure that oil and gasoline continued to be moved by trucks, as this increased the opportunities for diversion, theft, and smuggling.[20]

In some cases, those who were expected to protect the pipelines became the perpetrators of criminal or terrorist activities. The most blatant example of this involved Al Juburi, an influential tribal leader and former parliamentarian who in 2004 was employed by the Defense Minister to protect the Baiji to Kirkuk pipeline. The attacks intensified in 2005, not least because one of Juburi's commanders organized some of them. Moreover, Juburi put "ghost soldiers" on his payroll and kept the money that was supposed to be used for their salaries and equipment.[21] Although such blatant cases have become less frequent, the problem continues. According to the Northern Oil Company, which operates the Kirkuk field, one of its pipelines was tapped into 39 times between January and mid-September 2007.[22] The problem was equally acute in southern Iraq. In 2005, for example, one southern pipeline was found to have more than 20 illegal taps, allowing tanker trucks "to top up their loads at will."[23] In late 2007 it was estimated that there were at least 25 "holes" in the pipeline, which were being used to fill tanker trucks which would then illegally carry the oil to neighboring countries.[24]

A detailed analysis of the Iraqi oil industry and its vulnerabilities to diversion, theft, and smuggling was published by the Inspector General of Iraq's Oil

Ministry in the *Second Transparency Report*.[25] The most striking aspect of this report is its portrayal of the many vulnerabilities and the wide diversity of ways in which these vulnerabilities are exploited. Perhaps equally salient, although not discussed in the report, is the diversity of the perpetrators. As the UNODC report of 2003 noted, those involved in criminal activities in the oil sector make up "a complex and often overlapping network of former sanctions avoidance networks, tribal groups, and individual entrepreneurs."[26] To these could be added politicians, bureaucrats, sectarian factions, and criminal organizations. The exact mix differs depending on local conditions and the exact products being smuggled. One observer has suggested, in fact, that there are three distinct kinds of illicit activity which need to be differentiated from one another.[27] In addition, there are variations in diversions, theft, and smuggling in terms of routes and methods as well as the players involved.

IRAQI CRUDE

The smuggling of crude oil occurs in several different ways. The first is through the mingling of what might be termed official and unofficial oil. In effect, legal oil shipments are covertly topped up with additional oil for which separate illegal payments are made. The second is through illegal oil bunkering, which evades government control and surveillance of tanker-carried oil exports. Boats and small ships are filled with stolen oil which is later transferred to larger tankers at sea for long-distance transport. This method is extensively used in the Niger Delta in southern Nigeria and has also been used in southern Iraq. The third method is through the use of tanker trucks.

The first method requires a great deal of involvement by corrupt officials. Such involvement ranges from acquiescence through connivance or facilitation to the organization and control of smuggling. Regarding smuggling of crude through the Al-Basra oil terminal, for example, it has been suggested that "officials at Iraq's state-owned South Oil Company (SOC) that extracts the crude, and at SOMO that pipes the crude to the terminals, would have to know about smuggling, even if they were not benefiting."[28] In addition, "tanker operators would also have to be part of smuggling schemes. They would sign receipts for a lower quantity than they actually receive, and pay the extra directly to the smugglers."[29]

For the recipient of the stolen oil, such schemes can prove very lucrative. According to one oil tanker captain with extensive involvement in the smuggling trade, the profits from one trip with a rented tanker are enough to buy the tanker.[30] He added that deals are made in advance with members of a political party who ensure that "their" officials are manning the oil terminal when the tanker arrives. "Once the tanker is filled," according to this tanker captain, "another official usually arrives—a surveyor hired by the government to inspect the cargo—who is bribed to pass everything off as legitimate."[31] If official documentation is provided, the tanker can sail normally through the Gulf and, if stopped by American or British patrols, is allowed to proceed even if "carrying twice the stated shipment."[32] If official documentation is not supplied, the tanker sails through Iranian waters, carries an Iranian flag, and bribes the Iranian coastguard.[33] The oil tanker captain does not worry about the Iraqi navy, which is "involved in the party."[34] Such schemes have the virtue of simplicity, ease, and speed, while also involving significant amounts of oil.

In contrast, oil bunkering is messier and more complex but also allows the involvement of small-scale smugglers, including local fishermen who have found it difficult to maintain their livelihood in post-Hussein Iraq.[35] Often obtained from tapping the pipelines, the oil is "emptied into small makeshift tanks in the Abu al-Khasib area, the deep river that leads to the Gulf."[36] From this area, the oil is taken in minute quantities to tankers at the mouth of the Gulf on al-Faw peninsula. From there, it is carried to refineries in such countries as the United Arab Republic (UAR), Yemen, or even India. Such actions are risky, with the prospects for interdiction more acute. In one sting operation, for example, 24 outlets were closed, and 166 boats and ships were seized.[37] Overall, however, the sporadic enforcement has had little impact, not least because of the ability of smugglers to counter enforcement efforts and reduce risks by bribing the right people.

The third method is overland smuggling using trucks. In April 2006, for example, Iraqi police seized 400,000 barrels of crude oil that was being smuggled into Syria, often relying on forged documents and facilitated by the complicity of government officials in both countries.[38] Dawud al-Baghistani, head of the Commission on Public Integrity in Mosul, explained that "while the ring was connected to insurgents," those involved "included officials from customs and the ministries of oil, interior, and finance, as well as some private companies. Smugglers offered Baghistani, who coordinated the sting, one million dollars "to release the $28 million shipment."[39]

How much oil is stolen, diverted, or smuggled by these methods is impossible to determine. Indeed, estimates of oil smuggling as a whole are highly elastic and enormously controversial. Even the range of possibilities in terms of barrels per day varies from one expert to another. There are also important differences between the estimates provided by different departments and agencies in the U.S. Government as well as between U.S. and Iraqi figures. In 2007, for example, the U.S. Government Accountability Office (GAO) issued a report on Iraq's oil and electricity sectors in which it noted a discrepancy between the State Department's estimates of crude oil production (2.1 million barrels per day) and exports (1.5 million barrels per day) in 2006 and the estimates provided by the Department of Energy, which suggested a level of production that was between 100,000 and 300,000 barrels fewer per day.[40] A GAO official subsequently suggested that "inadequate metering, reinjection, corruption, theft, and sabotage account for the discrepancy, which amounts to $5 million to $15 million daily or about $1.8 billion to $5.5 billion per year."[41]

The GAO report, however, had been leaked to the *New York Times* prior to publication. In a careful analysis, James Glanz focused on the discrepancy of between 100,000 and 300,000 barrels per day, suggesting that smuggling was one possible explanation.[42] The Iraqi Ministry of Oil was incensed, with a spokesman noting that (1) the GAO report was based on "incorrect performance information that was published by the mass media away from all sources from the Iraqi Ministry of Oil"; (2) that it confused oil derivatives and crude oil; and (3) that it relied on "operational data" with "no relationship to financial accounting."[43] The Ministry also dismissed allegations of crude oil smuggling as based "on accounting discrepancies, not on forensic evidence of smuggling rackets."[44]

There was something to the Ministry spokesman's rebuttal. Discrepancies in production estimates, as such, are certainly not sufficient evidence of large-scale theft, diversion, or smuggling. Nevertheless, the rebuttal was not entirely credible.[45] Claims that "the smuggling of crude oil is very complex and is almost beyond the economic capabilities of smugglers" ignore the role played by corrupt officials and politicians in facilitating the trade.[46]

Anecdotal evidence — including press interviews with those directly involved as well as those trying to counter the problem — reveals that smuggling of crude oil is a serious problem which reduces Iraq's export earnings, adds to the challenges of reconstruction in the oil industry, lines the pockets of corrupt officials, and helps to fund at least some of the violence that has wracked Iraq since the large-scale uprising in April 2004. The difficulty comes in efforts to move from anecdotal evidence to precise or even imprecise estimates. This is true of most criminal markets and is particularly the case in an industry where gauges and meters to measure legitimate production and flows are absent or inadequate. As the Inspector-General for the Oil Ministry acknowledged, the lack of a central database as well as the absence of measurement and computational systems means that there is "no accurate information and reports on the values and quantities of smuggled crude oil and oil products."[47]

Such gaps not withstanding, it is clear that the theft and smuggling of oil is very lucrative — and is prized by competing groups and factions. Basra, in particular, witnessed an intense and often violent struggle over the distribution of spoils from oil smuggling. Violence has sporadically occurred among competing Shiite parties and factions seeking to control oil facilities and outlets. Indeed, during the years since the U.S. invasion, the struggle to control the port and to dominate theft, diversion, and smuggling opportunities has become intense. In what has been described as "a legal vacuum, where the state is absent, law enforcement is nonexistent, and the spoils are shared by politicians, militias, and smuggler gangs," violence is inevitable.[48] Conflict in Basra was reminiscent of that in the Ukrainian city of Odessa in the mid-1990s when the mayor and the oblast governor became locked in a struggle for the "rents" (smuggling and extortion profits) associated with the oil flows through the port. The dispute in Odessa was intensified by a proposed new oil terminal. Each political party was allied with a criminal organization, giving the struggle a distinctly violent quality.[49] Kidnappings, shootings, and beatings became part of the repertoire of political competition in the city, much as they have in Basra.

Port cities, such as Shanghai, Naples, Marseilles, and New York, have long been infamous as incubators of organized crime.[50] The main difference in Basra is that the prize is particularly lucrative. Not only are "nearly 80 percent of Iraq's 115 billion barrels of proven reserves, the third largest in the world, . . . buried in or around Basra," but also the port has become the single most important transshipment point for Iraq's oil exports.[51] Continued attacks on the northern pipeline have ensured that most of Iraq's oil exports go through the port in Basra.[52] Such realities make control over Basra key. Whoever controls the provincial government—and/or has strong enough militias—has charge over the oil industry there and holds sway over the unknown amounts of oil and fuel sidetracked to the smuggling racket.[53]

The main protagonists in Basra, however, were religion-based parties and factions, each of which has control over some of the local power structures.

In some ways there was considerable continuity with the Hussein regime. Although many of the players changed, the game remained much the same. As one smuggler commented, "We use the same methods we used during Saddam," but "instead of Ba'athists and generals, it is now Shia militias and their cronies who are doing the business."[54] It was also a business which continued to be assisted by Iraq's neighbors, particularly Iran. Numerous incidents occurred in which Iranian coast guard and naval vessels protected Iraqi smugglers, allowing them to take refuge in Iranian territorial waters in exchange for payment.[55] But whereas under Saddam Hussein oil smuggling had taken place under the auspices of the regime, the business in Basra became much more diversely sponsored and thus competitive. One report even suggested that:

> Basra is a case study of Iraq's multiple and multiplying forms of violence. These often have little to do with sectarianism or anti-occupation resistance. Instead, they involve the systematic misuse of official institutions, political assassinations, tribal vendettas, neighborhood vigilantism, and enforcement of social mores, together with the rise of criminal mafias that increasingly intermingle with political actors.[56]

Most important, the violence is "fundamentally related to the battle over oil," whether the legal trade or the smuggling business.[57] When the SOC director, for example, ordered his senior managers to avoid contacts with Mahdi army militias, the response was a bomb attack on a feeder pipeline.

It appears that the Fadhila Party, which won 21 of the 41 seats in the 2005 elections, developed considerable influence over smuggling operations in Basra. The Party not only controlled the Oil Ministry but also took control of the Oil Facilities Protection (OFP) service, which according to Kenneth Katzman put it "in a position to really control how much is or is not smuggled."[58] The OFP made oversight and investigation very difficult, regularly blocking "foreign contractors and military personnel from entering the Rumaila oilfields."[59] In addition, Fadhila controlled the Tactical Support Unit which, in 2005, was reportedly the best trained unit in the police. Fadhila supporters also controlled the port of Abu al-Khassib.[60] In May 2006, however, when al-Maliki announced his new cabinet, Fadhila lost control of the Oil Ministry.[61] Fadhila also faced growing competition from political and religious rivals increasingly aware of the profits to be made from oil smuggling and wanting a slice of the pie. The situation was complicated — at least until the government offensive in March 2008 — because Muqtada al-Sadr's militia dominated the local police force and made inroads into the Facilities Protection Service and the Basra port authority as well as the Abu Flus port traditionally used for illegal exports of crude oil.[62] The Supreme Islamic Iraqi Council's (SIIC) Badr militia was also a powerful force in the city.

Another player in the oil smuggling business was the Thaar Allah (God's Revenge) organization. Led by Yussif al-Mussawi, Thaar Allah has been described as everything from a political party to a warlord-run fiefdom to a death squad. Whatever description is used, it is clear that Thaar Allah had close ties to units in the Basra police force. Indeed, the Department of Internal Affairs, the Criminal Intelligence Unit, and the Serious Crimes Unit all had personnel working with Thaar Allah in carrying out contract killings and attacks on British forces.[63] Thaar Allah was also believed to be responsible for killing women who did not adhere strictly to Moslem dress codes. As the Iraq Oil Minister subsequently noted, Thaar Allah was involved in "kidnapping, extortion, and several smuggling rackets including oil."[64]

Part of the problem was that each of the parties and factions had its own power base in the city, but no one party was dominant. In effect, there were separate groups sharing power in a context where the rules were unclear and the profits immense. Moreover, each group was prepared to use violence to maintain or enhance its position. In effect, the parties were acting more like "criminal gangs than political forces, and the gap between political and paramilitary activity" was blurred.[65] Tensions sometimes erupted into violence, with triggers taking various and sometimes surprising forms. When Fadhila replaced a Sadr supporter with one of its own people as head of the local electricity department, for example, this sparked a series of violent clashes.[66]

The clashes between SIIC's Badr organization and elements of the Mahdi Army became particularly intense in the summer of 2007. In August, two SIIC governors were assassinated and 52 people killed in Karbala during clashes between Mahdi and Badr militias. In October, however, al-Hakim, leader of SIIC, and Muqtada al-Sadr, agreed to preserve and respect "Iraqi blood under any condition."[67] Even when these more overt clashes were avoided, however, "influential actors" engaged in violence and abduction on a daily basis.[68]

There were few constraints either on the violence or the theft and smuggling of oil. Law enforcement authorities in Basra were both divided and weak. The Iraqi Navy lacked the resources to catch oil smugglers, and was limited in its jurisdiction by the Coast Guard, which was controlled by the Ministry of Interior and infiltrated by the militias. Indeed, elements in both the Navy and Coast Guard were almost certainly complicit in smuggling operations. This was also true of the police. Indeed, the "web of different security forces with allegiances to different factions or militias" undermined law enforcement and extended clashes between the militias into the police and other agencies.[69] There were even instances in which police units fought one another on behalf of their respective militias. The situation was further complicated by militia members defecting to rival organizations for higher payments. Turf wars, attacks on party headquarters, and armed clashes were common in Basra. Although the city was largely spared the insurgency, it nonetheless "descended into chaos and violence that threatened to unravel the region's progress."[70]

In spite of claims that "influential political people and parties [were] running these smuggling operations" in Basra, tribes and clans were among the main smuggling groups, albeit with political protection and support.[71] Some tribes established protection rackets "co-located with major oil fields."[72] The involvement of others was more direct. The Ruwaymi, Ashur, and Yusif clans were among those believed to be heavily involved in smuggling.[73] The Ashur clan, consisting of about 50 families, took over the Abu Flas port after the invasion and "became the quasi-official authority there."[74] They also built underground oil tanks on their farms, where "fuel tankers [emptied] their cargoes to be pumped later into small pontoons."[75] One estimate suggests that they made about $5m a week from such bunkering, although at one point, when challenged by a rival clan, they were paying about $250,000 a week to gunmen for protection.[76] In addition, they had protection from both Fadhila and the Mahdi army which controlled Abu Flas and levied taxes on the smuggled oil—sometimes in exchange for false documentation which made the smugglers less vulnerable to arrest.[77] Significantly, in early 2008, the Ashurs were mentioned again as important smugglers along with the Kattan family and the Marwini family.[78]

It is therefore plausible that the oil smuggling was "run by clans and controlled by militias." [79] According to one estimate, the militias took about 30 percent of the profit.[80] Other reports, however, suggest that the political parties were more directly involved. Allegations were made, for example, that the Fadhila Party in the spring of 2007 was offering "pilfered oil for $10-12 a barrel."[81] It was typically resold by traders who shipped it to Dubai and sold it for $30 a barrel.[82] According to this report, traders could expect only a 4 percent return, with the rest of the money going to Fadhila and the militias.[83] Although it is not clear that Governor Muhammad Mosabeh al-Waeli, a member of the Fadhila Party, was directly involved in oil smuggling, his brother, Ismail al-Waeli, allegedly emerged as one of the most important smugglers in Basra.

It is not clear that the parties and militias confined themselves strictly to taxing the smuggling, when the profits from direct involvement were much higher. Certainly, party and militia involvement provided a high degree of impunity for those directly involved in the smuggling process and for those— including officials within the Oil Ministry providing false documentation—who facilitated the process.[84] Members of a local nongovernmental organization (NGO), the Basra Centre for Reconstruction, identified about 50 cases in which senior police officers facilitated smuggling operations which moved about $50 million worth of oil over a 2-year period.[85]

Although some arrest warrants were issued and cases sent to court, this had little impact. One member of the countersmuggling directorate explained simply that small smugglers had been arrested, "but we have been prevented from even watching the big gangs by verbal orders from our administration. . . . These big gangs are linked to government institutions and the parties."[86] In other words, theft and smuggling of oil in Basra was deeply entrenched within a web of political parties and militias which gave the smugglers high-level protection. Indeed, in Basra in 2007 it was not clear where politics ended and crime and oil smuggling began. The oil Minister described it as a "web of interrelations" in which gangs colluded with "local officials, powerful parties, or militias."[87]

The climate of impunity, however, began to change in early 2008, as the central government initiated an effort to regain control over Basra's oil wealth. The oil facilities protection force was replaced by a new unit in the Ministry of Interior. This was followed by a military offensive launched by al-Maliki in March 2008 known as Charge of the Knights. Prior to this assault, the government had a list of 200 smugglers it sought to arrest or put out of business. These included the governor's brother, Ismael al-Waeli, who reportedly escaped to Kuwait, as well as leading figures in Sadr's organization in Basra.[88] The governor retained his position in spite of suspicions of involvement in the illicit oil business.

Though the offensive was not an unqualified success, it appeared to have reduced the smuggling. Minister of Oil Shahristani claimed that the offensive "cleansed large swaths on both sides of Shatt al-Arab that were being used to smuggle oil products and other materials."[89] Portrayed by the Iraqi government as simply an attempt to clamp down on crime and smuggling, the offensive in Basra was, in part, a clash between the Badr organization, which had been integrated into the Iraqi army, and the Mahdi Army. It was perhaps an effort to influence who controlled and benefited from oil smuggling rather than to stop it altogether. Nevertheless, it had an impact—at least in terms of reducing the power and influence of the Mahdi Army and in establishing a greater degree of order and stability in the south. The offensive did little or nothing, however, to deal with other dimensions of the oil smuggling problem.

FRAUD, THEFT, AND SMUGGLING OF IMPORTED FUEL

Although Iraq is a major oil producer, in the period after the U.S. intervention, the limits to its refining capacity, the shoddy state of its infrastructure, and attacks by terrorists and insurgents on pipelines and facilities compelled the government to buy refined fuel from its neighbors. According to the SOC, for example, Iraq had to import daily more than 10 million liters of petrol, diesel, and kerosene from Iran, Kuwait, Saudi Arabia, and Turkey in order to meet its needs.[90] This was a novel experience for Iraq and was poorly managed. Supervision was lax and oversight was nonexistent, while the volume of imports and the number of tanker trucks coming into Iraq was overwhelming. In 2005, an estimated 200,000 Turkish trucks entered Iraq, a number that far exceeded the "supervisory and control capacities available."[91] This provided all sorts of opportunities for abuse and exploitation, especially theft, fraud, and smuggling.

The first set of problems was related to the imports themselves. In some instances, the oil deliveries were little more than phantom shipments. All the documentation was provided, and it appeared that the fuel shipments had been received when, in fact, they had not. A variant on this scheme was delivery (and acceptance) of less fuel than specified. To work effectively, the scheme required corruption and connivance at the distribution end and at the receiving warehouses. Indeed, export companies and transport contractors played an "essential role" in fraud of this kind.[92] According to the Oil Ministry Inspector General, this kind of fraud occurs in the two northern outlets (products imported from Turkey), and in the southern land outlet (products imported from Kuwait).[93]

The truck drivers themselves also devised a series of smuggling methods and scams to obtain illegal profits. In some instances, oil to be imported into Iraq was sold in Turkey, Syria, and Jordan, with the drivers then entering Iraq with a partial load that was subsequently topped off with cheap local fuel and delivered as imports.[94] In other schemes, drivers modified the container to ensure that there was oil product at the inspection opening while most of the tank was filled with water.[95]

Another option was for truckers to sell the imported fuel on the black market where they could receive a much higher payment. In effect, they were exploiting the arbitrage opportunities provided by a government distributing fuel at a highly subsidized and therefore artificially low price. As one commentary noted, in 2005 subsidized diesel was sold by the government for less than three cents a gallon, which meant that:

a 9,000-gallon tanker truck carried fuel officially worth around $250. But the same fuel was worth perhaps a dollar a gallon on the black market. Consequently, according to a report done for the oil industry, even after paying $500 for protection money or police bribes and $800 for the truck driver, a smuggler could make at least $7,450 by bringing in fuel from Jordan, Syria, or Turkey.[96]

Truckers were willing to cooperate with "smuggling gangs, pay bribes or use forged papers to inflate the value of their load, tamper with their fuel meters, or simply turn their loads over to the gangs."[97] Moreover, the whole process was lubricated by pervasive corruption at facilities and within ministries. This allowed truckers to obtain both access to the fuel itself and false documentation about the amount of fuel picked up or delivered.

Even when fines were imposed, these were very modest compared to the profits. In one case cited by the Oil Ministry Inspector General, between September 1, 2004, and February 15, 2005, 1,551 trucks carrying 56 million liters of oil products (gasoline, oil, and imported white oil), the import cost of which was $28 million, left Basra for the central and southern provinces but never arrived at their destinations.[98] Although the carriers were fined $4 million, this still left a profit of $24 million—even if the fines were paid.[99]

Money could also be made through reexporting the imported fuel. As one commentary noted, "smugglers siphon off a significant amount of the government subsidized fuel to sell back overseas at full price." The Ministry of Oil estimated the value of this trade at $800 million.[100] Estimates also suggested that "as much as 30 percent of imported gasoline [was] promptly stolen and resold abroad by smugglers."[101] Some of the gasoline was moved offshore while some was smuggled across Iraq's land borders with its neighbors. The distribution of fuel stations was skewed towards border regions, and this enhanced the capacity for smuggling. Whatever the methods, however, the Iraq government's reluctance to end fuel subsidies provided major incentives for theft, diversion, and smuggling.

Theft of Locally-Produced Gasoline.

Theft, diversions, and smuggling were not limited to crude and imported fuel. Products such as gasoline and kerosene refined in Iraq itself were also tempting targets for criminals. Iraq has three main refineries: the Daura refinery near Baghdad, the Basra refinery, and, most significant, the Baiji refinery. As the largest of Iraq's refineries, Baiji has been a target for corruption, infiltration, and attacks, as a result of which it has operated at well below capacity. The January 2007 Special Inspector General for Iraq Reconstruction (SIGIR) report indicated that at least some of the oil storage facilities in the Baiji refinery were under "insurgent control."[102] In June 2007, the Department of Defense (DoD) quarterly report on Iraq acknowledged that as much as 70 percent of the Baiji refinery output was diverted to the black market and that Strategic Infrastructure Battalions and Facilities Protection Services which had responsibility for the protection of the oil sector were believed to be complicit in theft and smuggling.[103] These diversions were estimated to cost Iraq two billion dollars per year. Efforts by the government to counter the activity seemed to have little impact. In 2005, the Oil Ministry fired 450 employees on suspicion of fuel theft; yet this did not staunch the illegal diversions and sales.[104]

As one commentary points out, the refineries are characterized by systemic corruption at almost all levels of operation.[105]

> Refinery workers routinely allow tankers to pick up fuel without any paperwork, which makes it easy to sell off the books. Police officers demand bribes of as much as $1,000 to let tankers pass through checkpoints or for 'protection' along routes, the officials say. And some government officials work directly with smugglers or secretly own gas stations and fuel trucks, giving them a share of money earned through illicit sales.[106]

In some cases, the smuggling is so blatant that the authorities feel compelled to act. In September 2006, the official in charge of the Baiji refinery's oil distribution was arrested after allowing 33 tankers in 1 day to receive fuel without authorization and paperwork.[107] In January 2007, a senior transportation official was arrested for trying to help smuggle out seven tankers of heavy fuel oil.[108] In February 2007, members of the 82nd Airborne and Iraqi forces became directly involved in overseeing operations at the refinery in what was named Operation Honest Hands.[109] This was followed by investigations of "senior officials from the Baiji city council, the local police force, and the provincial and national governments."[110] Senior Iraqi officials, however, continued to protect their clients, pressuring U.S. forces to abandon certain investigations and to release certain people.[111] Moreover, the risk of Iraqi military forces becoming corrupted and also accepting payoffs is very real.[112] Although some improvements have clearly been made at Baiji, the problems have not been solved. Moreover, the difficulties of providing security on the roads to and from the refinery, although less acute, have not been eliminated.

Indeed, it appears that a regional black market has grown up around Baiji. For example, the number of gasoline stations near Sharqat, a 1-hour drive from Baiji, has increased from 8 in 2003 to more than 50.[113] According to one official, the refined fuel "is not going to the stations" but to the black market. He explains:

> Gas stations are often built just to gain the rights to fuel shipments, at subsidized government rates, that can be resold onto the black market at higher prices. New stations cost more than $100,000 to build, but black market profits from six or seven trucks can often cover that cost, and everything after that is profit, said officials who have studied the scheme.[114]

Bribes of $20,000 were reportedly paid to the Ministry of Oil official who had to approve the documentation for the gasoline stations, while local and provincial officials demanded payment as well.[115] The regional officials also provide protection for those who divert and sell black market fuel.[116] Unlike the situation at Basra, those involved in the illicit oil business still operate with a high degree of impunity.

Oil Smuggling and Violence in Iraq.

In sum, the theft, diversion, and smuggling of oil and oil products became almost a national pastime in Iraq. Given the central role of oil in the Iraqi economy — much akin to the role of opium in Afghanistan's economy — the involvement of various actors who overlap and intersect in complex and often covert ways is almost inevitable. At some levels, oil theft and smuggling support family subsistence in an economy characterized by high levels of unemployment and economic dislocation. For example, "bakers, brick makers, and even fishing boat operators find it more profitable to sell fuel, which they receive at subsidized prices, to illicit traders rather than operate their businesses."[117] In addition, many young people are attracted to the smuggling business because it is seen as a relatively easy way of making money.[118] In many cases, however, powerful mafias quickly co-opt them, forcing them to cooperate or face the consequences.[119] At other levels, the beneficiaries are the entrenched political authorities. In the north of Iraq, for example, where until 2007 trucking was "the primary means of export due to pipeline closures, the two main Kurdish parties continue to draw extensive revenues from their historic trade in subsidized local oil sold on the external market at inflated prices."[120] Some of the tribes there also used pipeline sabotage as a not-so-subtle form of extortion for employment opportunities protecting the pipeline.

The illicit oil business is related directly to funding violence against the Iraqi government, U.S. forces, and political rivals. Diversion, theft, and smuggling are linked not only to criminal organizations, but also to insurgents and militias. As one analysis notes, attacks on the oil pipeline, "once thought to be only a tool for insurgents to undermine the government, . . . have evolved into a lucrative money-making scheme for insurgents and enterprising criminal gangs alike."[121] Similarly, the Inspector General's *Transparency Report* observes that the attacks were designed to force the government to import and distribute fuel using tanker trucks — which offer far more opportunities for smuggling.[122] In some cases, the attacks were timed precisely to allow the flow of sufficient oil to enable the Baiji refinery to operate but not enough to feed the export terminals to Turkey.[123] In a similar vein, the pipeline between the Baiji refinery and the al-Dura refinery was also a target for attack, requiring the government to use trucks to supply several Iraqi cities — once again providing opportunities for various thefts, diversion, and other money-making schemes.[124]

In 2006 Ali Allawi, Iraq's finance minister, estimated that insurgents were obtaining between 40 and 50 percent of the profits from oil smuggling.[125] He also claimed that insurgents had infiltrated senior management positions at Baiji and that intimidation of truck drivers was the norm. "This allows the insurgents and their confederates," he continued, "to tap the pipeline, empty the trucks, and sell the oil or gas themselves."[126] Allawi even claimed that the smuggling had gone "beyond Nigeria levels" and that "the insurgents are involved at all levels."[127] Other officials have made similar assessments. In January 2007, the Iraqi government announced that militants were taking most of the $1.5 billion a year stolen from the Baiji oil refinery through smuggling and corruption.[128] As one minister put it, "We are losing $1.5 billion at Baiji refinery alone, and most of this money is channeled to terrorists who are using it to target us and target our nation."[129] The governor of Salahaddin, the province in which Baiji is located, put it more graphically, claiming that "the fuel that is stolen comes back as bombs, mortar shells, and Katyusha rockets."[130] There have even been reports that Sunni insurgents, including al-Qaida in Iraq, have obtained funds through stealing fuel shipments "for re-sale in Jordan as a means of financing themselves."[131]

U.S. assessments have agreed on the importance to the insurgency of corruption, theft, smuggling, and extortion linked to Iraq's oil sector. A government report leaked to the *New York Times* in November 2006 estimated that Iraqi militants obtained $25 million to $100 million a year by stealing tankers full of fuel, smuggling oil to other countries, kidnapping oil-sector workers for ransom, and charging protection money from truckers and gas station owners.[132] The insurgents disrupted oil and fuel distribution by attacking depots and refineries, but also obtained payments in exchange for refraining from attacks. The Islamic Army in Yusifiya, for example, obtained protection money for not attacking the depots.[133] The implication was that the capacity for violence can sometimes be more effective than the violence itself, making oil-related extortion a lucrative activity. This is also true of the roads where insurgents demanded payments from tanker truck drivers for safe passage.

Sunni insurgents have not been the only armed groups to benefit from crimes linked to the oil industry. The gasoline retail sector, including filling stations, has also been criminalized by Shiite militias as well as Sunni insurgents. Although subsidies for gasoline were in effect, refinery problems and supply chain difficulties meant that fuel was "often unavailable at the state-mandated price" or required a very long wait.[134] With filling station owners typically receiving quotas of 100,000 liters of fuel a week and subject to little oversight, it was more profitable to sell gasoline on the black market.[135] One report in early 2007, for example, suggested that gas station owners often sold out of "jerrycans on the street" because "prices in these illicit transactions" could reach "almost three times the mandated price."[136]

Although this was very attractive for suppliers, it meant that ordinary Iraqis had to pay much higher prices for fuel. The payments also benefited "corrupted militiamen."[137] Many of the gasoline filling stations were dominated by Shiite militias which imposed "levies on fuel products sold to the public."[138] They were able to do this by "by placing their loyalists at the head of filling stations in major cities," including Baghdad.[139] It was also reported "some Iraqi National Guard troops" were involved in these rackets, taking a cut of the inflated profits in exchange for protection of the illegal activity."[140]

In addition, "diesel, kerosene, and liquid gas, which Iraqis use for cooking and heating," were sold primarily through the black market, yielding enormous profits.[141] According to an assessment carried out by the Central Organization for Statistics and Information Technology at the Ministry of Planning, about "40 percent of the gasoline consumed annually in Iraq was purchased on the black market."[142] In 2005, $1 billion was spent on black market fuel markets (which include gasoline, white oil, gas oil, and liquid gas) by Iraqi households.[143] The real cost of the fuels, however, was less than 20 percent of the sale price. In other, words, about $800 million "went straight into profits for those who run the illicit network."[144] These profits were shared among several levels of black market dealers. Their opportunities have since been constricted as the Iraq government—largely under pressure from the International Monetary Fund—has reduced subsidies for imported fuel oil. Nevertheless, continued problems with violence and corruption, which impede effective, efficient, and reliable distribution of fuel, mean that the black market will not disappear anytime soon.

The smuggling ecosystem has helped fund a significant part of the violence in Iraq.[145] In some cases — the killing or kidnapping of workers trying to repair damaged pipelines or the murder of members of the Oil Ministry's Inspector General's office investigating corruption and criminality in the oil industry — the violence is designed to protect the system. In others — as was clear in the discussion of Basra above — the issue has related more to the distribution of spoils in the system.

In all cases, however, the central government has been hurt. As one observer notes,

> The gravity of the smuggling phenomenon resides in the fact that the smuggled goods are either stolen (without any payment), or are obtained at the official rate (which does not represent 5% of the real cost, as a result of subsidies). Hence, the losses are sustained directly by the public treasury, unlike other countries where smuggling represents for the most part a loss of taxes and duties only with respect to smuggled goods and products."[146]

Corruption and crime in the oil sector deprive the Iraqi government of revenues while funding a significant portion of the violence and disorder in Iraq. Another observer notes, "While problems associated with subsidies and oil industry corruption may seem mundane amidst continued kidnapping and car bombs, until U.S. and Iraqi authorities manage to constrain Iraqi oil smuggling, violent crime and insurgency will continue to flourish."[147] This is not to suggest that oil smuggling is the only source of revenue for Iraq's armed groups. These groups have also excelled at kidnapping.

ENDNOTES - CHAPTER 3

1. For a good overview, see Amy Myers Jaffe, *Iraq's Oil Sector: Past, Present and Future*, Houston, TX: James A. Baker III Institute for Public Policy, Rice University, March 2007.

2. *Ibid.*, p. 38.

3. *Ibid.*

4. *Ibid.*

5. Government Accountability Office, *Rebuilding Iraq: Serious Challenges Impair Efforts to Restore Iraq's Oil Sector and Enact Hydrocarbon Legislation*, Statement of Joseph A. Christoff, Director International Affairs and Trade, Testimony Before the Subcommittee on the Middle East and South Asia and the Subcommittee on International Organizations, Human Rights, and Oversight, Committee on Foreign Affairs, House of Representatives, July 18, 2007. See pp. 4-5 for a brief but useful overview of the infrastructure. Hereafter cited as Christoff.

6. See Iraq Oil Ministry, Office of the Inspector General, *Second Transparency Report*, p. 14, sect. 2.2.3, available at *www. iraqrevenuewatch.org*.

7. *Ibid.*

8. For an excellent overview of investment in Iraq, see "Foreign investment in Iraq, Study by Dunia," March 12, 2009, available at *www.ameinfo.com/188298.html*.

9. Amy Myers Jaffe, quoted in "KTVT Investigation: Lack of Metering at Terminals Funnels Billions into Hands of Corrupt Officials and Insurgents," CBS News, February 10, 2007.

10. Policy Recommendations from Discussions at the London Conference, "Iraqi Oil Wealth: Issues of Governance and Development," Meeting Sponsored by the Open Society Institute, London School of Economics, June 29 to July 1, 2005, p. 16, available at *www.iraqrevenuewatch.org/reports/073105.pdf*.

11. See *Second Transparency Report*, p. 8, sect. 2.1.

12. Nikos Passas, "Globalization and Transnational Crime: Effects of Criminogenic Asymmetries," in Phil Williams and Dimitri Vlassis, eds., *Combating Transnational Crime*, London, United Kingdom: Frank Cass, 2001, pp. 22-56.

13. Pratap Chatterjee, "Mystery of the Missing Meters: Accounting for Iraq's Oil Revenue," March 22, 2007, available at *www.corpwatch.org/article.php?id=14427*.

14. Mike Morris, quoted in "KTVT Investigation."

15. The author is grateful to Dr. Lawrence Cline for this observation.

16. This comment was made by Alexandre Konanykhine, who also probably coined the term "mafiocracy." For his perspective, see Alex Konanykhin, *Defiance*, New York: Renaissance Publishing, 2006.

17. Robert F. Worth and James Glanz, "Oil Graft Fuels the Insurgency, Iraq and U.S. Say," *New York Times*, February 5, 2006.

18. Former Oil Minister Ibrahim Bahr al-Ulum, quoted in *Al Hayat. Ibid.*

19. One of the staff members was released sooner. See Reuters, "Kidnapped Deputy Oil Minister Freed in Iraq," August 28, 2007.

20. James Glanz and Robert F Worth, "Attacks on Iraq Oil Industry Aid Vast Smuggling Scheme," *New York Times*, June 4, 2006.

21. Worth and Glanz, "Oil Graft Fuels."

22. See "Oil and Corruption in Iraq," *Environment News Service*, September 21, 2007, available at *www.albionmonitor.com/0709a/iraqoilcorruption.html*.

23. Yaseen al-Rubai'I, "Corruption Draining Oil Industry," *Iraqi Crisis Report* No. 121, April 19, 2005, *Institute of War and Peace Reporting*, available at *iwpr.gn.apc.org/?s=f&o=244850&apc_state=heniicr200504*.

24. "Integrity Commission: Reveals Details About Oil Smuggling," *Badr Newspaper*, November 22, 2007.

25. *Second Transparency Report*, p. 7.

26. United Nations Office of Drugs and Crime (UNODC), *Addressing Organized Crime and Drug Trafficking in Iraq*, New York: UNODC, p. 6.

27. Chatterjee.

28. *Ibid.*

29. *Ibid.*

30. Ghaith Abdul-Ahad, "Oiling the Wheels of War: Smuggling Becomes the Real Economy of Iraq," *The Guardian*, June 9, 2007.

31. *Ibid.*

32. *Ibid.*

33. *Ibid.*

34. *Ibid.*

35. Haider al-Musawi, "Basra Fishermen Smuggle Subsidized Fuel," Iraqi Crisis Report No. 178, May 24, 2006.

36. Abdul-Ahad, "Oiling the Wheels of War."

37. *Second Transparency Report*, p. 5.

38. Wahab.

39. *Ibid.*

40. *Rebuilding Iraq: Integrated Strategic Plan Needed to Help Restore Iraq's Oil and Electricity Sectors*, Washington, DC: U.S. General Accountability Office, May 2007, pp. 24-25.

41. Christoff.

42. James Glanz, "Billions in Oil Missing in Iraq, U.S. Study Says," *New York Times*, May 12, 2007.

43. Iraqslogger, "Oil Official Slams GAO on 'Smuggling' Report. Ministry: Crude Racketeering Unlikely—If MNF Does Its Job," May 16, 2007, hereafter cited as "Oil Official Slams GAO."

44. *Ibid.*

45. Other estimates indicate that the figures might be higher. Mike Morris, for example, suggests that "between 200,000 and 500,000 barrels a day are probably unaccounted for." See "KTVT Investigation."

46. The quotation is from "Oil Official Slams GAO."

47. *Second Transparency Report*, p. 4.

48. Abdul-Ahad, "Oiling the Wheels of War."

49. See Phil Williams and John Picarelli, "Organized Crime in Ukraine: Challenge and Response," *Trends in Organized Crime*, Vol. 6, No. 3 and 4, pp. 100-142.

50. On this point, the author is grateful to Dr. Peter Lupsha, Professor Emeritus, University of New Mexico, Albuquerque, NM.

51. Ben Lando, "Shia Parties Battle for Control of Oil-Rich Basra Region," *UPI*, August 18, 2007.

52. *Ibid.*

53. *Ibid.*

54. *Ibid.*

55. See Abdul-Ahad, "Oiling the Wheels of War"; and Wahab.

56. International Crisis Group, *Where is Iraq Heading? Lessons From Basra*, Middle East Report No. 67, June 25, 2007, p. i.

57. Reidar Visser, quoted in Lando.

58. Kenneth Katzman, quoted in Lando.

59. "Iraq: Shia Factional Struggles Threaten Stability," *Oxford Analytica*, June 19, 2006, hereafter cited as "Shia Factional Struggles."

60. Ghaith Abdul-Ahad, "Welcome to Tehran—How Iran Took Control of Basra," *The Guardian*, May 19, 2007, available at *www.guardian.co.uk/Iraq/Story/O,,2083387,00.html*.

61. "Shia Factional Struggles."

62. International Crisis Group, *Where is Iraq Heading?* p. 12.

63. Max Fuller, "State-Sanctioned Paramilitary Terror in Basra Under British Occupation," Global Research, August 8, 2008, available at *www.globalresearch.ca*.

64. Oil Minister Sharistani, quoted in Sam Dagher, "Basra Strike Against Shiite Militias Also About Oil," *Christian Science Monitor*, April 9, 2008.

65. Anthony Borden, "Battling for Power in Basra," *Institute for War and Peace Reporting: Iraqi Governance Report,* Issue 2, August 2007, p. 2.

66. IWPR, "Basra's Struggle for Power and Wealth: Militias Compete like 'Mafia Families' over Oil Rackets and Public Resources," *Iraqslogger*, August 12, 2007.

67. "Iraq: Overlapping Conflicts Strain Unity," *Oxford Analytica*, October 8, 2007.

68. IWPR, "Basra's Struggle for Power and Wealth."

69. Abdul-Ahad, "Welcome to Tehran."

70. Raheem Salman and Borzou Daragahi, "Violence in Basra Rooted in Oil Smuggling: Shiite Militias Fighting for a Piece of the Lucrative Trade, Officials Say," *Los Angeles Times*, July 7, 2006.

71. Wahab.

72. *Ibid.*

73. Abdul-Ahad, "Oiling the Wheels of War."

74. *Ibid.*

75. *Ibid.*

76. *Ibid.*

77. *Ibid.*

78. "Moussa Faraj Accuses Parliament Integrity Committee Chief And Fadhila Party of Being Corrupt," *Al Mowaten Newspaper*, February 11, 2008.

79. "Oil and Corruption in Iraq" *Environment News Service*, September 21, 2007, available at *www.albionmonitor.com/0709a/iraqoilcorruption.html.*

80. Abdul-Ahad, "Oiling the Wheels of War."

81. Robert Baer, "Who is stealing Iraq's oil," *Time*, May 17, 2007, *www.time.com/time/world/article/0,8599,1622785,00.html.*

82. *Ibid.*

83. *Ibid.*

84. *Ibid.*

85. Institute for War and Peace Reporting, "Smuggling Thrives in Basra," *Iraqi Crisis Report*, No. 232, September 7, 2007, available at *www.iwpr.net.*

86. *Ibid.*

87. Dagher.

88. *Ibid.*

89. *Ibid.*

90. Institute for War and Peace Reporting.

91. Office of the Inspector General, Oil Ministry, Iraq, *Smuggling Crude Oil and Oil Products: Second Transparency Report.*

92. *Ibid.,* p. 28.

93. *Ibid.*

94. *Ibid.,* p. 30.

95. *Ibid.*

96. Glanz and Worth, "Attacks on Iraq Oil Industry Aid Vast Smuggling Scheme."

97. *Ibid.*

98. Office of the Inspector General, *Smuggling Crude Oil and Oil Products.*

99. *Ibid.,* p. 19.

100. Chatterjee.

101. Glanz and Worth, "Attacks on Iraq Oil Industry Aid Vast Smuggling Scheme."

102. EnerPub, *Iraq: Energy Profile,* September 14, 2007, available at *www.energypublisher.com.*

103. *Measuring Stability and Security in Iraq,* June 2007 Report to Congress in accordance with the Department of Defense Appropriations Act 2007, June 7, 2007, p. 13.

104. For the number of firings, see Wahab.

105. See Abdul-Ahad, "Oiling the Wheels of War."

106. Yochi J. Dreazen, "US, Iraq Launch Campaign To Cut Oil Smuggling," *Wall Street Journal,* March 15, 2007.

107. *Ibid.*

108. *Ibid.*

109. *Ibid.*

110. *Ibid.*

111. *Ibid.*

112. *Ibid.*

113. Richard A. Oppel, "Iraq's Insurgency Runs on Stolen Oil Profits," *New York Times,* March 16, 2008.

114. *Ibid.*

115. *Ibid.*

116. *Ibid.*

117. Glanz and Worth, "Attacks on Iraq Oil Industry Aid Vast Smuggling Scheme."

118. "Oil and Corruption in Iraq," *Environment News Service,* September 21, 2007, available at *www.albionmonitor.com/0709a/ iraqoilcorruption.html.*

119. *Ibid.*

120. "Iraq: Infrastructure Seizure Reflects Central Power Ebb," *Oxford Analytica,* August 29, 2007.

121. Glanz and Worth, "Attacks on Iraq Oil Industry Aid Vast Smuggling Scheme."

122. *Second Transparency Report*, p. 22.

123. Glanz and Worth, "Attacks on Iraq Oil Industry Aid Vast Smuggling Scheme."

124. Kathleen Ridolfo, "Iraq: Oil Woes Continue," *Radio Free Europe/Radio Liberty*, January 4, 2006, available at *www.rferl.org*.

125. Glantz and Worth, "Oil Graft Fuels the Insurgency."

126. *Ibid.*

127. *Ibid.*

128. "Iraq Says Rebels Make $1 Billion a Year from Refinery," *Reuters*, January 14, 2007.

129. *Ibid.*

130. Quoted in Dreazen.

131. "Iraq: Infrastructure Seizure Reflects Central Power Ebb."

132. John F. Burns and Kirk Semple, "Iraq Insurgency Has Funds To Sustain Itself, U.S. Finds," *New York Times*, November 26, 2006, p. 1.

133. Abdul-Ahad, "Oiling the Wheels of War."

134. "Fuel Prices Shift in Recent Weeks: Black-Market Prices Higher than Official Rates in All but One Sampled Province," *Iraqslogger*, October 1, 2007.

135. Dreazen.

136. "Baghdad's Black Markets in Fuel: Prices Can Be Nearly Three Times the Official Rate," *Iraqslogger*, March 12, 2007.

137. Abdul-Ahad, "Oiling the Wheels of War."

138. Nidhal al-Laithi, "Factions Vie for Oil Deals to Finance Activities," *Azzaman*, November 3, 2007. See also Ridolfo.

139. Naidal al-Laithi; *ibid*.

140. "Baghdad's Black Markets in Fuel."

141. Glanz and Worth, "Attacks on Iraq Oil Industry Aid Vast Smuggling Scheme."

142. *Ibid*.

143. *Ibid*.

144. *Ibid*.

145. On the notion of the ecosystem, see John Robb, *Brave New War*, New York, Wiley, 2007, pp. 176-179, although he uses it in relation to licit rather than illict business.

146. *Second Transparency Report*, p. 4.

147. Wahab.

CHAPTER 4

KIDNAPPING IN IRAQ

Nature of the Business.

As discussed in Chapter 3, criminal activities in Iraq related to oil are highly complex. Kidnapping in Iraq, if anything, is even more convoluted than oil and petroleum smuggling. Kidnapping is both a highly profitable activity and a form of asymmetric warfare for the weak against the strong; it empowers the perpetrator and demeans the victims; sometimes it garners international attention but most often it occurs in relative obscurity; it can end in death and tragedy or relief and celebration. In Iraq it is often unclear who is responsible for particular kidnappings, how and why specific individuals are targeted, or why some kidnap victims are killed while others are released unharmed. Furthermore, obtaining an accurate assessment of the scale and scope of the kidnapping industry in the country is well-nigh impossible since most kidnap victims are Iraqis, and the reporting of these abductions—either to the authorities or in the press—is fragmentary at best.

Similarly, identifying trends in Iraqi kidnapping is complicated by under-reporting, the absence of a centralized repository of kidnapping incidents, and what, with a few exceptions, appears as the indifference of the Western news media. Kidnapping of Iraqis, unlike the kidnapping of foreigners, rarely results in much publicity, let alone the headlines and outrage generated by the abduction of foreigners. Consequently, the gaps in information and knowledge are enormous. As one official at the U.S. Embassy in

Baghdad acknowledged, the most that can be done is a "tip-of-the-iceberg analysis."[1]

Nevertheless, it is indisputable that kidnapping in post-Hussein Iraq was both a major "growth industry" and a highly profitable activity for criminal organizations, indigenous insurgents, and terrorists associated with the global jihad.[2] Although there is a long tradition of kidnapping in Iraq and elsewhere in the Middle East, the phenomenon expanded enormously amid the chaos and disorder following the U.S. invasion in March 2003. The lack of a legitimate central government; the weakness, corruption, and sectarian infiltration of the police; the general sense of lawlessness; the spread of anomie; and ruthless opportunism, as well as the availability of a large and highly vulnerable target population or victim pool, contributed to the massive upsurge of kidnappings from mid-2003 onwards.

In one sense, kidnapping in Iraq became a fashion, creating bandwagon effects that were not entirely surprising given the lack of legitimate employment opportunities, the poverty of many Iraqis, and the potential for alleviating that poverty through kidnapping. To criminals concerned about money, kidnapping was a means of income redistribution in a society that had been subjected to massive economic dislocation and the constriction of licit opportunities. In 2004, it also emerged as a form of empowerment in the face of occupation, a way of getting the attention of foreign governments while elevating the offending group's status in the resistance to the occupation.

Western views of kidnapping in Iraq, however, have been distorted by an overly narrow focus on the high profile kidnapping of foreigners and a lack of attention to the daily kidnappings of significant numbers of Iraqis. Yet Iraqis are the primary victims, and, although it is impossible to provide an accurate estimate of how many Iraqis have been abducted, even in the most conservative estimate they vastly outnumber foreigners.[3] Indeed, there appears to be an almost inverse relationship between the pervasiveness and impact of the kidnappings and the attention given to them in the western press. Certainly for kidnapping organizations concerned about profit rather than politics, seizing Iraqis is the bread and butter business that yields substantial profit with very low risk. It is important, therefore, to go beyond the kidnapping headlines and to look at the realities on the ground — which include multiple motives, perpetrators, and targets.

Kidnapping in Iraq has several distinct dimensions. First is motivation. Different kinds of kidnapping are determined largely by the motivations of the perpetrators. Although the main focus in this chapter is economic or for-profit kidnapping rather than political kidnapping, the distinction between the two is not as clear as it initially appears. Sometimes it is impossible to determine whether a kidnapping is primarily about money or about politics. Indeed, it is often apparent only in retrospect — and sometimes not even then — as to which category of kidnappings a particular abduction belongs. As one commentary noted, "Abductions are sometimes lucrative criminal enterprises, sometimes brutal aspects of sectarian violence, and sometimes a tangled mix of the two."[4]

Kidnapping occurs in a world of smoke and mirrors characterized by violence, brutality, duplicity, arbitrary decisions, large and small payoffs, and enormous human misery. Activities which initially appear to be politically inspired sometimes turn out to be primarily about profit, while ransom demands have frequently been made even though the person kidnapped has already been killed. In some instances—such as that of Baghdad businessman Abu Sufiyan whose family paid $120,000 for his freedom—the ransom made no difference, and he was killed anyway.[5]

Many kidnapping groups display enormous cruelty, yet some give gifts to their victims as they are being released. In some cases, victims are kept in absolute squalor and constricted confinement, and are subjected to frequent beatings; in others, they are treated with a degree of compassion and, within the bounds of confinement, are allowed to participate in the domestic lives of their captors. In some cases, a kidnap victim is passed from one group to another, usually for payment. In many instances where ransom payments are involved, there is a remarkable degree of flexibility on the part of kidnapping gangs who start off with exorbitant demands yet accept much less. In other words, kidnapping like most other criminal activities and criminal markets, is subject to enormous variations in both form and content.

After looking at different kinds of kidnapping, this study focuses on the perpetrators, highlighting not only the variety of participants in the kidnapping business but also the way in which different kidnapping groups sometime make strange bedfellows. It then traces the evolution of kidnapping in the period from mid-2003 to the present, noting the ways in which patterns have changed over time. The focus then moves to what might be termed the anatomy of kidnapping, zeroing in on the process itself and the key steps involved, while taking into account variations resulting from divergent objectives and the nature of the victims. An assessment is also made of the profits that have been obtained through kidnapping, recognizing that an important counterpoint to the relatively few high-profile, large-payment instances of kidnapping and ransoming of foreigners is the large number of kidnappings of Iraqis for much smaller payments. In effect, the kidnapping business is like any other, with some income streams coming from high volume with low payoffs and others coming from low volume with high payoffs.

Types of Kidnapping.

Kidnapping in Iraq, traditionally linked to tribal rivalries, forced marriages, and business disputes, has a long pedigree. On occasion, kidnappings are "used to solve tribal and commercial disputes," in the process becoming little more than a forcible extension of business negotiations.[6] Since 2003, however, kidnappings have largely fallen into one of two categories — economic or political.[7] Yet, even within each of these categories, there are several variations. Keeping this in mind, we can identify the following types of kidnapping:

- Kidnapping for profit. This is the simplest and probably most common form of kidnapping in Iraq. Initially it was directed at Iraqis and simply involved seizure, payment, and release. In some instances, wealthy families have been victimized more than once, with sequential kidnapping of family members. Not surprisingly, this form of kidnapping eventually spread to foreigners and led to some large ransom payments.
- Kidnapping for profit plus. In some cases, kidnapping was done for profit, but the victim was also told to leave the country or face death. This seems to have been particularly prevalent in kidnappings of scientists, university professors,

and doctors. Although the primary motive was profit, a political motive—typically related either to sectarian cleansing or to the elimination of secular professions and the transformation of Iraq into a theocracy—overlay the profit motive.

- Kidnapping as prelude to murder. In Iraq, many kidnappings—especially mass kidnappings—are preludes to murder. In these cases, the purpose is not kidnapping as such but sectarian cleansing, revenge, and retribution.[8] A number of cases of mass kidnappings have been followed some time later, for example, by the discovery of mass graves. Individuals have also been kidnapped off the streets and taken to another location to be killed (sometimes preceded by torture), with their bodies then dumped at the abduction location. This is psychologically important as a demonstration of the perpetrators' immunity to punishment. It is a far more forceful and effective method of sectarian cleansing than a simple drive-by shooting. In some instances, groups within the police have been responsible for very blatant actions of this kind. Although mass kidnappings and mass killings have added a great deal to the pervasive insecurity of the Iraqi population, they are really outside the focus of this analysis, having far more to do with sectarian cleansing than with organized crime.
- Kidnapping for political purposes. Political kidnapping can target both Iraqis and foreigners. It can be a powerful intimidation tactic within a sectarian cleansing strategy: victims of kidnapping are clearly frightened

and, when released, will often move to a safer neighborhood or try to leave Iraq altogether. Sometimes creating fear is more important than obtaining money—although it is preferable to succeed in both. Abduction can also be used to protect criminal activities such as oil smuggling from anti-corruption officials who are trying to reestablish the rule of law. More generally, kidnapping is an excellent weapon for both insurgents and terrorists since it has multiple functions. Kidnappings help to create a climate of fear (especially if they end in the videotaped execution of the hostages); they offer a way of exercising coercive pressure against selected targets who are subject to political demands (such as the withdrawal of soldiers or workers from Iraq); they highlight the continued inability of the government to protect its citizens and establish law and order; and they can be a lucrative and important source of funding for the cause. In addition, kidnapping can be a powerful boost for the groups engaged in the business. At its most basic level, kidnapping provides a sense of affirmation and importance: I kidnap, therefore, I exist—and you need to acknowledge me. In effect, kidnapping groups with a clear political agenda and which target foreign nationals demand—and receive—attention. In this sense, kidnappings are a powerful psychological leveler. Kidnapping foreign nationals ensures the attention of their governments. Even if the governments reject ransom payments (and some do not), they might still engage—explicitly or tacitly—in protracted negotiations in efforts to have the victims freed.

In post-Ba'athist Iraq, kidnapping has come to possess an almost contagious quality: the importance of emulation in the growth of kidnapping is difficult to overestimate. After the chaos of the looting morphed into organized criminal activities, kidnapping gangs became prominent, initially focusing only on Iraqi targets. Success bred imitation, lending to the spread of kidnapping a viral quality. The result was an epidemic that inevitably extended to foreigners in Iraq. In a sense, Baghdad simply came to resemble Mexico City and Metropolitan Manila, where foreigners had long been a prime target of kidnapping gangs. What distinguished Iraq, however, was that kidnapping of foreigners became a political device intended to influence or coerce governments or companies with a military or civil presence in Iraq. Kidnapping became a way of increasing risks and costs for those involved in the occupation, and had some success in making companies and even governments decide to leave. Many kidnappings, of course, were about both politics and profit, with mutually reinforcing objectives. In some respects, the result was unprecedented, with one commentary claiming that kidnapping had never before been "made into a system and employed as a military and political weapon as is being done in Iraq."[9] Although insurgents in both the Philippines and Colombia had also made extensive use of kidnapping, in Iraq for a short time at least, hostage-taking became almost "an independent front" in the conflict between insurgents on the one side and the coalition forces and Iraq government on the other.[10]

The Kidnappers.

The perpetrators of kidnappings in Iraq are sometimes as elusive as the motivations. Nevertheless, we can tentatively identify several kinds of groupings that were or are involved. It seems likely that the market in hostages is very similar to other criminal markets with a wide range of different participants, from small and rather amateur groups on the one side to very sophisticated and large organizations on the other. These included:

- *Former regime elements.* In the immediate aftermath of the collapse of the regime, as kidnapping became more common, some of it was based on targets of opportunity, while in other cases targets were very carefully selected. This selectivity suggested that former regime elements were deeply implicated in the kidnapping business. Those who had worked for the Saddam Hussein regime had access to personal profiles and were able to identify victims whose families would be able to afford very substantial ransom payments. Some victims, for example, claimed initially that they had very little money only to find that their kidnappers had detailed information about their personal finances.[11] The regime elements had a long history of predatory behavior towards the population, the skill, training, and resources to continue this behavior, and the incentive to raise money either to enrich themselves (and maintain the lifestyles to which they and their families had become accustomed) or to fund opposition to U.S. efforts.

- *Former convicts.* Equally predatory were kidnapping gangs consisting of convicts who had been released by Hussein prior to the invasion. Many had a long history of violence, and it is unlikely that prison had increased their scruples about victimizing innocent people. Although they had the inclination and the ruthlessness to enter the kidnapping business, they lacked the intelligence resources of the former regime elements. Consequently, their activities focused on targets of opportunity such as children, businessmen, or anyone who displayed the outward trappings of wealth and a degree of vulnerability. On occasion, they linked up with members of the former regime, thereby obtaining the intelligence to identify high-value targets.

- *Unemployed youths and young men.* Other groups which came into the kidnapping business were driven by a desire to find ways out of the poverty and unemployment traps that seriously constricted legitimate career opportunities in Iraq. The same impulse that led people to plant roadside bombs and to carry out other paid activities for insurgents also encouraged kidnapping. The potential payoffs, combined with the absence of entry barriers and a low learning curve, made it a very attractive option.

- *Opportunistic amateurs.* In one sense, all kidnapping is opportunistic. Yet it also seems likely that some kidnappings involved unscrupulous family members trying to exploit their relatives. In other cases, the kidnapping group consisted of only two or three people, often including a woman who played a major role in the initial abduction. Women are typically seen as less threatening than men and are able to get closer to the victims without arousing suspicion.

- *Insurgents and jihadist groups.* Although it appears unlikely that Sunni insurgents and extremist groups from outside the country were deeply involved in the initial burst of kidnappings in Iraq, they gradually embraced kidnappings as both a funding source and a strategic weapon.
- *Militias and militia factions.* Shiite militias in Iraq are involved in all sorts of criminal activities, including kidnapping and killing high-level Sunni officials. Although militias are also responsible for mass abductions and killings, more selective kidnapping is used by them as a revenue source. It is often unclear whether such kidnapping is a result of a high-level strategy or the work of rogue factions. It is equally uncertain if these actions earn the grudging respect or the disapproval of the leadership.

Delineating the separate kinds of group in this way is an important starting point, but analysis does not end here. Some groups are almost certainly hybrids, and some kidnappers probably move from one group to another in what might be a constantly shifting kaleidoscope of allegiance, membership, and motives. Another key issue concerns relationships among the various groups. Although it is hard to obtain details of specific cases of cooperation, it is clear that cooperation has occurred. Whether the cooperation is the result of political affinity or is simply a business transaction, "there are many credible reports suggesting that hostages, in particular foreign nationals, taken by criminal gangs are then handed over to armed political groups in exchange for money."[12]

In sum, kidnapping in Iraq involves a variety of groups operating in the same space, constantly interacting with one another in a dynamic mix of conflict, competition, and cooperation, while responding to varied opportunities and pressures. Kidnapping is a constantly evolving industry that adapts to changing circumstances. New firms enter the business, while others leave. Sometimes kidnapping victims are traded from one group to another at the behest of the initial kidnappers; at other times, kidnappings of particular targets are carried out by for-profit groups in response to tacit or explicit requirements from political groups. According to one analysis, "As the kidnap industry has matured, investigators have seen cooperation evolve among criminal groups, and between them and the insurgency. Victims are sometimes sold and resold, gaining value each time."[13] The growth of cooperation has been accompanied by a trend towards greater sophistication and division of labor within groups, with "members specializing in duties like surveillance, abduction, transportation, guarding, and negotiations."[14] Although details are sparse and the picture is often confused and incomplete, it is possible to detect certain patterns and to trace how they change over time.

The Evolution of Kidnapping in Iraq.

Patterns of kidnapping in Iraq can be understood in terms of kidnapping streams, each of which has its own origin, expansion, and continued flow or contraction. Sometimes these streams run in parallel with one another, sometimes they merge, and at other times they overlap and intersect. On occasion, one kind of kidnapping can even morph into another kind. Targets change over time, and there is sometimes a degree of unpredictability in particular abductions which start as one kind of kidnapping and end as another. One of the major kidnapping streams in Iraq has been criminal in nature, has targeted Iraqis, and has predominantly involved ransom payments—although even this stream is complicated by the fact that some ransom payments have funded insurgent or sectarian groups. A second stream developed in April 2004 with the seizure of foreigners. Compared with the number of Iraqis abducted, this stream was minuscule. Yet, it succeeded in attracting global attention—not least because several victims were beheaded or shot and videos of their execution posted on jihadist web sites. Although the immediate impulse for the abduction of foreigners was political rather than financial, on occasion it proved lucrative. With some governments willing to make large ransom payments for the release of their citizens and companies ready to pay for the release of their employees, foreigners became attractive targets. By the time this came about, though, the kidnapping of Iraqis had already become a major concern.

The U.S. invasion and the collapse of central authority in Iraq provided ideal conditions for the growth of a kidnapping industry. Yet, even prior to U.S. military intervention, in February 2003 the State Department issued a warning to American citizens about the danger of kidnappings in Iraq.[15] The trickle of kidnappings prior to March 2003, however, soon became a flood. This was partly a manifestation of the underlying anarchy and disorder created by the U.S. invasion. Yet, often it was very calculated—whether the calculations concerned the proceeds that could be obtained or the impact on rival sectarian communities. Once again, there was considerable continuity with the Ba'athist era. "Kidnappings driven by ransom or sexual motives — both of which were formalized tools of the Ba'athist security apparatus"[16] — became what Robert Looney terms an "institutionalized criminal activity."[17] If the involvement of former regime elements ensured continuity, the scale of kidnapping was totally unprecedented. One report even suggested that while kidnappings under Saddam Hussein provided only about 1 percent of the cases for the Iraqi police, in the aftermath of the collapse of the regime they accounted for "70 percent of reported crime."[18] By summer 2003, kidnapping was already acknowledged as a central if unfortunate characteristic of post-Hussein Iraq. In August, for example, the new police chief in Basra noted that "every kind of crime known in the world" was evident in the city.[19] Kidnappings in particular had risen sharply, and of seven kidnappings in July 2003, six were for ransom and one for "tribal reasons."[20] The police chief added that, according to the victims, "the kidnappers pray and consider the 'profession of kidnapping' a respectable profession."[21] The growing phenomenon was acknowledged in a report in the *Los Angeles Times* by Robyn Dixon.[22]

At this stage, however, kidnapping targeted children and teenagers, especially "the only sons of large middle-income or wealthy families," including but not limited to Iraq's "tiny Christian community," most of whom were Assyrian Christians and easily identifiable.[23] Well-dressed children were obvious targets. In one case, a 6-year-old mute child was released after his family paid a $15,000 ransom, while in other instances ransoms as high as $75,000 were paid.[24]

Other early targets included the Sabean-Mandeans, a "small monotheistic community," many of whom were goldsmiths and jewelers.[25] "Their reputation as wealthy merchants," according to Elizabeth Ferris and Matthew Hall, "put the community at heightened risk for ransom kidnappings. Following the 2003 invasion, they quickly became targets for both armed gangs and radical groups (the two often blurring), both in Baghdad and in Basra."[26] As a result, many left Iraq for Syria.

Human Rights Watch reported that "some gangs specialized in kidnapping girls," who were then sold to Gulf countries.[27] Although this crime had sometimes happened "before the war," it intensified as it became possible "to get them in and out without passports."[28] In some cases, abductions were of short term, simply the occasion for rape, and the women were subsequently released. In other cases, however, sexual violence was a prelude to selling the women and girls to traffickers. Police in Iraq gave apprehension of sexual abductors a low priority and usually failed to follow up reports of such crimes with a serious investigation.[29] Consequently, the issue received only sporadic attention.

In September 2006, Yanar Mohammed, head of the Women's Freedom Organization, claimed that about 2,000 women had been kidnapped during the previous 3 years.[30] Other authorities believed this figure was too conservative. It also appeared that women were still being trafficked out of Iraq. In a climate characterized by anomie, women were seen as "cheap and exchangeable goods."[31] In a case in February 2007, a 13-year-old girl was abducted and beaten. She was "held in a room with 15 other girls for 7 hours before being released by police who raided the house."[32] It turned out she had been abducted by an "elderly woman" who "asked her to help her carry some plastic bags across the road to find a taxi."[33] The woman then forced the girl into the taxi, anesthetized her, and tied her up.

Few police units took kidnapping very seriously. The perpetrators were therefore able to act with enormous freedom and little risk, though there were occasional exceptions. In early August 2003, a nine-member kidnapping gang was arrested, and several victims were freed—although one of them was killed by the kidnappers during the police operation.[34] Three other gangs had reportedly been arrested, and it appeared that some of the members had posed as policemen.[35] Successfully disrupting kidnapping gangs, however, was the exception rather than the rule, and in most cases little help was given by either the police or coalition forces.

Consequently, families of kidnap victims were on their own. Often they were able to bargain over the ransom. For example, the kidnapping of a 17-year-old—an only son of a restaurant owner—was followed by a demand for a $120,000 ransom. When family members convinced the kidnappers that they could not pay this amount—and that their home was rented—the demand was reduced to $15,000, and the victim was subsequently released.[36] This result was fairly typical. According to one report, "those demanding ransoms typically ask for up to 300,000 dollars, but often accept payments of under 5,000."[37] Other sources suggest that the payment was more typically about 10 percent of the initial demand.[38] Clearly, bargaining was common. In fact, if the initial demands were met without bargaining, the implication was that the family was very wealthy—and the ransom demand could be increased or the family targeted a second time.[39] Kidnapping for profit was a ruthless business, but was characterized by a degree of pragmatism about the level of profit that could realistically be obtained.

Based on this pragmatic approach, and with kidnapping proving to be highly lucrative, the target pool was extended from members of small minorities, children, and women who might be trafficked, to merchants, jewelers, bankers, doctors, university professors, and government officials. To some extent, this expansion was a response to increased precautions taken by many parents to minimize the vulnerability of their children to kidnapping. Some schools, for example, experienced a significant drop in attendance as parents kept children home rather than put them in harm's way. Yet the expansion of the victim pool was not simply a response to the increased difficulty of abducting children. Targeting businessmen and professionals was a natural progression in an environment where lawlessness and disorder thrived. It was also an activity in which former regime elements were again able to pre-select targets.

The kidnapping of professionals, scientists, doctors, and university professors also attracted those who wanted the occupation and reconstruction of Iraq to fail and be replaced by a religion-based society in which modern science, medicine, and secular teaching had no place. By May 2004, one commentary noted that kidnappings had taken a very serious turn, targeting key segments of Iraqi society such as doctors, scientists, and professors, and no longer confined to ransom demands.[40] Typically, even after a large ransom had been paid and the victim released, he was told to "leave the country or face a second abduction or even be killed."[41] The family of an internationally known Iraqi scientist paid $30,000 for his release, but he was still ordered to leave Iraq.[42] The same happened to a leading organ transplant surgeon, although the ransom payment for him was $1 million.[43] The Iraqi Ministry of Health in 2005 claimed that 130 Iraqi doctors had been abducted in the previous 2 years, but the Iraqi Medical Association claimed the figure was almost 300.[44] About 50 of the doctors had been killed and many others forced to leave Iraq. Clearly they remained vulnerable targets.[45]

Another target was business leaders. In one well-documented case, the owner of a hotel was released for $40,000, but his son was abducted when he delivered the money and was released only after an additional payment of $60,000.[46] This ruse was not uncommon. The kidnapping gangs at the time were "made up of both former secret service members and of criminals" who induced victims to expose other rich people by promising to reduce the ransom.[47] In effect, a snowball sampling process was being applied to identify potential targets or victims. Bankers were a particularly tempting target; in one case, a ransom of $6 million was reportedly obtained for the safe return of Ghalib Kubba, the chairman of the Basra International Bank, and his son, Hassan, the bank's executive manager.[48] In addition, kidnapping gangs also focused on Iraqis who worked closely with the United States or with coalition forces — on the grounds that these people were being paid more money than most Iraqis.[49] The gangs also targeted families with relatives in the United States and elsewhere outside Iraq — on the grounds that these relatives could contribute towards the ransom.[50] Several businessmen born in Iraq but with Canadian citizenship returned to Iraq for business, but were kidnapped and in some cases killed.[51]

Although the growth of kidnapping was evident immediately following the downfall of Saddam Hussein, it was not until June 21, 2004, that the abduction of Iraqis was mentioned in the Iraq Index maintained by the Brookings Institution.[52] Moreover, it was not until September 2005 that the Index included its first table summarizing the number of Iraqis kidnapped per day. And even then the figures were very crude, offering static snapshots rather than a differentiated and dynamic picture. Nevertheless, the trend was clearly upward, with an estimate of two Iraqis per day kidnapped in Baghdad in January 2004, rising to 10 per day in December of the same year.[53] According to the Iraqi Ministry of the Interior, throughout Iraq 5,000 Iraqis were kidnapped between December 2003 and late April 2005.[54] By March 2006, according to the Iraq Index, the kidnapping rate had increased to somewhere between 30 and 40 people per day throughout the country as a whole. A spokesperson for the U.S. Embassy in Iraq described the business as "huge," acknowledging that there were a "lot more Iraqis being held hostage . . . than most people are aware of."[55] Ransoms averaged "between $20,000 and $30,000."[56] In a country in which poverty and unemployment were endemic, this level of payoff gave the business considerable momentum.

It is difficult to establish unequivocally that the kidnapping of Iraqis has diminished. It seems likely, however, that kidnapping rates declined in 2007 and 2008 because of improvements in the security situation and the fact that much of the sectarian cleansing in Iraq had run its course.[57] There might also be a diminishing target set. As suggested above, many professionals have left the country.[58] Kidnapping has also had indirect effects: its pervasiveness generated enormous concerns about the safety of family members, especially children, and this too contributed to the large exodus of people from Iraq. Those who remain have taken greater precautions. Yet the kidnapping phenomenon has not disappeared—nor is it likely to do so any time soon. Even with diminishing returns, kidnapping remains attractive, especially with the lack of more legitimate economic opportunities. And even if many of the more lucrative targets have disappeared, some are left, ensuring that kidnapping remains profitable—especially given the minimal investment. Indeed, anecdotal reports suggest that kidnapping remains an important source of continued feelings of insecurity. In one commentary in September 2007 on Mosul, it was noted that "kidnap operations are on the rise" and that security agencies in Nineveh had registered 40 kidnappings in August alone.[59] A very similar point was made by Joel Simon, Executive Director of the Committee to Protect Journalists, who noted in November 2007 that "armed groups continue to abduct Iraqis, including members of the press, at an alarming rate."[60] This is particularly the case in those provinces characterized by continued unrest and instability. As long as the situation remains unsettled in a few provinces and cities, then kidnappings in those areas will continue.

The kidnapping of foreigners which began in April 2004 seems to have occurred largely in response to the assault on Fallujah. Prior to this, foreigners had typically been targets of violence but not abduction. This changed dramatically. According to one persuasive analysis, there were several components of this new kidnapping focus. The most important cause was the broadening base of opposition to the United States and its coalition partners in April 2004.

Prior to this month, resistance was primarily carried out by a dedicated core of Sunni insurgents, who invariably killed foreigners either during attacks or immediately afterwards, in part because the taking and holding of hostages is impractical for such cells, whose modus operandi requires them to be able to merge back into the population. Instead, hostage-taking emerged from the brief popularization of armed resistance that occurred at the height of fighting in Fallujah and during Muqtada al-Sadr's uprising.[61]

An additional factor was "the collapse of road security," especially in the Sunni triangle.[62] Another consideration that almost certainly fed into the targeting of foreigners was the release of photographs of prisoner abuse at Abu Ghraib. This confluence of factors resulted in foreigners becoming a key part of the target pool for kidnapping. The evolution of this phenomenon is summarized in Figure 1. There were few, if any, indications in early 2004 that kidnapping of foreigners would soon become a major issue in Iraq. As Figure 1 shows, however, in April 2004, 43 foreigners were kidnapped. This initial surge was followed by a relative lull, with only two foreigners kidnapped in May and three in June. Another upsurge occurred in the following 3 months with 26 foreigners kidnapped in July 2004, 30 in August, and 31 in September. August also saw the peak of killings of victims, with 15 hostages being killed. After September 2004, the number of foreigners kidnapped declined into single digits before briefly spiking again at much lower levels in January (13) and February 2005 (10)—a spike that might have been related to the Iraqi elections held on January 30. In August 2005 (as the Iraqi draft constitution was completed by Shiite and Kurdish negotiators and rejected by Sunnis), the number climbed to 25 before dropping to three in both September and October. In November 2005, 11 foreigners were kidnapped, and in December there were 13. In January 2006, the figure dropped to five, and in February it rose to 12 before dropping back to five or below for the rest of the year—a decline that was probably connected to the death of Zarqawi on June 8, 2006.[63]

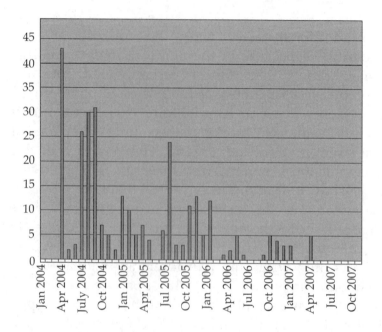

Source: Brookings Iraq Index.

Figure 1. Number of Kidnappings of Foreigners in Iraq, 2004-07.

Possibly as retaliation for Zarqawi's death, six foreign hostages were killed in June 2006, a monthly total second only to the 15 killed in August 2004. Between July 2006 and the end of 2007, according to the Iraq Index, only one more foreign hostage was killed —

in November 2006. In 2007 only 11 foreigners were kidnapped, three each in January and February and five in May. According to the March 2009 Iraq Index, there were no additional kidnappings of foreigners in 2007 and only one such kidnapping in February 2008.

It is worth emphasizing that the worst month on record for foreigner kidnappings was not much higher in numbers than the high-end count of daily kidnappings of Iraqis. This is not to make light of the kidnapping of foreigners. There were, of course, several distinct categories targeted for kidnapping. Members of the coalition forces were among them, but as the hardest targets they did not figure prominently. Foreign workers, including truck drivers, construction workers, and service providers, were seen as supporting the occupation and therefore legitimate targets. So too were journalists, whose work typically put them in dangerous situations. Members of NGOs were perhaps the easiest targets, but they were also the most controversial as some were clearly engaged in providing critical humanitarian assistance.

A particularly prominent aspect of kidnappings in this period was the video recordings of the victims.[64] These typically included messages pleading for their governments to change policy and the subsequent beheadings of the hostages. The posting of execution tapes on the Internet began with the release of a video on May 11, 2004, showing the execution of American citizen Nicholas Berg—an action which Berg's captors directly linked to Abu Ghraib.[65] Subsequent videos showed the killings of other American contractors, including Jack Hensley and Eugene Armstrong (posted in September 2004) as well as British aid worker Kenneth Bigley (posted in October 2004). The tactic was designed to mobilize support and strengthen recruitment efforts, to arouse public opposition to the occupation in coalition countries, and to spread fear in the foreign community in Iraq. The brazen nature of the execution videos made clear that those carrying out the executions were able to act with impunity, and that the United States was powerless to do anything about it.[66] In addition, by targeting foreign workers providing help in economic reconstruction, the kidnappers were seeking to undermine both the reconstruction efforts and the legitimacy of the government.[67] Particularly puzzling, however, was the case of Margaret Hassan, the head of the relief organization CARE operating in Iraq. Although a videotape of her killing was sent to Al-Jazeera, no group claimed responsibility, and the kidnapping and killing were widely condemned, as Hassan had been deeply involved in humanitarian activities to help Iraqis.[68] Some speculated that rogue terrorist elements were involved in her abduction and killing.

The group behind most of the Internet beheadings was Tawhid and Jihad, subsequently known as al-Qaeda in Iraq (or, more formally, the al-Qaeda Organization) in the Land of the Two Rivers, led by Abu Musab al Zarqawi. If Zarqawi's group was the most infamous for its treatment of hostages, it shared the kidnapping space with a bewildering array of other groups, some of which were spinoffs from larger factions, and some of which operated under several different names. These groups often made political demands for governments with a military presence in Iraq to withdraw and for companies providing logistic support for the occupation to leave the country. These demands were dramatized and accentuated by brutal killings. The Ansar al-Sunnah Movement, for example, abducted 12 Nepalese on August 23, 2004, and subsequently killed them all to advertise the dangers to foreigners working in Iraq.[69] The execution of South Korean Kim Il, kidnapped in May 2004 and killed in June, seems to have had the same objective.[70]

Sometimes, the political demands were a cover for more mercenary objectives. The Black Banners Group, for example, kidnapped three Indians, two Kenyans, and an Egyptian, all of whom worked as truckers for Kuwait and Gulf Link Transport Company (KGL). According to one assessment, their "aim was to compel the company to stop its activities in Iraq. The hostages were later released."[71] In fact, however, the situation was more complicated than this brief recitation makes it appear. The kidnappers initially demanded that Indian troops immediately leave Iraq, even though India had no troops in Iraq. This could suggest that political objectives were a pretext for financial gain (or that the kidnappers were stupid). Subsequently, the Group demanded a ransom payment—ostensibly as compensation for bereaved families in Fallujah. The Indian government employed a three-man team to negotiate for the release of the hostages through mediators, including Sheikh Hisham al-Dulaimi. "But even after 15 days of negotiations, there was no breakthrough. The kidnappers, who had initially demanded $5 million as ransom, later scaled it down to $2.5 million. But KGL said it could not pay more than half a million. Dulaimi slowly pulled out of the negotiations."[72]

One of the Indian team members began to focus instead on local people, leaving his card at a barber shop.[73] This led to another kidnapper intermediary visiting the Indian embassy and the subsequent resumption of negotiations. KGL agreed to pay $500,000 and to end its activities in Iraq.[74] In return, the hostages were released. As one commentary subsequently noted, "The negotiations to secure the release of the hostages were protracted, not because the issues . . . were intractable political ones but because of hard wrangling over money."[75]

In cases like this, it appears that political objectives are subordinate to financial gain.

> The groups that are engaged in hostage-taking might all be opposed to the presence of the U.S.-led occupation forces in Iraq, but not all of them are in the kidnapping business for political reasons. Some are mere criminal gangs who have seen the immense possible prospects of profit that hostage-taking holds out. These abduct foreign workers in Iraq, cloaking conditions for their release with political issues. It is money finally that secures the release of the hostages.[76]

Even in such cases, the assessment is clouded because the money could be for personal enrichment or for financing the insurgency — or indeed for some mix of the two.

Even killings of hostages, which are seen as purely political, could have an ulterior financial motive in that such actions establish the credibility of threats made by the kidnappers, thereby pressuring governments and companies to pay larger ransoms to save the lives of their citizens and employees. Moreover, "kidnappers whose only aim is to make money often pretend to be fighting the occupation."[77] In one case, Iraqi security forces captured a kidnapping gang with a Lebanese hostage. "In their hideout," according to Andrew Cockburn, "the police found banners with religious and political slogans. The head of the gang said they were to be used as a stage backdrop if they made a video of their victim in the hope that it would be shown on television."[78] The leader noted that if the kidnapping was on television, it meant more money.[79]

If kidnapping in Iraq is complicated by the multiple motives of the group, as well as their deception and denial activities, the relationships among them add another layer of complexity:

> Senior figures within Iraq's Interior Ministry believe that insurgents have begun working with criminal organizations, "outsourcing" kidnappings to criminal groups, thereby allowing them to seize a specific demographic of captive when they have the opportunity and then sell the captive to the insurgent group. It is believed that Jack Hensley and Eugene Armstrong, two American contractors seized from their Baghdad residence in September 2004 and beheaded by radical insurgents, were the targets of such an arrangement.[80]

The arrangements can be the result of tacit communication between the criminals and the insurgent or terrorist group, i.e., with the insurgents simply letting it be known what kinds of targets they are seeking. Alternatively, the arrangements can be the result of specific agreements between insurgents and a particular kidnapping gang. In yet other cases, it is possible that the initiative comes from the kidnappers. Some authorities suggest that the kidnapping gangs are

> . . . made up of criminals, unemployed soldiers, and former . . . regime intelligence and security service agents with little to lose and much to gain in Iraq's security vacuum. Some go straight to the hostage's family or employers demanding a ransom; others feel that they can achieve a more satisfactory price selling their hostages to militant groups.[81]

In some cases, the group responsible for the initial kidnapping might decide that it can benefit from a bidding war between insurgents on the one side, and governments, companies, or even wealthy families on the other. It is also plausible that in some instances, a kidnapping gang will transfer a victim to the custody of an insurgent group — which then does the negotiating — with the understanding that the gang will obtain a certain portion of the ransom. However the dynamic operates in specific cases, there was for some time a flourishing trade among kidnapping groups in Iraq.[82]

That the kidnapping of foreigners had two distinct but overlapping dimensions — politics and profit — was perhaps best illustrated by the kidnapping of Filipino truck driver Angelo de la Cruz in July 2004. The initial assessment seems to have been that this was a political kidnapping, with a threat from the kidnappers that de la Cruz would be beheaded unless the Arroyo government agreed to withdraw its 51 peacekeepers from Iraq.[83] In response, Arroyo agreed to withdraw the force a month earlier than had been planned.[84] Many reports, however, suggest that this was not enough for the kidnappers, who turned down an offer of $1 million for the victim's safe release before subsequently accepting a much higher payment.[85] According to reports in a Filipino newspaper which were picked up by conservative bloggers in the United States, the release of Cruz was obtained with the payment of a $6 million ransom.[86]

The Malaysian government reportedly provided $5 million of this, with the other $1 million coming from the Landbank of the Philippines.[87] Though Malaysia denied that such was the case, it appears that some kind of large ransom was indeed paid.[88] One Iraqi newspaper even suggested that in the de la Cruz case, the Arroyo government initially thought the issue was the withdrawal of the Philippine contingent from Iraq, only to find out later that the issue also included money.[89] Specifically, the release of Angelo de la Cruz probably required both a political concession and a substantial ransom. As it turned out, such an approach was not uncommon: "In many cases armed political groups seem to have made the release of their victims conditional on payment of money even when they [made] political demands such as the withdrawal of foreign troops."[90] Thus for at least some kidnapping groups, profits and politics were complementary to one another rather than alternatives. Even if this were not the case, there were benefits from making it appear that the price of release went beyond inflating the ransom. Such an approach maximized uncertainties, keeping both the Iraq government and the occupying forces off balance, and complicated the task of rescuing the hostages. It also added an additional layer of cover to the kidnapping organization, making it harder to identify and apprehend. The downside was that by mixing political and financial objectives, the kidnappers were more likely to provoke involvement by coalition forces.

Although the Philippine government was subject to severe criticism from the United States and other countries for capitulating to the kidnappers (by agreeing to remove its military forces), there is some suggestion that Japan had earlier paid for the safe release of three hostages captured and released in April 2004.[91] During the next 2 years, substantial ransom payments in the millions of dollars were made by both governments and companies. Some of them also agreed to stop operating in Iraq, confirming that the line between political and economic kidnapping was often crossed and that some

133

groups combined financial and political demands. In some instances, company payments were made as a result of pressure from national governments. It is also likely that in some cases, governments might have made the payments while hiding behind the fiction that the ransoms were coming from the companies. In yet other cases, the families of the victims seem to have paid ransoms with some assistance from the companies for which the victims worked. A Cypriot, for example, was released after 4 months in captivity following the payment of $200,000 by his family and his employer, Geto Trading, which supplied food rations for U.S. forces.[92]

The United States and Britain continued their traditional policy of refusing to pay ransoms and were very critical of governments and companies that did acquiesce to the kidnappers' demands. A spokesman for the Interior Ministry in Iraq indeed claimed that "the reason for the acceleration in kidnappings is simply because ransoms are being paid."[93] Perhaps the most surprising aspect about the kidnapping of foreigners is that it was both clustered and relatively short-lived. In part, this is because the Internet videos of beheadings proved counterproductive, which was pointed out by Zawahiri to Zarqawi. Another consideration is that after a spate of kidnappings, foreigners tended to take greater precautions against putting themselves in harm's way.[94] The improvements in the security situation, especially in the latter half of 2007, also restricted opportunities for kidnappers. In addition, some foreigners who were part of the NGO community simply left the country, thereby effectively reducing the number of available targets. Even so, the decline is somewhat surprising, given the large ransom payments that were made. It suggests that in some ways the capacity of kidnappers was limited.

The Anatomy of Kidnappings.

The essence of kidnapping is selection of victim, abduction, movement, captivity, negotiations (sometimes), and release of the victim on payment of a ransom or deposit of the remains. The first stage in the kidnapping process, identification of a potential victim or victims, can be done in several ways. One approach is territorial, involving what might be termed mobile victims. Iraqi roads have become highly profitable for kidnappers, who typically target truckers on the Amman-Baghdad Highway (especially near Fallujah), as well as the road between Syria and Mosul. Here, a favorite target is foreign truck drivers, whose high wages imply a lucrative payoff from their employers or governments. Another approach is what might be termed active searching for targets afoot, for example, by cruising through neighborhoods looking for children out alone or Christians exiting banks.

Yet another approach is careful selection of individual targets, based on information about their financial circumstances (pre-selection) or their vulnerability to abduction (targets of opportunity). Many Iraqi reports suggest that some targets are chosen on the basis of wealth, while others are seized simply because they are in the wrong place at the wrong time. Target identification can be based on dress, especially a well-dressed school child. In some cases, the abduction will be preceded by a period of surveillance; in others, identification of a potential victim and their physical capture will be almost simultaneous. Indeed, there are indications that some kidnapping gangs have informants for the express propose of pointing out potential targets. The ubiquity of the cell phone has meant that informants can contact kidnappers who then react quickly in abducting targets of opportunity.

In the case of several foreign journalists in Iraq, there are indications that they were set up, that is, they had an appointment with an Iraqi politician or cleric who failed to show. This was the case with journalist Jill Carroll, who had come for an appointment with Adnan al-Dulaimi, head of the Iraqi Accordance Front. He did not make the meeting, and Carroll was abducted from her car as she was leaving the location. As she subsequently wrote, "Within minutes of my capture, I had suspected Dulaimi. . . . The kidnappers were waiting for us when we left his office. They must have known about my appointment ahead of time."[95] The kidnapping of Italian journalist Sgrena was very similar. She was going to interview an Islamic religious leader and waited for over 3 hours near the al-Mustafa mosque. This was a mistake: "A foreigner in a public place for that long is vulnerable. All it takes is one person with a mobile to phone a kidnap gang."[96]

Although there is more uncertainty in the case of French correspondent Florence Aubenas, it is quite possible that she too was seized while awaiting a meeting.[97] Where foreigners have bodyguards, usually several cars converge on the victim. Bodyguards and drivers are typically shot. In cases where they survived, they were suspected of helping to plan the kidnapping or at least pointing out the target. With Iraqi children and adults, usually only one car is needed, and the victim is either bundled into the trunk or pushed into the car interior and covered up. This often occurs in daylight and with many witnesses, most of whom know that any interference would result in their deaths. Another approach sometimes used is based on theft of uniforms and vehicles from Iraqi police or military and subsequent impersonation of these officials. On occasion, kidnappers have even set up false check points to stop vehicles whose occupants are then abducted.

Abduction is usually followed by the transfer of the victim to a safe house where he or she is held in captivity or killed. When obtaining money for the cause is deemed more important than making a statement, the victim has to be maintained in captivity until the ransom is agreed upon and paid. For several women hostages, including Jill Carroll, the conditions were relatively good. Carroll, for example, was allowed to mingle with some of the kidnappers' families, being the only hostage. She was regularly moved among six different locations during her period in captivity. For some of the foreign men, in contrast, conditions were deplorable, so much so that it was surprising they survived. Some of the kidnapped Iraqis who were eventually freed note that other hostages were held in the same place. In some cases, they heard some of their fellow victims being beaten, tortured, or killed.[98]

Unless the kidnapping is intended as a prelude to beheading or political assassination or is part of sectarian cleansing, the next stage of the process involves contact, communication, and negotiation. When a member of an Iraqi family is kidnapped, the family typically posts its telephone number on the outside of the house so that the kidnappers can make contact. Initial contact is followed by an opening demand. This is usually the beginning of a bargaining process in which the family seeks to convince the kidnappers that it is impossible to meet the demand. Sometimes the negotiations are protracted as the kidnappers give the family time to turn to relatives or tribal members to round up the money for the payment. In many cases, however, the kidnappers recognize that they will have to settle for far less than the initial figure.

Parents will often be too distraught to negotiate and will pass the task on to another family member to act as the intermediary. The intermediary sometimes has to deliver the money and will be made to walk from one place to another before finally dropping off the money. An immediate money-for-hostage exchange is rare; it is sometimes the next day or even a few days before the victim is released close to home. In some cases, ransoms have been paid when the hostage is already dead or is killed after the money has been delivered. The paying of ransoms took on a somewhat bizarre quality in 2007 when, after several kidnappers were captured while collecting the payments, others began to drop homing pigeons outside family dwellings along with instructions for attaching money to the pigeon's legs and then freeing it to return to its owner.[99]

The ransoming of foreigners has a much more opaque bargaining process, the contacts between the kidnappers and the family, government, or employer of the victim often being indirect. These contacts and the negotiations are facilitated by people who have become almost professional intermediaries. These intermediaries include the members of the Association of Muslim Scholars, also known as the Muslim Ulema Council. According to one Iraqi newspaper, the Association became "the only door for contact with the ghosts of the resistance concerning kidnapped Arab and foreign nationals," while the Umm-al-Qura mosque became the focus of "world firms operating in Iraq and foreign governments whose personnel have been kidnapped, as well as the center for holding talks, clinching deals, setting prices demanded by kidnappers, and sending messages to them."[100]

Whether intermediaries are usually bonafide or are linked to—and even beneficiaries of—the kidnapping gangs is hard to determine. So too is the degree of influence of the Association. In some cases, such as that of Italian aid workers Simona Torretta and Simona Pari, the Association's public statements and private entreaties seem to have had a positive impact,[101] although it was probably less important than the ransom paid by the Italians, itself probably also arranged through the Association. In other cases, when the Association has been particularly vociferous, its statements might have been counterproductive.[102] The head of the Association, Harith Al-Dhari, insists that the Association has no special or illegal connections with the kidnapping gangs. Rather, he claims, "We address them and ask them to release the hostages. If they are of groups that respect us, they would listen and respond to us; if they are not, they would not."[103] In one instance, a member of the Association received a message about the location of freed detainees, who were picked up and brought back to the Association's headquarters. In other instances, hostages were given a note saying they were released at the Association's behest.[104]

It is also necessary, of course, to distinguish between the Association and its individual members. It is possible that in some cases the relationship between a member and one or more kidnapping gangs was closer than publicly acknowledged. Nor is it out of the question that there was occasional collusion. Norman Kember, the British aid worker who was eventually rescued by British forces, for example, had just visited the Association when he was abducted.[105] The evidence seems to point at Sheikh Abdel Salam al-Qubaisi, who acted as intermediary in several cases involving Italian citizens and became the conduit—and perhaps even the recipient—of the ransom payments handed over by Italian military intelligence and the Italian Red

Cross.[106] Al-Qubaisi is believed to have been involved in several abductions of Italians as well as British aid worker Margaret Hassan.[107] It is possible that his dual role—part perpetrator, part intermediary—was reenacted by other clerics.

At times, Iraqi politicians have also played the role of intermediary. A good example is that of Sheikh al-Dulaimi, leader of the Iraqi Accordance Party, the largest Sunni party in Iraq's parliament. In the case of American journalist Jill Carroll, al-Dulaimi was both a suspect—at least in the planning of the kidnap—and possibly the engineer of her release. Reports suggested that al-Dulaimi met with the leader of the kidnappers at least twice, and he has claimed that he paid $1.5 million to her kidnappers for Carroll's release—$500,000 the day of her release and the rest a few months later.[108] If so, the money could well have been passed to the kidnapping gang through Sheikh Sattam al-Gaood, who not only claimed to have acted as a middleman but also emphasized that he had refused demands for "eight million dollars."[109] Whatever the truth of this particular case, however, it is clear that intermediaries have become a crucial part of the kidnapping and ransoming process.

In the case of governments inclined to negotiate with kidnappers, they designate teams to work on the release of the hostages. These teams—generally small—typically include a national official already in Iraq and a representative of the country's foreign ministry or the intelligence agencies. Sometimes contacts are established through the intermediaries described above. Negotiations can then proceed, often for widely varying periods.

The final stages, in at least some cases, are payment and return. Although negotiations for the release of hostages are often obscured by secrecy, when compared to the subterfuge and denials surrounding ransom payments they appear almost transparent. Indeed, ransom payments have become a major issue, creating tensions and acrimony among the members of the coalition in Iraq as well as among members of the North Atlantic Treaty Organization (NATO) and the European Union (EU). At root, however, ransom payments are what most kidnappings in Iraq are really about. As one commentary notes, "Kidnapping is very much a business. Many of the kidnappings seem to have been carried out by criminal gangs with no particular ideological platform. Put simply, most kidnappers seem to be in it for the money."[110] It is useful, therefore, to examine the whole issue of ransoms and the amount of money they generate.

Criminal Proceeds and Insurgent War Chests.

One of the problems with efforts to determine the gross global proceeds of a particular generic crime is that they are highly dependent on assumptions and typically end up in the billions of dollars. For example, the global annual drug trade was estimated for a long time at $500 billion per year, while after 2001 the criminal and terrorist global economies were estimated to be about $1.5 trillion.[111] These are big numbers, and the main problem with them is that their accuracy depends critically upon too many assumptions that enter the calculations. Making accurate estimates at the micro-level (i.e., within a single nation such as Iraq) while focusing on a specific set of criminal activities such as kidnapping should therefore be somewhat easier. Yet, even at this level there are many imponderables and uncertainties. It is not clear, for example, how many Iraqis are kidnapped each day, and the figures that have emerged are crude estimates at best. The bigger danger, however, is the tendency to overestimate the monetary proceeds of kidnapping activity. At the same time, there is also a danger that the profits from kidnapping of foreigners in Iraq will be underestimated since governments, very naturally, are anxious to hide any ransom payments they might make. It is also extremely difficult to determine what percentage of the final figures is purely criminal proceeds as opposed to funding for insurgency and terror in Iraq.

Against this background, the most that can be done is to establish the assumptions on which any estimate is based, and where possible to offer a range of possibilities within which the bottom line might fall and then suggest why one option might be more compelling than others. The initial figure for Iraq kidnappings in 2004 of 10 a day (approximately 3,600 a year) is likely to be a considerable underestimate given the degree of chaos, the lack of reporting, and the failure of the occupation forces to recognize what a pervasive phenomenon kidnapping had become. To suggest that the average for the 5 years since the United States moved into Iraq is 20 per day is not inappropriate, given that U.S. estimates suggest that by March 2006 it was up to between 30 and 40 per day, with an average ransom payment of $20,000 to $30,000 per victim.

Realizing that not all kidnappings resulted in successful ransoms, we reach a reasonable estimate of about 6,000 victims ransomed each year. With a low average of $15,000 per ransom, the profits from domestic kidnapping (a business with minimal or no investment costs) were at least $90 million. But if we take the high figure for 2006 of 40 a day (that is, 14,000 hostages during the year) and the high figure for ransoms of $30,000 at the height of the kidnapping epidemic, the proceeds could have reached as high as $420 million in 1 year. We may conclude, therefore, that the domestic kidnapping business (as opposed to the kidnapping of foreigners) brought criminals and insurgents somewhere between $100 million and $150 million per year. How this money was divided between kidnapping gangs looking for self-serving cash and insurgent and jihadi groups looking for funding for their causes must remain uncertain.

One of the attractions of the kidnapping of Iraqis was that it provided a steady flow of criminal proceeds. The kidnapping of foreigners, in contrast, was far less reliable but brought in spectacular profits in some cases and little or nothing in others. Once again there is a large area of uncertainty. Most governments deny having paid anything to ransom their nationals. Yet this is partly because to do otherwise would be irresponsible. As one foreign diplomat in Iraq acknowledged: "In theory we stand together in not rewarding kidnappers, but in practice it seems some administrations have parted with cash and so it puts other foreign nationals at risk from gangs who are confident that some governments do pay."[112] The British and U.S. governments have been particularly steadfast in rejecting ransom demands, and it was even suggested in one British newspaper that the government had stifled an attempt by a wealthy businessman in Britain to pay for the release of Margaret Hassan.[113] Former British Conservative Member of Parliament Matthew Parris claims "frighteners" were put on the man, and he was warned that his family could be kidnapped next.[114]

Other countries—including Italy, Germany, and France—have been far more willing to make concessions. Although this has led to vociferous condemnation, it has been met with outright denials, with a refusal to release details of negotiations, or with quibbles such as the comment by a German official that the problem is not paying ransoms but [public] reporting of ransom payments.[115] As Daniel McGrory reported,

> A number of other governments, including those of Turkey, Romania, Sweden, and Jordan, are said to have paid for their hostages to be freed, as have some U.S. companies with lucrative reconstruction contracts in Iraq. At least four businessmen with dual U.S. and Iraqi citizenship have been returned, allegedly in exchange for payments by their employers. This money is often disguised as "expenses" paid to trusted go-betweens for costs that they claim to incur.[116]

The issue really came to the fore in May 2006 when *The Times* in London published an article detailing the payments made by France, Germany, and Italy.[117] According to this report, France led the pack in ransom payments, followed by Italy, then Germany. Specific allegations included the following:

- France paid $25 million for the release of three hostages: $15 million was handed over for Christian Chesnot and Georges Malbrunot, who were freed in December 2004, and an additional $10 million was given for the release of Florence Aubenas in June 2005 after 157 days in captivity.[118]
- Italy paid $11 million for the release of three hostages. Reportedly $5 million was paid for the release of two aid workers, Simona Pari

and Simona Torretta.[119] Abducted in September 2004, they were freed 20 days later. In February 2005, journalist Giuliana Sgrena was abducted. After intense negotiation, she was released in March 2005 for a reported ransom payment of $6 million. One of the Italian intelligence agents involved in her release was killed when their car refused to stop as it approached U.S. forces while en route to the airport. Although the Italians strenuously denied making payments, a subsequent report by the Caribinieri's anti-terrorism unit confirmed the payments.[120]

- In comparison, Germany paid less for its three hostages, although there is disagreement over whether it was $8 million or $10 million. Archaeologist Susanne Ostloff was abducted in late November 2005 and then released after 3 weeks in captivity. Although *The Times* put the ransom at $3 million, some German sources, including the *DDP News Agency*, claimed the figure was closer to $5 million.[121] Just over a month after Ostloff's release, two German engineers, Rene Braunlich and Thomas Nitzschke, were kidnapped in Baiji. This sparked enormous speculation that the Ostloff payment had encouraged this second kidnapping, especially as it became clear almost from the outset that the kidnapping was about money, not politics. German Deputy Foreign Minister Gernot Erler even went so far as to acknowledge the abduction was not political but was simply part of Iraq's "kidnapping industry."[122] Nevertheless, after Germany reportedly paid another $5 million on May 2, 2006, the engineers were released.[123]

Although these three European countries, along with the Philippines, are widely seen as participators in the most egregious cases of capitulation to terrorism and kidnapping, as suggested above they are not alone.[124] Governments also in some cases used companies employing victims of kidnapping as fronts for payment. Alternatively, they pressured the companies to meet the ransoms that were demanded, allowing the safe return of the hostages without making it appear as if the government itself had succumbed to blackmail. The relationship between India and the Kuwaiti company, KGL, probably fell into one of these categories.

Clearly, the kidnapping of foreigners has garnered much attention; it has also yielded some large one-time payments or in some cases successive large payments. If the calculations above are correct, however, the profits from this activity, although significant, are smaller than those from kidnapping Iraqis. The kidnapping of Iraqis has been more sustained and systematic than the kidnapping of foreigners. The success of the initial kidnapping groups bred a significant number of imitators. In tipping point terms, kidnapping as an activity was attractive to emulate and had a stickiness that ensured its durability.[125] Kidnapping of foreigners, in contrast, was a relatively short-term activity. Moreover, it seems to have developed in clusters. The sporadic nature of foreigner kidnapping suggests that kidnappers had a limited capacity to manage the logistic and bargaining sides of their business. And although it was lucrative, the risks involved were greater than with domestic kidnappings.

In the final analysis, however, it is important to beware of distinctions that are overly sharp in relation to an environment that is inherently fuzzy. As one commentary notes,

Criminals masked as insurgents have abducted people for ransom or for sale to insurgent groups. Likewise, some insurgent groups apparently engage in common crimes, such as kidnapping and robbery, to obtain funds for their military operations. In the lawlessness of today's Iraq, the line between the political and criminal is often blurred.[126]

Kidnapping, whether political or criminal, has been a very good source of money both for those seeking wealth and for those seeking money to fund their struggle—whether against rivals, the United States, or the Iraqi government. But as Chapter 5 will reveal, kidnapping still provided only one of a variety of revenue streams generated by criminal activities in Iraq.

ENDNOTES - CHAPTER 4

1. Erik Rye, quoted in Kirk Semple, "Kidnapped in Iraq: Victim's Tale Of Clockwork Death and Ransom," *New York Times*, May 7, 2006, p. 1.1.

2. Charles Recknagel, "Kidnapping becomes Iraq's Growth Industry," September 30, 2004, available at *www.albionmonitor. com/0410a/iraqhostagemoney.html*.

3. Vanessa Arrington, "Most Likely Kidnap Victims in Iraq Are Iraqis," *Associated Press*, March 30, 2006.

4. Semple.

5. Anthony H. Cordesman, *Iraq's Evolving Insurgency and the Risk of Civil War*, Washington, DC: Center for Strategic and International Studies, (CSIS), June 22, 2006, p. 185.

6. Semple.

7. I am grateful to Colonel Alex Crowther for this distinction.

8. Colonel Alex Crowther provided much helpful discussion on this issue, based on his experience in Iraq.

9. "Paying Ransom to Terrorists May Result in Greater Demands," Copenhagen *Information* (Internet Version-WWW) in Danish, September 30, 2004.

10. *Ibid.*

11. For the importance of imitation, see Malcolm Gladwell, *The Tipping Point*, New York: Back Bay, 2000.

12. AI report, July 25, 2005, quoted in Home Office, (UK) *Country of Origin Information Report: Iraq*, October 31, 2006.

13. Semple.

14. *Ibid.*

15. U.S. Department of State travel warning announcing lack of consular services for Americans in Iraq, February 8, 2003.

16. "Iraq: Serious Crime Thrives on Instability," *Oxford Analytica*, March 17, 2004.

17. Robert E. Looney, "The Business of Insurgency: The Expansion of Iraq's Shadow Economy," *The National Interest*, September 22, 2005.

18. "Iraq: Serious Crime Thrives on Instability."

19. Ahmad Jawdah, "Trip to Al-Basrah; Observations of People and Places; Machine Guns, Pistols, and Hand Grenades Sold Openly in the Al-Basrah Market," *Al-Sharq al-Awsat*, August 14, 2003, p. 6.

20. *Ibid.*

21. *Ibid.*

22. Robyn Dixon, "Kidnapping Gangs Add to Iraqis' Sense of Insecurity," *Los Angeles Times*, August 7, 2003.

23. *Ibid.*

24. *Ibid.*

25. Elizabeth Ferris and Matthew Hall, *Update on Humanitarian Issues and Politics in Iraq,* Berne, Switzerland: Brookings-Bern Project on Internal Displacement, University of Bern, July 6, 2007, p. 7.

26. *Ibid.*

27. Human Rights Watch, Iraq, *Climate of Fear: Sexual Violence and Abduction of Women and Girls in Baghdad,* Vol. 15, No. 8, July 2003, p. 1.

28. *Ibid.*

29. *Ibid.*, p. 1.

30. Duraed Salman, "Baghdad Kidnappers Target Easy Prey: Women and Children Increasingly Falling Victim to the Capital's Kidnapping Gangs" IWPR, October 9, 2006.

31. *Ibid.*, quoting Women's Freedom Organization.

32. Aseel Kami and Ahmed Rasheed, "Dreams of Bombs, Bad Guys Haunt Baghdad's Children," *Reuters*, March 16, 2007.

33. *Ibid.*

34. Dixon.

35. *Ibid.*

36. *Ibid.*

37. "Iraq: Serious Crime Thrives on Instability."

38. Interview with Colonel Alex Crowther.

39. *Ibid.*

40. Iyad al-Dulaymi, "After Paying a Large Ransom, A Scientist Is Told to Leave Iraq or Die," London *Quds Press* (Internet Version-WWW) in Arabic, May 7, 2004.

41. *Ibid.*

42. *Ibid.*

43. *Ibid.*

44. Sahar al-Haideri, "More and More Physicians Leave the Country, Saying Their Lives Are in Danger," ICR No. 132, July 12, 2005.

45. *Ibid.*

46. Jean-Pierre Perrin, "We Were Saddam's Hostages, Now We Are Those of the Terrorists," Paris *Liberation* (Internet Version-WWW) in French, August 2004.

47. *Ibid.*

48. Reportedly the ransom was paid by the family, not the bank. See James Glanz, "Violence in Iraq Creating Chaos in Bank System," *New York Times*, July 29, 2006, p. A1.

49. They sometimes killed those who worked with the United States which suggests that at least some of these kidnappings were political rather than economic in motivation. See Sam Knight, "In the Face of Death: The Iraqis Who Signed Up to Help the Americans Are Losing Faith—And Often Their Lives. One Family's Story," *Newsweek*, September 24, 2007.

50. Gina Chon and Joel Millman, "Iraqi Abductors Find Deep Pockets in U.S.: Militants and Criminals, Seeking Ransom, Target Iraqi Christians with Family Overseas; 'Trust Me, I Swear I Do Not Have Much Money'," *Wall Street Journal*, July 29, 2006, p. A1.

51. Simon Doyle, "Passport Cited in Iraq: Canadian Sold 'Forbidden' Technology Such as Computers," *The Gazette*

(Montreal), August 17, 2005.

52. Michael E. O'Hanlon and Jason H. Campbell, *Iraq Index: Tracking Variables of Reconstruction and Security in Post-Saddam Iraq*, Washington, DC: Brookings Institution, March 12, 2009, available at *www.brookings.edu/iraqindex*.

53. *Ibid.*

54. Haifa Zangana, "Blair Made a Pledge to Iraqis Once," *The Guardian*, April 22, 2005, June 30 2005; Samir Haddad and Mazin Ghazi, "Who Resists and Who Kidnaps," *IslamOnline.net*, September 14, 2004; and Peter Beaumont, "Kidnappers Target Youth of Baghdad," *Observer*, February 29, 2004, available at *observer.guardian.co.uk/international/story/0,6903,1158675,00.html*, March 10, 2004.

55. Elizabeth Colton, quoted in "At Least 10 Hostages a Day, Mostly Iraqi," *Chicago Sun-Times*, March 31, 2006.

56. *Ibid.*

57. "Baghdad Security Clampdown Curbs Abductions," *Gulf News*, March 1, 2007, Financial Times Information (Global News Wire — Asia Africa Intelligence Wire).

58. Doug Struck, "Professionals Fleeing Iraq As Violence, Threats Persist; Exodus of Educated Elite Puts Rebuilding at Risk," *Washington Post*, January 23, 2006, p. A1.

59. Adel Kamal, *Iraq Politics and Constitution*, Mosul, September 17, 2007.

60. "Abducted Iraqi Reporter Freed," Committee to Protect Journalists, November 5, 2007, available at *www.cpj.org*.

61. "Iraq: Kidnapping Poses New Security Threat," *Oxford Analytica*, April 22, 2004.

62. *Ibid.*

63. All figures are drawn from O'Hanlon and Campbell.

64. Pete Lentini and Muhammad Bakashmar, "Jihadist Beheading: A Convergence of Technology, Theology, and Teleology?" *Studies in Conflict & Terrorism*, Vol. 30. 2007, pp. 303–325.

65. See Dexter Filkins *et al.*, "The Struggle for Iraq: Revenge Killing; Iraq Tape Shows the Decapitation of an American," *New York Times*, May 12, 2004.

66. For a good analysis of the goals of the insurgent groups, see Human Rights Watch, "A Face and a Name: Civilian Victims of Insurgent Groups in Iraq: III Insurgent groups in Iraq," available at *www.hrw.org/reports/2005/iraq1005/3.htm*.

67. *Ibid.*

68. See "Family Heartbreak over Hassan Fate," *CNN.com*, November 17, 2004.

69. "Web Site Posts Statement on Kidnapping of 12 Nepalese in Iraq," *Al-Jazeera TV*, Doha, in Arabic, August 20, 2004.

70. "Seoul Blames Washington for Withholding Information on Kidnapping of National in Iraq," *Xinhua*, June 22, 2004.

71. Samir Haddad and Mazin Ghazi, "An Inventory of Iraqi Resistance Groups: Who Kills Hostages in Iraq?" *Al Zawra*, September 19, 2004.

72. "A $500,000 Exchange," *India.com*, February 4, 2008.

73. *Ibid.*

74. *Ibid.*

75. Sudha Ramachandran, "Iraq Held Hostage to Terror," *Asia Times Online*, September 25, 2004, available at *www.atimes.com/atimes/Middle_East/F125ak01.html*.

76. *Ibid.*

77. Andrew Cockburn, "Kidnap-For-Cash Is the One Growth Industry in Iraq's No-Go Areas," *The Independent*, September 30, 2004.

78. *Ibid.*

79. *Ibid.*

80. Mark A. Steliga, *Why They Hate Us: Disaggregating the Iraqi Insurgency*, Monterey, CA: Naval Postgraduate School, March 2005, p. 62; Anne Barnard, "Lethal Alliance Fuels Kidnappings, Iraq's Militants, Criminals Team Up," *Boston Globe*, September 25, 2004.

81. Looney, p. 70.

82. *Ibid.*

83. "Arroyo Defends Decision to Pull Out Troops in Iraq, Keeps Commitment to Allies," Quezon City *National Broadcasting Network* July 23, 2004. See also "Indonesian Editorial: Arroyo's Troop Withdrawal 'Domestic Political Compromise'," Surabaya *Jawa Pos* (*Internet Version*) in Indonesian, July 22, 2004.

84. For the global news media reaction to this, see "Iraq: Philippine Troop Withdrawal a Grave Mistake," July 28, 2004, at *www.globalsecurity.org*.

85. See Anthony Spaeth, "Giving In," *Time*, July 18, 2004.

86. Michelle Malkin, "The $6 Million Cutthroat Payoff," July 18, 2004. The article also contains the excerpt from the *Philippines Daily Tribune*, available at *michellemalkin.com/2004/07/18/the-6-million-cutthroad-payoff*.

87. *Ibid.*

88. "Daily Dismisses Reports Malaysia Pays Ransom to Free Filipino Hostage in Iraq," Kuala Lumpur *New Straits Times* (Internet Version-WWW), July 23, 2004.

89. "Iraqi Newspaper Says Kidnapping Becomes Profitable Trade," *Al Shira* (Baghdad) in Arabic, October 2, 2004, supplied by BBC Worldwide Monitoring.

90. AI Report, July 25, 2005, quoted in Home Office (UK) *Country of Origin Information Report: Iraq*, October 31, 2006.

91. "Article Hints Japan Paid Ransom for Hostages in Iraq, Manipulated Public Opinion," Tokyo *Gendai*, June 1, 2004.

92. See "George Psyllides, Iraqi Kidnappers Release Cypriot Hostage After Four Months," *Associated Press Worldstream*, January 1, 2006.

93. Quoted in Charles Recknagel, "Iraq: Latest Kidnappings Raise Questions about Motives of Hostage Takers," *RFE/REGIONAL* October 1, 2004.

94. On establishing this point, I am grateful to Colonel Alex Crowther.

95. Jill Carroll and Peter Grier, "Hostage: The Jill Carroll Story—Part 7, False Hopes," *Christian Science Monitor*, August 22, 2006, p. 1.

96. Sabah Kadhim, a spokesman of the Interior Ministry in Baghdad, as quoted in Patrick Cockburn, "I Have Children! Don't Kill Me!: The Kidnapping Gangs of Baghdad," February 7, 2005, available at *www.counterpunch.org/patrick02072005.html*.

97. *Ibid.*

98. Semple.

99. Aqeel Hussein, "Kidnappers Leave Pigeons and Ransom Money Flies In," *The Sunday Telegraph* (United Kingdom), August 5, 2007.

100. "Iraq's Sunni Ulema Said 'Torn Apart' Under Kidnappers' Pressure," *Al-Shira* (Baghdad), in Arabic, September 20, 2004.

101. Borzou Daragahi "Hassan Kidnapping Shakes Resistance Supporters," *The Globe and Mail* (Canada), October 27, 2004, p. A20.

102. *Ibid.*

103. Shaalan Ahmed, "Interview: Iraqi Cleric Says Kidnapping Tarnishes Resistance," *Xinhua*, September 27, 2004, at *www.xinhua. org.*

104. *Ibid.*

105. Daniel McGrory, "How $45m Secretly Bought Freedom of Foreign Hostages," *The Times* (London), May 22, 2006, p. 8.

106. "Italy Paid Ransom for Hostages in Iraq: Police" *Agence France Presse*, January 30, 2006.

107. *Ibid.*

108. Scott Peterson and Dan Murphy, "Ransom Claims Abound in Carroll Case; New Evidence Indicates That the UAE Tried to Negotiate for Her Release," *Christian Science Monitor*, August 25, 2006, p. 1.

109. "US Reporter's Kidnap A Mistake; Ransom Paid: Iraqi Insurgent," *Agence France Presse*, April 13, 2006.

110. AKE Group, *State of Iraq 2004*, p. 6, available at *www. Noozz.com.*

111. Loretta Napoleoni, *Terror Incorporated*, New York: Seven Stories Press, 2005.

112. McGrory.

113. Maurice Chittenden, "Hassan Ransom Payment 'Blocked by Foreign Office'," *Sunday Times* (London), January 1, 2006, News, p. 2.

114. *Ibid.*

115. Frank Walter Steinmeier, quoted in Kate Connolly, John Hooper, and Julian Borger, "Germany May End Ransom Payments for Kidnap Victims: Number of Hostages in Iraq and Afghanistan Growing. Willingness to Pay Out Believed to Increase Risk," *The Guardian*, July 31, 2007, p. 14.

116. McGrory.

117. *Ibid.*

118. *Ibid.* See also "French Government Denies Report That It Paid Secret Ransom for Iraq Hostage Releases," *Associated Press Worldstream*, May 22, 2006.

119. McGrory.

120. On the denial, see "Italy Foreign Minister Denies Country Pays Ransoms for Iraq Hostages," Associated Press, *Worldstream*, January 30, 2006. Details of a Carabinieri report investigating the payments which undercuts the denials are in "Italy Paid Ransom for Hostages in Iraq."

121. "German Iraq Hostage Carrying Ransom Money on Release—news magazine," *Text of report by German news agency DDP on January 21, BBC Worldwide Monitoring*, January 23, 2006.

122. Nathalie Waehlisch, "Iraq Hostages Expected in Berlin: German Hostages' Release in Iraq 'May Well' Have Involved Ransom Payment, *Berlin DDP in German*, May 3, 2006.

123. "Germany Accused of Paying Large Ransom for Release of Hostages: Two Men Freed Following 99 Days in Captivity in Iraq: Critics Say Payments Encourage Kidnapping," *The Guardian*, May 4, 2006. See also Luke Harding, "Western Countries Reject Claims of Iraq Ransom Payments," *Deutsche Presse-Agentur*, May 22, 2006.

124. McGrory.

125. On the notion of stickiness, see Gladwell.

126. "A Face and a Name," p. 8.

156

CHAPTER 5

EXTORTION AND OTHER CRIMINAL ACTIVITIES

Extortion and Skimming.

Several commentators during the last several years have suggested that one of the best ways for soldiers to prepare for their experience in Iraq is to watch *The Sopranos*, the U.S. television series about the Mafia. Although the term tends to be used often as a synonym for organized crime, a more precise definition of mafia has been provided by Diego Gambetta, who has argued that mafias are essentially in the business of private protection.[1] If this is the case, then Iraq has a lot of mafia organizations. Indeed, extortion in Iraq has become pervasive—partly because of the inability, until late 2007 or 2008, of either U.S. forces or the Iraqi government to provide security. In an insecure environment, especially one characterized by sectarian or ethnic conflict, nonstate actors often emerge as protectors—at least of their particular sect or ethnic group. One problem with protectors, however, is that they rarely remain on the defense, but rather sometimes form "death squads" targeting other groups. Another problem is that protection and predation are two sides of the same coin.[2] Protectors often extort money from those they are protecting. Consequently, in the anarchy of post-Ba'athist Iraq, extortion has become a major funding source for militias, insurgents, and terrorists.

Broadly speaking, there are two kinds of targets of extortion—the stationary victims and the mobile.[3] Stationary victims are typically small businesses which pay protection money to avoid attack. In Mosul, insurgents reportedly extort "5 to 20 percent of the value of contracts local businessmen get from the government."[4] Larger businesses are also subject to extortion and generally find it preferable to make payoffs than to incur the risks and costs associated with resistance. In addition, militias—because they provide protection to particular segments of the population—have enormous opportunities for both extortion and black market activities. Markets in Baghdad resemble those in Moscow in the 1990s when even small market stallholders were required to make protection payments—often under the guise of ostensibly legitimate fees—in return for which they were allowed to continue selling.

In the spring of 2004, as opposition in Iraq developed into a full-blown insurgency, the occupying forces lost control of the highways.[5] This allowed insurgents to extort money from contractors (both American and Iraqi) involved in the reconstruction business, and from commercial truck drivers, whether carrying legal loads such as food and reconstruction materials or engaged in theft and smuggling. For Sunni insurgents, the legality or illegality of the load was irrelevant. Indeed, they not only subjected drivers to extortion, but confiscated "a portion of the harvests and goods transported through the areas they control" as a tax for safe passage.[6] One contractor noted that the insurgents would sometimes "hijack a truck or kidnap a driver" to illustrate their power and establish their credibility.[7] Gradually, however, the process became institutionalized and, as with extortion elsewhere, the threat itself was sufficient. The going rate for allowing oil trucks to pass was typically $500.[8] The huge volume of truck traffic made the practice highly lucrative. With rail and air service inoperable in most of the country, many areas, especially Baghdad, relied on truck convoys for basic goods and reconstruction materials. The dilemma for transportation services was multiple tolls in different locations exacted by different actors—although for those involved in the smuggling of oil and petroleum derivatives there was often enough money to cover all these tolls.

For contractors and subcontractors, of course, these payments became simply the cost of doing business in an environment where security and law had been lacking and were almost certainly factored into contract bids to U.S. authorities in Iraq. Knowing that extortion payments are required for the movement of supplies and people, contractors inflated their bids accordingly. While the scale of extortion is impossible to determine, in a culture where baksheesh and "fixers" have long been necessary and in which the United States has spent enormous amounts on reconstruction, it is almost certainly in the millions of dollars. Parasitic taxes on commerce, reconstruction, and the transportation of oil (whether it is part of the licit trade or stolen and diverted) are highly profitable. Extortionists have few, if any, start-up costs, especially if they already have a reputation for violence; payments tend to be recurring; and, in Iraq, the number of businesses which could be targeted grew as the reconstruction process gradually became more effective.

In some cases, protection money will go to locals who have or pretend to have some contact with armed groups of one kind or another and are trying to cash in on this affiliation or are exploiting the brand name. This certainly happened in Moscow in the 1990s, and a similar opportunism is evident in Iraq. In most cases, however, payments are paid to insurgents, militias, or criminal groups willing to use the violence necessary to establish credibility. The tragic if ironic consequence of this is that the United States has indirectly funded the very people who are killing American soldiers. Businessmen in Baghdad and Mosul, for example, have paid insurgents sometimes out of sympathy but more often because of fear. Businessmen in Basra have claimed that anything connected to the state requires payments to Shiite militias and parties—often in the form of kickbacks. One businessman involved in construction noted that there were two options: "one, they give you the contract for a price but then you have to provide your own security; the other deal is that for a certain percentage of the contract they will provide you with gunmen. No other militia will attack you."[9] In his last four contracts, the businessman had paid $500,000 in bribes.[10]

In some cases, the targets of extortion have simply been minorities rather than businessmen. Reports have suggested, for example, that "in areas controlled by Sunni militias" Shiite and Christian residents "have only secured their 'right' to remain in the areas" by paying tributes and fees extorted from them.[11] In other instances the Shiite militias have expelled Sunnis from their homes and have then taken control of the property. Although they have sometimes allowed displaced Shiites to take refuge in these homes, they have also sold or rented the homes for profit. Sectarian cleansing often has an underlying financial motive not yet fully appreciated. Moreover, it can sometimes feed directly into violence. At least one car bomb detonated in the Bayya district of Baghdad seems to have targeted the local Directorate of Properties in an attempt to destroy the property registries and thus "weaken the claims of those displaced from the area."[12] At the very least, the destruction of the directorate strengthened the position of the "new landlords" who "go to the trouble of generating forged deeds proving their ownership of the property."[13]

Nor has extortion been confined to obvious targets with considerable wealth or simply readily available resources such as real estate or cars. Some groups have even targeted refugee camps in which the situation is dire because nongovernmental organizations (NGOs) have found it difficult to provide a steady supply of drinking water, so that many displaced families have little choice other than using contaminated water. In 2007, a report from the Integrated Regional Information Networks (IRIN) suggested that even internally displaced people were subject to extortion by men who brought in much needed drinking water, but in return demanded money or sexual favors. In one camp in southern Iraq, two men were killed for challenging "militants demanding sex for water."[14] Although the deaths and the extortion were reported, little seems to have been done about it.

All this highlights what for at least 4 years was one of the central problems in Iraq: neither the United States nor the Iraqi government was able to provide adequate levels of security for citizens of Iraq. As a result, people had little choice other than to pay for "protection" or accept expulsion if they were lucky and violence or murder if they were not. In turn, the proceeds from protection fees and confiscated property sales and rentals have strengthened nonstate groups and provided resources for their continued challenge to the Baghdad government.

Whereas extortion is involuntary on the part of the target, some businesses provided money for the insurgents or militias as a result of sympathy with the cause rather than fear. This occurred in Mosul and is discussed more fully in Chapter 7, which looks closely

161

at insurgent criminal activities. The key point here is simply that extortion and skimming are so pervasive that, like oil smuggling and kidnapping, they are real moneymakers in Iraq. Profits were clearly extensive, enduring, and highly lucrative—both to criminals and to other violent actors in Iraq's post-Hussein conflict milieu. Other criminal activities provided additional revenue streams for criminal and political groups alike.

Armed Robberies.

Since the fall of Saddam Hussein, Iraq has been rife with criminal activities ranging from bank robberies and drug trafficking to kidnapping, oil smuggling, and extortion. Because of its cash economy, there are many opportunities for robberies, and it has been estimated that, on average, about a million dollars a month are stolen at gunpoint.[15] As one report noted, Baghdad has become the bank robbery capital of the world. This appeared to be underlined in the summer of 2007 when three guards at the Dar al-Salam Bank in Baghdad stole what was widely reported to be $282 million but in fact was the far more modest amount of $282,000. More substantial robberies took place at al-Rafidian Bank ($1.2m), the Industry Bank, ($784,000), the Iraqi Trade Bank, ($1.8m), the Bank of Baghdad ($1.6million), the al-Warka Bank, ($750,000), and the Middle East Investment Bank ($1.32 million).[16] In addition, as discussed in Chapter 4, "bank executives have been kidnapped from their homes for ransoms as high as $6 million."[17] In effect, both banks and bankers have become targets in what for the perpetrators has been a highly "rewarding" activity.

In addition to bank robberies, criminals have also robbed those transporting money. This practice has extended well beyond Baghdad. In one robbery in Diala, armed men stole one billion Iraqi dinars ($860,000) from government accountants as they left a Diala bank with "bags of cash" to be used for social welfare payments for poor families.[18] Identifying the perpetrators is difficult, but it seems likely that policemen and security guards are almost certainly involved in at least some of the robberies. Fortunately, it also appears that the number of bank robberies in which large amounts of cash are stolen has been diminishing, particularly since 2007 and 2008. Such a trend could reflect enhanced protective measures by the banks themselves, as well as the more general improvement in security.

Commodity Smuggling.

Smuggling between Iraq and its neighbors is a time-honored way of life which is culturally and economically embedded in border communities and, therefore, resistant to interference by governments or occupying forces. This is understandable given a country which shares 3,650 kilometers of borders with six different neighbors: Iran (1,458 km), Jordan (181 km), Kuwait (240 km), Saudi Arabia (814 km), Syria (605 km), and Turkey (352 km). Multiple borders have combined with the nature of the terrain, the itinerant Bedouin tradition, and the difficulties of policing to create a legacy of contraband smuggling which, in most border regions, is simply regarded as an extension of legitimate trade. One well-informed observer even argues that calling "the unofficial cross-border trade between Syria and Iraq 'smuggling' is to do it a considerable disservice. Such "smuggling" is long-standing and has been vital to the welfare and prosperity of the populations of western Iraq and eastern Syria since the two states were formed."[19]

Much the same could be said about Iraq's other borders, especially that with Iran and that with Turkey. The border with Turkey, for example, is dominated by Kurdish networks based on a common sense of identity which transcends national borders. It too is "dominated by the tribes, whose relationships to the national capitals . . . is historically uneasy."[20] The border with Iran has a similar porosity, partly because of the common Shiite identity. Smuggling through the marsh region and across the Shatt al-Arab also has a long tradition. In other words, Iraq has long been characterized by porous borders, while those involved in cross-border trade, both licit and illicit, had accumulated knowledge and resources about routes and methods and developed personal, social, and business networks which greatly facilitated their activities.

Thus smuggling has long had considerable significance as a coping mechanism for border communities. Saddam Hussein's creation of a large-scale infrastructure enabling the regime to circumvent sanctions, to continue to export oil and other proscribed commodities, and to import weapons technologies, simply formalized and extended activities which were an integral part of the history and geography of the region. Since the collapse of the regime, however, smuggling has been driven by market forces rather than sanctions. It has functioned through traditional networks and cross-border connections outside the state apparatus, resulting in distributed rather than centralized financial gains.

The Coalition Provincial Authority's (CPA) disbanding of the Iraqi Army, including the Iraq Border Army, left the borders almost completely open. And, as Robert Bateman notes, "The Coalition did not have enough military units to replace these disbanded forces in guarding the 2,281 miles of Iraq's borders. Coalition forces assigned to border security had their hands full concentrating on the land-based ports of entry, leaving the hundreds upon hundreds of miles between the official crossing points exposed."[21] Limited manpower was one problem. Another was the inexperience of CPA officials assigned the responsibility for border control. The official given this responsibility was deployed to Iraq because of his political and ideological support for the Bush administration rather than because he offered the kinds of skill, expertise, and experience needed for border security. Although this situation improved as the U.S. military took on greater responsibility, the difficulties of revitalizing the Ministry of Interior and the Ministry of Defense retarded the development of an effective border force with adequate training and logistic support.[22] The Iraqis themselves have a very limited capacity to patrol large areas, while customs officers, given their modest wages and the lack of oversight, are highly susceptible to bribery and corruption. Moreover, border checkpoints are relatively few in number and have modest inspection capabilities.

The result was an easily exploited vacuum, seized upon by both terrorists and criminals. This allowed an influx of al-Qaeda members — most of them from Saudi Arabia, Libya, and Morocco — who came into Iraq, mainly through Syria, to fight against Coalition forces or to carry out suicide attacks. The smuggling of commodities which were not illegal in themselves but which were subject to rules and tariffs also became endemic. Post-Ba'athist Iraq experienced increased demands from segments of the Iraqi population for consumer goods long denied them. This was driven in part by the replacement of state-controlled television with multiple and diverse channels, which made Iraqi consumers much more aware of what they had been missing during the sanctions era. In response, electronics and other consumer goods, cars, computers, cigarettes, and a wide array of other commodities were all smuggled into Iraq. In some cases, payoffs were made to customs to allow safe passage; in other instances, however, traders chose to circumvent customs posts and smuggle goods across the border because corrupt customs officers were demanding large bribes.[23]

Price differentials in the region also encouraged smuggling out of Iraq. Commodities which were moved across the border included minerals, oil, antiquities, and sheep, which brought twice the price in Syria they fetched in Iraq.[24] In 2004, for example, over 13,000 sheep were seized while en route to Syria.[25] Such seizures reflect the importance of livestock in the cross-border trade between Jordan, Syria, and Iraq. Indeed, "cattle, goats, and sheep intended for sale in urban markets, are moved in large flocks, usually by Bedouin shepherds, who move their charges across borders in very remote areas, where they are picked up and moved to market by trucks owned by or contracted to the importing syndicate."[26]

This trade, along with that in electronics, gold, and consumer products, can be understood as a blend of traditional activities, especially on the part of many tribes, coping strategies developed during the 20 years or so of economic decline, the maintenance of informal trade linkages with Iraq's neighbors, and a response to both new imperatives and new opportunities. Unfortunately, these opportunities also included smuggling to fund insurgency as well as the trafficking of drugs, arms, and people.

Drug Trafficking.

Analyzing the drug business in Iraq is extremely difficult. The Iraqi police, who understandably give drug trafficking and abuse a low priority, appear to have done few, if any, serious studies. Similarly, with the health service in disarray and overwhelmed by continuing, if declining, levels of violence, there is no systematic assessment of drug abuse. Nevertheless, anecdotal evidence suggests that there is little room for complacency. Some of the problems are already evident, and Iraq has many of the conditions which typically facilitate an expansion of the drug business.

This is not intended to exaggerate the problem— clearly, drug trafficking in Iraq is relatively modest when compared both with other criminal activities besetting the country and with the scale of trafficking in many other countries. Moreover, "a strong cultural undercurrent against drug abuse in Iraqi civil society" remains evident.[27] "Drug abuse is stigmatized quite heavily."[28] In part this reflects the attempt by religious groups to maintain a degree of social control, particularly over young people. Even so, controls and inhibitions are weakening. Indeed, during the next several years, it seems likely that Iraq will suffer from a significant growth in both drug trafficking and drug abuse. Iraq has almost all the preconditions for an increasing drug problem. There are at least three distinct, if reinforcing, dimensions to this problem: drug abuse, transshipment through Iraq and trafficking within Iraq.

Drug abuse in Iraq has already taken a variety of forms, ranging from glue-sniffing by children to the abuse of pharmaceuticals such as captagon (a stimulant very similar to methamphetamine), benzhexol (relaxant), benzodiazepine (can act as a stimulant when abused), valium, and both synthetic and botanical illegal drugs.[29] Cocaine, methamphetamine, heroin, and hashish are all being smuggled into the country either for transshipment or local sale. In July 2008, U.S. Marines and Iraqi highway patrolmen seized approximately 500 pounds of narcotics, largely methamphetamine-type stimulants, and arrested three individuals.

Although this was described as "a major disruption of the drug trafficking in Western Al Anbar," experience elsewhere suggests that at best such disruption has only a short-term impact.[30] Not only are various drugs readily available in Iraq, it also appears that insurgents, terrorists, and militia members have used narcotics to help them in combat. Members of Zarqawi's organization reportedly used drugs, while the 2005 uprising in Najaf seems to have been fuelled in part by drug-intoxicated combatants.[31] In addition, reports suggest that Khanaqin, a small Iraqi town near the Iranian border, has become an outlet for cheap drugs which many locals believe are provided by Iranian traffickers.[32]

What makes all of this particularly disturbing is the absence of serious health and education programs to help reduce or restrain market demand—which appears to be growing. Assessments suggest that the domestic market, although small in absolute terms, has expanded significantly. One official in the Ministry of Health estimated in March 2006 that "more than

5,000 Iraqis are consuming drugs in the south today, especially heroin, compared with 2004, when there were only around 1,500."[33] He also acknowledged that "the number could be as high as 10,000 countrywide."[34] It is likely that the numbers have grown since then. Nevertheless, prevention and rehabilitation programs continue to have a very low priority in a country where reconstruction efforts remain halting and uneven and governance mechanisms are only partially effective at best.

The irony is that preventive/rehabilitation programs will be increasingly needed. The demographics of Iraq seem likely to feed the burgeoning drug problem. Of the population of Iraq, 38.8 percent (or 5.7 million males and 5.5 million females) is aged 14 years or under.[35] As this cohort ages, it becomes a major market for criminal organizations looking for profitable markets. Moreover, a context of continued upheaval, widespread unemployment and poverty, and anxiety and uncertainty about the future will make many of these young people more susceptible to drug abuse and to involvement in the drug business. Drugs in Iraq will offer users an escape from desperate conditions and pushers an escape from unemployment. This situation is likely to be worsened by the large number of orphans in Iraq. According to an assessment by the Iraqi Ministry of Labor and Social Affairs, Iraq has 4.5 million orphans, with half a million of them living on the streets.[36] Even if this figure is exaggerated, it suggests a very large recruitment pool for both consumption and trafficking. According to one Iraqi official, there are already signs: drugs which come in from Iran are "sold at the Saudi border. Smugglers are young, and they use motorcycles or animals to cross the desert late at night."[37]

Drug use is also likely to increase as a result of growing transshipment through Iraq which has become an increasingly important route for opium and heroin from Afghanistan en route to the Gulf States. When countries are on transshipment routes, they almost inevitably develop local markets as a result of product leakage. This has happened in Mexico, as well as many other countries, and seems to be happening in Iraq. Such a process is insidious, especially in a country where public health and education capacity are limited.

Transshipment countries, as Richard Friman points out, have two particularly important characteristics: access to target or market countries, and ease of transshipment.[38] Iraq qualifies on both counts. It is strategically located for access to Kuwait, Saudi Arabia, and the Gulf states, and offers few serious obstacles to the movement of narcotics. Iraq's borders remain highly porous and difficult to patrol. Shiite pilgrimages to Najaf and Kerbala also offer opportunities for unscrupulous traffickers to enter and exit Iraq with an apparently legitimate purpose.[39] This makes border control even more problematic, not least because of the importance of maintaining free movement for the pilgrims.

Cross-border linkages and relationships which have been so important for smuggling of oil and other commodities are equally suited to the smuggling of drugs. This is important in a number of areas of Iraq, but perhaps nowhere more so than those controlled by the Kurds. The Kurdish Worker's Party (PKK), a terrorist organization, as well as the Kurdish and Turkish diasporas, have been extensively involved in heroin trafficking to Western Europe, including Holland and Germany.[40] The use of Iraq as a transshipment country by drug trafficking networks affiliated either with the PKK or Kurdish and Turkish criminal organizations seems likely to increase. In this connection, it is worth noting that "the Commander of the Iraqi Drug Squad in the northern Kurdish province of Sulaymaniyah reported 117 arrests for drug smuggling over the past 2 years. His squad sees opium, heroin, and cannabis coming over the border in mule trains, cars, and trucks operated by Iranian gangs. He reports that the drugs are moved on to Turkey, where the opium is refined into heroin."[41]

As well as going northwest through Iraq from Iran, heroin shipments also come through Iraq going south. In this connection, one of the more vulnerable areas is Maysan province, where the marshes along the border with Iran are very difficult to control. The provincial capital of Amara has become a way point for what one Iraqi police commander described as a "huge amount of drugs heading for the Gulf countries."[42] Even if we acknowledge that "huge" is relative, the problem is serious. Other important transshipment points include Safwan near Iraq's border with Kuwait and Samawa city in Muthanna province, from where drugs are smuggled into Saudi Arabia.[43] It is worth noting that several hundred Iraqis have been arrested in Saudi Arabia in recent years, most of them for drug offenses. According to September 2008 reports, of 340 Iraqi citizens convicted of criminal activities by Saudi courts (with another 93 awaiting trial), 306 were found guilty of either drug possession or drug trafficking.[44] Although few details have been made public apart from the numbers, this suggests that Iraqi involvement in regional drug trafficking might be growing.

Trafficking within Iraq also appears to be increasing not least because the opportunities in the licit economy remain limited. Some people have entered the drug business as pushers, simply as a means of feeding their families. Once they have fallen under the control of a drug trafficking group, it is very difficult for them to extricate themselves from the business. Moreover, as security is gradually restored in Iraq, so the major criminal revenue stemming from oil smuggling, kidnapping, and extortion will diminish significantly; in such circumstances, there will a shift to other crimes as criminal organizations are compelled to adapt. As one criminal market contracts, others will expand. Furthermore, as long as the criminal and war economies in Iraq remain deeply intermeshed, combatant organizations will look to criminal activities for funding. In sum, drug trafficking, which could increasingly offer a highly dependable and lucrative form of revenue generation, is set to expand.

It is worth noting that as early as 2004, elements of the Mahdi Army were caught by Polish forces in possession of significant amounts of heroin.[45] Although the Mahdi Army subsequently broadened its portfolio of criminal activities and has not been implicated further, the incident suggests that the drug business is certainly not taboo. It is possible that as Muqtada al-Sadr has sought to be integrated into the political process, Mahdi Army inhibitions against involvement in the drug business have increased. Nevertheless, splinter factions of the Mahdi Army will almost certainly look to drug trafficking as a major moneymaker. Reports that farmers were cultivating opium poppy and that AQI might even control some of the opium farms have not been substantiated.[46]

It seems clear, therefore, that the overall scale of the problem remains modest, at least for now. The Department of State's March 2008 International

Narcotics Control Strategy Report (INCSR) contains few details in the section on Iraq. In its analysis of Syria, however, the INCSR notes that captagon is smuggled through Syria and into Iraq for use by foreign fighters and insurgents.[47] As always, the difficulty lies in determining how much illicit activity is visible and how much remains covert. Given all the difficulties Iraq faces, however, under-reporting of the drug problem seems more likely than inflation of the figures. Indeed, what are by most standards very modest assessments take on an added significance in a country characterized by high levels of violence and instability with limited government capacity for accurate appraisal of social, political, and economic problems. In the final analysis, it is difficult to disagree with Paul Kan's assessment that the instability in Iraq has facilitated "the emergence of a robust drug market."[48]

Weak government and economic upheaval provide an ideal environment in which drug trafficking and drug use can flourish. None of this should be exaggerated. As Kan notes, Iraq is still in the "incipient stage" of the drug problem, and both its scope and impact remain limited. Indeed, the 2009 INCSR noted that military check points and subversive activity outside military-controlled areas act as major inhibitors, ensuring that the amount of narcotics smuggled in and through Iraq remains low.[49] The Report also notes that most Iraqis would find it difficult financially to support a drug habit.

At the same time, Kan's argument about the potential for the growth of the drug problem in Iraq is very compelling. This was evident in 2009 which highlighted some of the seizures and arrests made by Iraqi authorites.[50] Moreover, the conditions outlined above suggest that Iraq is ripe for a significant expansion of drug trafficking and use and that countervailing forces which might inhibit such an expansion are weak. Consequently, criminal organizations and other violent groups are almost certain to diversify their illicit businesses into the drug trade in the years ahead. Such a development, however, is much easier to predict than to forestall.

Antiquities Theft and Smuggling.

Another important area of criminal activity in Iraq is the theft and smuggling of antiquities. Here, there are two separate activities which need to be kept distinct: the initial plunder of Iraq's National Museum, and the subsequent looting, theft, and trafficking of antiquities from Iraq's 12,000-plus archaeological sites, most of which are either unguarded or guarded very poorly. The first received a great deal of attention, provoked enormous criticism of the United States, and generated a lot of misinformation. The second has been largely neglected.

Much of the debate over the museum looting has revolved around the issue of whether it was organized or spontaneous. Matthew Bogdanos, a Marine Colonel and assistant district attorney who investigated the looting, concludes that there was "not one but three thefts at the museum by three distinct groups: professionals who stole several dozens of the most prized treasures, random looters who stole more than 3,000 excavation-site pieces, and insiders who stole almost 11,000 cylinder seals and pieces of jewelry."[51] He also notes that initially the extent of the theft was greatly exaggerated, with claims that 170,000 pieces had been stolen when in fact the figure was around 15,000.[52] Part of the initial difficulty of making an accurate assessment was that prior to the Coalition invasion sections of the museum were already in disarray, while cataloguing and accounting procedures were not up to international standards.

Some of the looted pieces were returned to the museum in the days and weeks after the looting spree by local people, while other pieces were returned by museum employees who had removed them for safekeeping. In addition, 465 artifacts were recovered at a checkpoint in Kut—although the smugglers escaped.[53] Subsequently Syria confiscated looted items including golden necklaces, daggers, and other artifacts that had been smuggled out of Iraq and returned them to Baghdad.[54] Another 1,450 artifacts turned up in Jordan.[55] In contrast, "few of the randomly looted items appear to have made their way into the hands of the kinds of established smugglers who have developed the sophisticated strategies necessary for evading border seizures on a regular basis."[56] Some of the more select items which were taken by professionals or insiders did start to appear very quickly in Europe and the United States, leading one of the curators to conclude that this portion of the looting "was an organized crime."[57] It was also a crime with transnational linkages, although whether the thefts were actually executed to order remains uncertain. Nor is it clear who the perpetrators were, although it is certainly conceivable that some of them were closely connected to the regime.

Important as they were, the thefts from the Museum were simply part of a systematic and continuing process of looting antiquities from archaeological sites throughout Iraq. Such looting predated the U.S. invasion and has continued since. During the 1990s, with the regime under international pressure, it "had difficulty policing and securing the sites."[58] As one antiquities expert notes, "sites get looted because of the lack of political stability, lack of security, and poverty."[59] In Iraq all three factors were at work during Saddam Hussein's last years in power. During subsequent years, however, looting seems to have become even more systematic and more organized. According to one report, the excavations are "planned and executed by organized bands—200 to 300 per site—with heavy machinery at many of the 12,000 sites. And the payout is big. The average Iraqi makes the equivalent of $1,000 per year, yet a cache of looted antiquities can sell for $20,000. And looters can sell two or three such caches every week."[60]

Those in charge of the business, of course, make much larger profits, and it has been alleged that "there are dozens of antiquities kingpins who organize large-scale looting, moving thousands of objects out of Iraq each year."[61] Reports suggest that in some instances as many as 200 looters were working at night using electrical generators at sites such as Umma.[62] The route for smuggled Iraqi antiquities goes from the museums or archaeological sites in Iraq overland to Jordan or Syria and from there to Beirut, Dubai, or Geneva where they are assigned false provenance and then sold "to private collectors or even well-known auction houses."[63]

In March 2008 Bogdanos claimed that some of the profits from antiquities trafficking were finding their way to the insurgents.[64] This conclusion was partly based on the discovery in 2006 of antiquities which had been stolen from the National Museum "in bunkers alongside weapons, ammunition, and uniforms."[65] He also suggested that antiquities were playing the same kind of role for the insurgency in Iraq as opium was for the Taliban in Afghanistan and that they had even generated "an underground tariff system."[66] Others were skeptical. The remarks were dismissed by one journalist/documentary-maker. As he put it, "Looting is not about terrorism. It's about money. It's a criminal activity. It's like the drug trade."[67] The problem with this argument is that it is undermined by the analogy that is used. In Colombia and Afghanistan, the drug trade is fully exploited by the Revolutionary Armed Forces of Colombia (FARC) and the Taliban, respectively. Indeed, insurgents and terrorists need funding and will use whatever source is available — including the drug trade and the theft and smuggling of antiquities.

Bogdanos acknowledges that initially the insurgents in Iraq were not "sophisticated," but claims that by 2004 the Sunni insurgents and al-Qaeda were using antiquity theft and trafficking for funding and that the Shiite militias subsequently followed suit.[68] Insurgents and militias need funding and are unlikely to remain aloof when others are making money, either legally or through illicit activities. As with oil smuggling, even if they are not directly involved they are almost certainly imposing some kind of tax or demanding a slice of the profits in return for allowing the trade to operate.

Car Theft and Car Smuggling.

Another criminal activity that appears to be linked to the insurgency in Iraq is car theft and smuggling — including from sources as far away as the United States, though few details have been publicly acknowledged. However, the *Boston Globe* in October 2005 reported that "the FBI's counterterrorism unit has launched a broad investigation of U.S.-based theft rings after discovering that some of the vehicles used in deadly car bombings in Iraq . . . were probably stolen in the United States."[69] In November 2005, U.S. troops raiding a bomb-making factory in Fallujah "found a sport utility vehicle registered in Texas that was being prepared for a bombing mission."[70] Further investigations found other cases in which automobiles stolen from the United States were smuggled to "Syria or other Middle East countries and ultimately into the hands of Iraqi insurgent groups—including al-Qaeda in Iraq."[71] Although no authoritative figures have been released, one FBI agent later acknowledged that the figure was in the dozens.[72] It was also suggested that large sport utility vehicles (SUVs) like the Chevrolet Suburban were particularly attractive to terrorists and insurgents for car bombs as they resembled American security vehicles, therefore arousing less suspicion than other vehicles.[73] Another advantage was that more explosives could be packed inside them, generating more death and destruction.

This seems to have been confirmed by a private investigator who claims that "numerous used car dealers in Tampa from Iraq and Gaza . . . are sending vehicles to the Middle East (Dubai) and then into Iraq in what appears to be in support of terrorism. . . . [B]oth the Mahdi army and al-Qaeda in Iraq rely heavily upon profits from [selling] the vehicles to continue with their terrorist activity."[74] Other reports have suggested that elements in the Mahdi Army in Basra were deeply implicated in the smuggling of cars into Iraq from Dubai and paying for them with the proceeds obtained from oil smuggling.[75] Although this appears to be a for-profit activity rather than for car bombs, the profits in turn are almost certainly used to support both JAM's military activities and its provision of social welfare.

The United States is not the only source of stolen cars that ended up in Iraq. There were hints in several

Canadian news reports that some vehicles stolen from Canada might also be appearing in Iraq. With an estimated 20,000 to 30,000 "higher-end stolen vehicles leaving Canada every year . . . worth $50,000 each," this is clearly big business.[76] How many of these vehicles are destined for Iraq is not known, but it is probable that some are. More substantive and less speculative reports indicated that cars from Norway were also being smuggled to Iraq. It was estimated that approximately 10,000 cars are stolen each year in Norway, and only about 20 percent of them are recovered.[77] Moreover, it appears that some car thefts in Norway are executed systematically rather than randomly. Many of the cars targeted for theft "carry large loans, meaning their theft amounts to a swindle against the lender financing them or the car's insurance company. Nearly 60 stolen cars worth as much as NOK 20 million are believed to have been sent to northern Iraq via Syria and Turkey as early as 2004."[78]

One Norwegian investigator claimed that "some of the cars were then smuggled into southern Iraq" where they were "used in suicide bombings or in other terrorist operations."[79] In November 2006, some of the cars stolen in Norway and appearing in Iraq were noticed with the European license plate "covered by an Iraqi plate" but without additional modification.[80] If cars from Norway are being stolen and smuggled to Iraq, then it is likely that cars from elsewhere in Western and Central Europe are also smuggled into Iraq. Car theft in Europe is big business, and even if only a small percentage of stolen vehicles end up in Iraq, the profits for the recipients are significant.

Stolen cars also arrive in Iraq from elsewhere in the Middle East. It has been reported, for example, that in the first 2 months of 2007, 90 cars stolen in Lebanon were smuggled through Syria into Iraq, entering through the al-Walid crossing in Anbar province.[81] There are some claims that Hezbollah is involved in this trade. Other cars from the Saudi Arabian border and Kuwait come into Southern Iraq. In the incident in March 2007 in which British sailors were captured by the Iranian navy, the ship they boarded was carrying smuggled cars — suggesting that the car smuggling into al-Basra was under the protection of the Iranian navy.[82] There has also been a trade in stolen car parts that are smuggled out of Israel into Jordan, and from there to Iraq, the purpose being unclear.[83] The whole business of theft and smuggling of automobiles to Iraq is only dimly understood — at least in open sources. One of the uncertainties is whether particular vehicles are stolen and smuggled specifically for sale for use as weapons in Iraq or simply as one outcome of an extended transactional process for making money illegally.

Of course, there is also car theft within Iraq itself. This became a problem almost immediately after the occupation began, with an upsurge of violent carjackings. In August 2003, for example, the *Washington Post* noted that in postwar Baghdad, a Mercedes Benz was easy to get and easy to lose.[84] Initially, the carjacking was almost always a disorganized, opportunistic crime, facilitated by the widespread availability of firearms, targeting the influx of luxury automobiles, some legally imported, some smuggled through Basra and across the Turkish and Jordanian borders. The thefts took place in a low-risk environment in which the police and military forces were seriously over-stretched. Stopping car theft was not a high priority. By the time the *Washington Post* article was written, an estimated 70 cars a day were being stolen and carjacking was described as "Baghdad's number one crime problem," with cars being taken "by gunmen who surprise drivers at busy traffic stops, on lonely stretches of road, or just outside homes and garages."[85] There were also suggestions that carjacking was becoming organized, with "gangs following potential victims and learning their driving routes, and even offering to find and return stolen cars to their owners for a hefty fee."[86] This transition from disorganized to organized crime in the car theft business almost certainly increased in years after the collapse of the Saddam Hussein regime. This was perhaps best illustrated in Maysan Province where British forces noted not only that "kidnapping for ransom, carjacking, and drug smuggling" were "the staples of local employment," but also that auto theft had become "so regular that victims know where to go to buy back their car when it's taken."[87]

There are several other dimensions worth noting. First, car smuggling into Iraq and car theft problems within Iraq have occasionally intersected: stolen cars which were brought into Iraq simply for commercial purposes were not immune to theft or to subsequent use in suicide bombings. Second, as "death squads" in Baghdad became particularly active in kidnapping people for torture and murder, car theft became a bonus and even a form of funding for the atrocities. The authoritative website *IraqSlogger* outlined what it described as "an important but often overlooked financial aspect of the torture squad operations" carried out by Mahdi Army members; it noted that the death squads typically financed their operations by stealing anything of value from the victims and often the most valuable things were their cars.[88] Reportedly, stolen cars are sold on the black market for roughly 50 percent of their fair-market price, although the most typical price was in the range of $2,000 to $2,500, depending on condition and model.[89]

The exploitation of stolen cars was not limited to Shiite militias. Sunni insurgents also used it as a funding mechanism. In November 2006, U.S. forces captured six insurgents who had not only carried out car-bomb attacks but also were "responsible for criminal activities including extortion, murder, kidnapping, and car theft in the Haswah and Baghdad areas."[90] The group had even provided other insurgents with financial support obtained through its criminal activities. Recent reports about al-Qaeda in Iraq reveal that this organization too has been deeply involved in car theft, an issue discussed more fully in Chapter 7.

Smuggling and the Black Market in Arms and Ammunition.

Another area of criminal activity is weapons smuggling and black market sales. In Iraq, however, this tended to be a disorganized rather than organized market, partly because of the ready availability of weapons. Iraq has long been a country with widespread gun ownership. Moreover, under Saddam Hussein, weapons stockpiles were widely distributed through the country. U.S. forces in Iraq, partly because of insufficient troop levels, failed to secure these stockpiles. As one report notes, "Conventional munitions storage sites were looted after major combat operations and some remained vulnerable as of October 2006."[91] Indeed, there does not appear to have been a survey of these sites throughout Iraq, and it is unclear how many weapons and how much ammunition were looted. Nevertheless, it was clearly significant. The U.S. Central Command (CENTCOM) commander, who testified before the U.S. Senate Committee on Appropriations on September 24, 2003, acknowledged that there was "more ammunition in Iraq than any place I've ever been in my life, and it is [not all] securable."[92] Although more than 417,000 tons of munitions were destroyed or secured, significant amounts of conventional munitions had fallen into the hands of resistance groups or remained unsecured.[93] The amount of unaccounted-for munitions "could range significantly from thousands to millions of tons."[94] Even though the scale of the problem is uncertain, these munitions almost certainly contributed to both the insurgency and the more general violence in Iraq.

A second reason for the lack of organization in the weapons market is that individuals in the Iraqi police and military have frequently sold their weapons.[95] Although the evidence here is anecdotal, *IraqSlogger* notes cases in which Iraqi policemen sold the weapons issued to them: in one instance, which is cited, an Iraqi policeman sold his Glock pistol and protective vest for $1,500.[96] The low salaries paid to policemen are, of course, a contributing factor. It is particularly disturbing, however, since several hundred thousand weapons have been purchased by the United States for the Iraqi police and military. By 2006 an estimated 14,000 weapons of the 370,000 the United States had provided in the previous few years were unaccounted for.[97]

In part, this was because strict control had been sacrificed in order to get weapons where they were needed as rapidly as possible. Though this was understandable, it meant that police weapons became available for purchase in Iraqi markets. Indeed, *IraqSlogger* even provides a list of black market prices for weapons. AK-47s, for example, can be purchased in Iraq for around $500 (a significant increase since 2003, when the price was only $50); launchers for rocket-propelled grenades (RPGs) cost $150, while the explosive charges are $50 each; Glock and Walther pistols cost between $900 and $1,100; Dragunov sniper rifles with rudimentary scopes cost over $1,000; and Krinkov short barrel rifles with folding stock cost $2,000.[98] The price of the Krinkov is high because it can easily be concealed and used from cars. Bullets remain relatively cheap and once again seem to be sold by policemen looking to augment their salaries. More control over weapons has been imposed, however, with serial-numbered individual weapons matched to individual Iraqi soldiers and policemen by name.

Human Smuggling, Women Trafficking, and Document Fraud.

One area of criminal activity in Iraq that has been little explored in open literature is the issue of human smuggling and the associated document fraud that is an essential facilitator of such activities. The massive refugee problem, with an estimated two million Iraqis having fled to neighboring countries where job opportunities are very limited, provides a powerful incentive for people to try to resettle completely outside the area, especially in Western Europe. Pressure has mounted on businessmen, in particular, as they have had to face a barrage of violence and theft.[99] The same is true of the internally displaced people in Iraq. In many cases, however, families will not have the means even to consider the possibility of resettlement. But sometimes the desire is accompanied by sufficient funds either to buy false or real documentation or to pay human smugglers the high fees they charge for facilitating illegal emigration. Some "companies" or middle men offer visas to the United Arab Emirates (UAE), while others assist with visas to the European Union (EU).

The latter visas increased in price, costing anywhere from $8,000 to $15,000 per person, on top of which are the costs of transportation and accommodations.[100] Some of the facilitators are little more than confidence men, taking the money, disappearing, and never delivering the goods. Others actually provide legitimate visas, although in many cases this requires some level of bribery. Once the visa is obtained, people leave, often from Syria or Jordan. Italy tends to be the initial destination, but in some cases people move on to Holland where they destroy their passports and request political asylum.[101]

An alternative to the visa process is to become involved in human smuggling. Indeed, both internally displaced people and refugees in Syria and Jordan who have the money look to criminal enterprises to smuggle them into Western Europe. One of the most surprising elements of this trend is the boost it has given to the human smuggling business in Sweden, which has emerged as one of the major destinations of Iraqis immigrating to Europe. In 2006 almost 9,000 Iraqis applied for asylum; in 2007 the number more than doubled to almost 18,600.[102] Many of the Iraqis arrive via Germany.

In fact, in 2006, German authorities "arrested a 48-year-old Iraqi and a 36-year-old Syrian" who had not only smuggled in people from both countries using forged passports, but were suspected of having links with the Ansar al-Islam terrorist network.[103] In the first 3 months of 2007, German Federal Police detained 444 Iraqis smuggled through the borders with the Czech Republic and Poland.[104] Another route goes through the Czech Republic into the EU. In March 2007 Czech police arrested six Iraqi emigrants as well as two Slovaks involved in the smuggling business.[105] In May 2007, police arrested nine human smugglers, including the Lebanese leader, and detained nine Iraqis who had no passports.[106]

In still another case, arrests were made in Greece.[107] Perhaps the most extensive arrests in Europe, however, came in June 2008 as part of what was called Operation Baghdad. At least 75 people—mainly Iraqi Kurds—were arrested, 24 of them in Paris.[108] Arrests were also made in Germany, Belgium, Britain, Greece, Ireland, Norway, the Netherlands, and Sweden, disrupting what was described as a "well-structured transnational cell."[109] The emigrants from Iraq were "generally taken through Turkey and several southern European countries" and then to Sweden or elsewhere in Scandinavia.[110] They usually paid between $9,300 and $21,000.[111] In addition, the United States is the destination for some smuggled Iraqis using fake European passports, sometimes via Central or South America. Unfortunately, little is known about the smugglers including the relationship between the parts of the networks within Iraq and those outside.

Although illegal migrants are often exploited, essentially the decision to become involved in illegal migration is a voluntary one. This is not the case with people—especially women and children—who are trafficked and often coerced into lives of sexual servitude or forced labor. Reports that this was becoming a problem surfaced soon after the U.S. invasion, and in July 2003 Human Rights Watch (HRW) claimed that the number of abducted women and girls sold abroad in the Gulf and elsewhere had increased.[112] According to the Middle East Director of HRW, gangs were "going around the capital, looking for girls" who were then "abducted and even sold. There is trafficking taking place. And . . . with lack of law and order, it's coming much more to the fore."[113] Around the same time, documents were found in Kirkuk providing evidence of the abduction of 18 Iraqi girls for dispatch to bars and nightclubs in Egypt.[114]

In spite of NGO efforts to highlight the trafficking of women, the issue received little attention, partly because of the rapid deterioration in the security situation, partly because trafficking was not blatant enough to be a high priority, and partly because of the shame attached to the loss of chastity even when it was coerced. By 2006, however, the Organization for Women's Freedom in Iraq estimated that more than 2,000 Iraqi women had gone missing since the fall of Saddam Hussein—a figure that subsequently rose even higher.[115] It was believed that young women and girls had been sent to Yemen, Syria, Jordan, and the Gulf for commercial sexual exploitation and that they were sold for as much as $10,000 each.[116] In some cases, this was accomplished under the guise of marriage; in others, women thought they were entering domestic service only to find themselves in sexual servitude.

In some instances, families sold their daughters to traffickers who arranged marriages to men in Dubai. Although the traffickers provided assurances to the families about the husbands, this was rarely, if ever, accompanied by due diligence concerning the motive of the purchaser. In some cases, women were even sold by their husbands. Some of those who by virtue of their office were charged with providing support to vulnerable young women and girls also joined in the exploitation; for example, it appears that "some trafficking victims were taken from orphanages and other charitable institutions by employees of these organizations."[117] In one particularly tragic case, a female journalist, Sahar al-Haideri, who reported in 2007 that in Mosul "girls and young women from poor and illiterate families" were "particularly vulnerable to sexual exploitation," was murdered shortly after her report was filed.[118]

The trafficking of humans was not limited to women being "exported" from Iraq to other countries; it also involved people being brought into Iraq. According to the U.S. State Department 2007 report on human rights practices,

> non-Iraqi males were reportedly brought from Georgia and South Asia, in some cases under guise of a work contract in Kuwait or Jordan, and forced to work under abusive conditions that constituted involuntary servitude. There were also reports of girls, women, and boys trafficked within the country for sexual and other exploitation.[119]

Some boys were forced into prostitution by criminal gangs who kept them in line with threats of violence or shaming them by informing their families of what they were doing.[120] Once again, anomie dominated: the only thing that appeared to matter to the gangs was money, and if it required deception or violence, so be it.

In sum, it is hard to disagree with the comment from one Iraqi blogger who observed:

> Iraq has become a business venture. Fake IDs, fake passports. Tailors selling army/police uniforms. Police renting out their cars to militias and insurgents. Arms being sold in mini stores. Kidnappings out of the blue taking place for ransom money. Black market fuel, black market visas. You name it, everyone is making a living out of it, the Baghdad Money Making Machine.[121]

The variety and depth of criminal activities in Iraq certainly support such an appraisal. These activities are both facilitated and protected by rampant corruption. Indeed, the relationship between organized crime and corruption is the theme of Chapter 6.

ENDNOTES - CHAPTER 5

1. Diego Gambetta, *The Sicilian Mafia*, London, United Kingdom: Harvard University Press, 1993.

2. William Reno, "Protectors and Predators: Why Is There a Difference Among West African Militias?" Louise Andersen, Bjorn Moller, and Finn Stepputat, eds., *Fragile States and Insecure People? Violence, Security, and Statehood in the Twenty-First Century*, New York: Palgrave Macmillan, 2007, pp. 99-122.

3. This distinction draws on that between stationary and roving bandits. See Mancur Olson, *Power and Prosperity: Outgrowing Communist and Capitalist Dictatorships*, New York: Oxford University Press, 2000.

4. Richard A. Oppel, Jr., "Iraq's Insurgency Runs on Stolen Oil Profits," *New York Times*, March 16, 2008, p. 1.

5. See "Iraq: Kidnapping Poses New Security Threat," *Oxford Analytica*, April 22, 2004.

6. Alexandra Zavis, "Iraqi Militants Feed on Corruption," *Los Angeles Times*, October 26, 2007.

7. Hannah Allam, "Iraqi Insurgents Taking Cut of U.S. Rebuilding Money," Washington, DC: McClatchy Washington Bureau, August 26, 2007.

8. James Glanz and Robert F. Worth, "Attacks on Iraq Oil Industry Aid Vast Smuggling Scheme," *New York Times*, June 4, 2006.

9. Ghaith Abdul-Ahad, "Oiling the Wheels of War: Smuggling Becomes the Real Economy of Iraq," *The Guardian*, June 9, 2007.

10. *Ibid.*

11. "Stolen Cars Finance Militia Operations; Fenced Autos Fetch $2,000 on the Black Market; Few Live to Complain," *IraqSlogger*, June 28, 2007.

12. "Car Bomb Targets Official Registries? Slogger's Sources Get the Word on the Street in Southwest Baghdad," *IraqSlogger*, November 12, 2007.

13. *Ibid.*

14. "Militants Using Water to Extort Displaced," Report, IRIN, August 8, 2007, available at *electroniciraq.net/news/aiddevelopment/ Militants_using_water_to_extort_displaced-3172.shtml.*

15. Kim Sengupta, "Baghdad Revealed as Bank Robbery Capital of the World," *The Guardian*, September 19, 2007.

16. *Ibid.*

17. *Ibid.*

18. "Diyala Bank Heist Nets $860,000: Gunmen Seize Social Security Money Intended for Poor Families," *IraqSlogger*, May 18, 2007.

19. Anonymous, "On the Ground from Syria to Iraq," Brian Fishman, ed., *Bombers, Bank Accounts and Bleedout: Al Qa'ida's Road In and Out of Iraq*, West Point, New York: Combating Terrorism Center, July 2008, p. 86.

20. *Ibid.*, p. 85.

21. Robert Bateman, "Iraq and the Problem of Border Security," *SAIS Review*, Vol. 26, No. 1, Winter-Spring 2006, pp. 41-47.

22. *Ibid.*

23. Interview with military officer, Gettysburg, PA, March 2008.

24. Monte Morin, "Policing a No Man's Land between Iraq and Syria: Troops Work Against Decades-Old Smuggling Tradition," *Stars and Stripes*, Mideast edition, December 11, 2005.

25. "Boats, Cows, Tasty Lamb: Iraq Battles Smuggling," *New York Times*, March 26, 2005.

26. Anonymous, p. 86.

27. Paul Rexton Kan, "Drugging Babylon: The Illegal Narcotics Trade and Nation-Building in Iraq," *Small Wars and Insurgencies*, Vol. 18, No. 2, June 2007, pp. 216-230, particularly p. 227.

28. *Ibid.*

29. *Ibid.*, p. 220.

30. Corporal Ryan L. Tomlinson, "Marines Deal Blow to Drug Traffickers," U.S. Central Command, August 11, 2008, available at *www.centcom.mil/en/what-we-do/marines-deal-blow-to-drug-traffickers.html.*

31. Kan, p. 222.

32. Barry Newhouse, "Iraqi Border Town Struggles with Violence, Drugs, and Little Government Help," *Voice of America*, March 3, 2007.

33. "Iraq: Officials Complain of Rising Drug Use, Trafficking," available at *stopthedrugwar.org/chronicle-old/429/iraq.shtml.*

34. *Ibid.*

35. *The 2008 World Fact Book*, Washington, DC: Central Intelligence Agency, updated April 2009.

36. "4.5 Millions Orphans in Iraq, A Tragic Situation," Baghdad, *Voices of Iraq*, January 25, 2008, available at *www.mhrinet. splinder.com/post/15607775/4.5+millions+Orphans+in+Iraq%2C+.*

37. "Iraq Emerging as Key Route in Global Drugs Trade," *news.yahoo.com*, July 6, 2008. This was evident in the 2009 INCSR which highlighted seizures and arrests made by Iraqi authorities.

38. Richard Friman, "Just Passing Through: Transit States and the Dynamics of Illicit Transshipment," *Transnational Organized Crime*, Vol. 1, No. 1 1995, pp. 69-83.

39. Robert E. Looney, "The Business of Insurgency: The Expansion of Iraq's Shadow Economy," *The National Interest*, September 22, 2005, p.5.

40. On Kurdish and Turkish smuggling networks, see Cyrille Fijnaut *et al.*, *Organized Crime in the Netherlands*, The Hague, The Netherlands: Kluwer, 1998; and Frank Bovenkerk and Yucel Yesilgoz, "The Turkish Mafia and the State," in Cyrille Fijnaut and Letizia Paoli, eds., *Organized Crime in Europe*, Dordrecht, The Netherlands: Springer, 2004, p. 6.

41. Bureau for International Narcotics and Law Enforcement, *International Narcotics Control Strategy Report (INCSR): Vol. 1: Drug and Chemical Control*, Washington, DC: U.S. Department of State, March 2008, p. 578.

42. Abigail Hauslohner, "Where Iraq and Iran Meet, Uneasily," *Time Magazine*, July 10, 2008.

43. "Iraq Emerging as Key Route in Global Drug Trade," *news. yahoo.com*, July 6, 2008.

44. Turki al-Suhayl, "Saudi Arabia Hands Over to Iraq a List of Names of 434 Detainees," *Al-Sharq al-Awsat website*, London, United Kingdom, in Arabic, BBC Worldwide Monitoring, September 4, 2008.

45. Kan.

46. For the claims, see Patrick Cockburn, "Iraq's Deadly New Export," *The Independent*, London, United Kingdom, May 23, 2007; and Patrick Cockburn, "Opium Fields Spread Across Iraq as Farmers Try to Make Ends Meet," *The Independent*, January 17, 2008, p. 30.

47. INCSR, p. 618.

48. Kan, p. 220.

49. INCSR, p. 575.

50. *Ibid.*, p. 576.

51. Matthew Bogdanos, "The Casualties of War: The Truth about the Iraq Museum," *American Journal of Archaeology*, Vol. 109, No. 3, pp. 477-526, especially p. 477.

52. *Ibid.*, p.477.

53. *Ibid.*, p. 499.

54. Lawrence Van Gelder, "Syria Returns Iraqi Loot," *New York Times*, April 30, 2008.

55. Bogdanos, p. 514, n. 144.

56. *Ibid.*, p. 516.

57. "Robbing the Cradle of Civilization, Five Years Later," *Salon News*, March 20, 2008, available at *www.salon.com/news/feature/2008/03/20/iraq_roundtable/*, hereafter cited as "Robbing the Cradle."

58. Susan Breitkopf, "Lost: The Looting of Iraq's Antiquities," *Museum News*, January/February 2007, available at *www.aam-us.org/pubs/mn/MN_JF07_lost-iraq.cfm.*

59. *Ibid.*, quoting Patty Gerstenblith.

60. Breitkopf.

61. *Ibid.*, quoting Micah Garen and Marie-Hélène Carleton

62. "Robbing the Cradle."

63. "Investigator of Baghdad Museum Looting Says Antiquity Smuggling Finances Terror," *Associated Press*, March 19, 2008.

64. *Ibid.*

65. "Antiquities from Iraq: Funding for Insurgents?" March 19, 2008, available at *lootingmatters.blogspot.com/2008/03/antiquities-from-iraq-funding-for.html?showComment=1205952540000#c799346 7084302644406.*

66. "Investigator of Baghdad Museum Looting Says Antiquity Smuggling Finances Terror."

67. "Robbing the Cradle."

68. "Investigator of Baghdad Museum Looting Says Antiquity Smuggling Finances Terror."

69. Bryan Bender, "US Car Theft Rings Probed for Ties to Iraq Bombings," *Boston Globe*, October 2, 2005, available at *www.boston.com/news/world/articles/2005/10/02/us_car_theft_rings_probed_for_ties_to_iraq_bombings/*.

70. *Ibid.*

71. *Ibid.*

72. Bryan Bender, "Auto Theft Database Is Left to Languish. Tool Against Terror Lost to Poor Compliance," *Boston Globe*, July 16, 2007, available at *www.boston.com/news/nation/washington/articles/2007/07/16/auto_theft_database_is_left_to_languish/*.

73. *Ibid.*

74. Bill Warner, *From Shiite Used Car Dealers In Tampa, Florida to Iraq Via Dubai: Cars to Fund Terrorism*, November 24, 2007, available at *atlasshrugs2000.typepad.com/atlas_shrugs/2007/11/global-islamic.html*.

75. "Basra-Iraq's Second Largest City Controlled by Militias and Mafias," *Al-Sharq al-Awsat*, November 11, 2007; and Ghaith Abdul-Ahad, "When Night Falls, The Assassins Gather in Hayaniya Square," *The Guardian*, November 17, 2007.

76. Richard Dubin, "Stolen Cars Linked to Terror Attacks Overseas," CTV, July 17, 2007, available at *www.ctv.ca/servlet/ArticleNews/story/CTVNews/20070717/stolen_cars_070717/20070717?hub=CTVNewsAt11*.

77. "Stolen Cars Found in Iraq," *Aftenposten*, October 23, 2006, available at *www.aftenposten.no/english/local/article1505622.ece*.

78. *Ibid.*

79. *Ibid.*

80. *Ibid.*

81. "Iraq: Syria's Role in Smuggling—and Insecurity," *Stratfor Today*, March 26, 2007.

82. On the incident, see "U.K.: 15 Sailors Detained by Iranian Navy," *Associated Press*, March 23, 2007.

83. Yaakov Katz, "Car Parts Smuggled from Israel to Iraq," *The Jerusalem Post*, March 12, 2006.

84. Pamela Constable, "In Postwar Baghdad, A Benz Is Easy to Get, Easy to Lose; Theft of New and Luxury Cars Becomes Rampant in Capital," The *Washington Post*. August 10, 2003, p. A 18.

85. *Ibid.*

86. *Ibid.*

87. Doug Struck, "No Exit for British in Poor Corner of Iraq. Despite Progress, Old Scores Still Unsettled and Local Problems Unresolved," *Washington Post* Foreign Service, February 12, 2005, p. A01.

88. "Stolen Cars Finance Militia Operations."

89. *Ibid.*

90. "Iraq Police Capture Members of Insurgent Cell," *The Advisor*, available at *www.mnstci.iraq.centcom.mil/advisor/2006%20 Issues/20061118.pdf.*

91. Davi M. D'Agostino, "DOD Should Apply Lessons Learned Concerning the Need for Security over Conventional Munitions Storage Sites to Future Operations Planning," Testimony before the Subcommittee on National Security and Foreign Affairs,

Committee on Oversight and Government Reform, House of Representatives, GAO-07-639T, March 22, 2007, p.2.

92. Quoted in *Operation Iraqi Freedom: DOD Should Apply Lessons learned Concerning the Need for Security over Conventional Munitions Storage Sites to Future Operations Planning*, Washington, DC: U.S. Government Accountability Office, Report GAO-07-639T, March 22, 2007.

93. *Ibid.*

94. *Ibid.*

95. Adam Schreck, "The Conflict in Iraq: Shiite Muslim Rivalries; Looted Weapons Stockpiles; Study Looks at Arms Security Gaps; U.S. Military Is Said Not to Know the Scope of Theft from Prewar Iraqi Stockpiles and How Many Caches Are at Risk," *Los Angeles Times*, March 23, 2007, p. A4.

96. "Iraqi Police Sell Weapons: Black Market Relies on Issued Weapons," *IraqSlogger*, February 2, 2007.

97. *Ibid.*

98. *Ibid.*

99. Ghazwan Muhammad, "Who Is Responsible For the Migration of Large Numbers of Iraqi Traders?" Baghdad, *Al-Bayyinah* in Arabic, August 8, 2006, p. 5.

100. See *neurotic-iraqi-wife.blogspot.com/2007/01/baghdad-money-making-machine.html*.

101. *Ibid.*

102. See Nicholas Keung, "Help Sought for Iraq's Refugees: UN members Asked to Open Doors and Donate Funds," *Toronto Star*, April 17, 2007; and Peter Beaumont, "Sweden Closes Its Doors as Refugee Debate Rages," *The Observer*, March 30, 2008, p. 44.

103. DDP, "German Police Arrest Two Alleged 'Islamist human traffickers'," May 11, 2006.

104. DPA, "Iraqi Refugees Entering Germany Illegally," *Die Welt*, May 2, 2007.

105. CTK, "Czech Police Detain Six Iraqis, Two Suspected Slovak Human Smugglers," March 15, 2007.

106. CTK "Czech Police Arrest Human Smuggling Ring," May 16, 2007.

107. "Iraqi Held After Police Bust Migrant 'Prison'," Athens, *Kathimerini Online*, October 25, 2008.

108. Ingrid Rousseau, "European Police Nab Iraq Immigrant Ring," *Associated Press Online*, June 23, 2008.

109. Ingrid Rousseau, "European Police Detain 50 Suspected of Funneling Illegal Iraqi Kurd Immigrants to Europe," *Associated Press Worldstream*, June 23, 2008.

110. *Ibid.*

111. *Ibid.*

112. See "Iraq: Climate of Fear: Sexual Violence and Abduction of Women and Girls in Baghdad, "*Iraq*, Vol. 15, No. 7, July 2003.

113. Nick Grimm, "Rape and Trafficking of Women Prevalent In Post-War Iraq," July 17, 2003, available at *www.abc.net.au/pm/content/2003/s904673.htm*.

114. Sonja Wolte, *Armed Conflict and Trafficking in Women: Desk Study*, GTZ, January 2004, p. 26, available at *www2.gtz.de/dokumente/bib/04-5304.pdf*.

115. Tracy Clark-Flory, "Roommaids, Brawlers, and Sex Slaves: Time Magazine Reveals the Many Flattering Faces of the Female Gender," May 2, 2006, available at *www.salon.com/mwt/broadsheet/2006/05/02/time/print.html*.

116. *Country Reports on Human Rights Practices 2007*, Released by the Bureau of Democracy, Human Rights, and Labor, U.S. Department of State, March 11, 2008.

117. *Ibid.*

118. Sahar al-Haideri, "Women Looking For Work Are Being Tricked into Sexual Slavery, With Some Trafficked Abroad," *ICR*, No. 225, June 29, 2007.

119. Country Reports on Human Rights Practices, 2007.

120. IRIN News Service, "Iraq: Boys Trapped in Commercial Sex Trade," August 8, 2005, available at *pageoneq.com/news/2005/ IRAQ_Focus_on_boys_trapped_in_commercial_sex__0808.html.*

121.See *neurotic-iraqi-wife.blogspot.com/2007/01/baghdad-money-making-machine.html.*

CHAPTER 6

CORRUPTION AND ORGANIZED CRIME IN IRAQ

The Relationship between Organized Crime and Corruption.

Organized crime in Iraq is both facilitated and protected by corruption. Although organized crime and corruption are often treated as separate and distinct phenomena, they are often intertwined in complex ways. This is certainly the case in Iraq, where the fragmented nature of the society made it extremely difficult to establish a viable and legitimate central state after 2003. The legacy of Saddam Hussein, the debilitating consequences of sanctions, particularly the deterioration of administrative and technical capacity, and the rise of anomic conditions after the collapse of the Ba'athist regime, perpetuated a culture of corruption. What had hitherto been centrally controlled suddenly became diffused and democratic. In addition, the U.S. presence brought with it a massive injection of cash for reconstruction, much of which was handled in an ad hoc manner with little oversight. The reconstruction program provided enormous opportunities for corporate malfeasance on the U.S. side and skimming and personal profiteering on the Iraqi side. A narrowly legalistic and bureaucratic approach emphasizing the compelling need to free the market was accompanied with little understanding of the disruption that would accompany the liberalization process. Although shock therapy had been largely discredited in Russia, during the 1990s it was alive and well in Iraq—albeit without the name—after the U.S. occupation. And it proved even more disastrous. The result was that Iraq rapidly metamorphosed into one of the most corrupt countries in the world. According to Transparency International's Corruption Perceptions Index for 2007, Iraq was ranked number 178, below Haiti, and above only Somalia and Myanmar.[1] This was inevitable, given the nature of the previous regime and the rapidity of its collapse, the prevalence in Iraq of a tribal and patrimonial culture, the vacuum of state norms and legal rules after Saddam Hussein, the high levels of insecurity and uncertainty which encouraged an emphasis on immediate or short-term gains, and the prevalence of criminal organizations and criminal activities, both of which are buttressed and protected by corruption in government.

Corruption in Iraq.

Robert Harris suggests that political corruption is better regarded as an extension of political activity than as a radical departure from it.[2] He also draws on Mark Summers' definition of political corruption as being both the use of public position for private advantage or exceptional party profit, and the subversion of the political process for personal ends.[3] As Robert Klitgaard and others have observed, these traits are inherent in authoritarian regimes characterized by monopoly control of political and administrative power and an absence of oversight and accountability.[4] Opportunities are widely available, and constraints and safeguards are weak. This is even more marked in the absence of any notion of collective or public interest to inhibit the untrammeled pursuit of individual, tribal, or factional interests.[5] William Reno's argument that "the absence of collective versus private interests is a major distinguishing feature of warlord politics" is equally applicable to corruption.[6] As another astute observer notes, corruption "is a symptom that the political system is operating with little concern for the broad public interest."[7]

The rule of Saddam Hussein not only involved the subordination of collective interests to the private interests of Saddam, his family, and the Ba'ath party, but was also a prime example of what Jean Bayart termed the "criminalization of the state."[8] Although Bayart focused on Africa, his criteria for categorizing a state as criminalized are readily met by Iraq under Hussein. He suggests that a criminalized state uses the legitimate organs of state, including the capacity for violence, as an instrument in strategies to accumulate wealth; that the power structure benefits from the privatization of the legitimate means of coercion or access to an illegitimate apparatus of violence; that this structure participates in economic activities considered criminal; that these activities become intermeshed with transnational criminal networks; that historical culture specific to the conduct of such activities in any given society enters transnational cultural repertoires related to globalization through a process akin to osmosis; and that these activities are of central importance to the power holders and to the process of "accumulation in the overall architecture" of the society.[9]

The Ba'ath Party had a long tradition of creating slush funds and using its elitist position for privilege of all kinds. Violence was also used to protect this position. As for Saddam Hussein, he seems to have drawn no distinction between himself and the state. The identity of the two was never more evident than in his building additional palaces with some of the proceeds from oil smuggling and the oil-for-food program.

At one level, the changes in corruption patterns in Iraq since the fall of the regime are enormous. Private interests have become more diverse and more competitive. Unfortunately, the jostling for private power has not been accompanied by widespread acceptance of collective identity or shared rules of the political game. The structure of politics and patterns of corruption have changed, but many of the embedded attitudes and forms of behavior persist in a zero-sum conception of political power. Saddam Hussein's regime had winners and losers; with the regime's collapse the former losers became the new winners at the expense of the Ba'athist and Sunni elites. Moreover, the Iraqi state—hollowed out as it was—remained the prize of politics. As Shiite politicians took control of a state apparatus stripped bare by the looting, they saw this as an opportunity to obtain resources and benefits long denied them. That Iraq retained its centralized governmental services and even food distribution system created more opportunities for rent-seeking.

In other words, since 2003 the United States has had to contend with a very corrosive legacy: the over-reliance of the Ba'athist regime on coercive power and its failure to establish authority and legitimacy transcending local, tribal, and sectarian loyalties. U.S. efforts to transform the politics of exclusion into inclusion, narrow sectarianism into broad tolerance, and enmity into cooperation had only limited success.

A second corrosive legacy of the Ba'athist regime, combined with the impact of sanctions, was the loss of professional and technological expertise, the decline of state infrastructure, and the loss of state capacity. All of these problems were intensified in 2003 by the decapitation of the regime, the looting which followed the invasion, and the exodus of professionals from Iraq, as well as by efforts to impose a free market doctrine which was rapidly and uncritically applied. Of course, there is no denying that rapid efforts to reconstruct a state apparatus were essential. Although safeguards against corruption were put in place—through an Inspector-General system, an independent Commission on Public Integrity, and the Board of Supreme Audit— inhibitions against corruption were far outweighed by the incentives for it.

Part of the problem lay in a salient difference between modernized societies and those of developing countries. The former draw clear distinctions between the legal and illegal, and between the public and the private. But in developing countries, these distinctions are either absent or hazy. Culture also plays into this. As one study, in a very different setting, notes, "The role of culture in corruption continues to be the focus of controversy, although most scholars are of the view that culture is a determining or at least conditioning factor."[10] This partly comes down to the focus of group loyalties and the extent to which they are based on family, kin, tribe, and clan affiliation as opposed to loyalty to the state. Indeed, "in many cultures, mutual obligations in many sorts of transactions, embodied in social networks and kinship relationships, remain paramount."[11] In such cultures, positions in government or law enforcement are seen not as opportunities for public service but as opportunities to meet family, tribal, or clan obligations. The distinction between private and public is not simply absent in more traditional societies; it is explicitly contradicted by the nature of obligations that are far more important than those to the state or the collectivity. Patronage and political power are inextricably intertwined. As David Ronfeldt notes, "What modern analysts regard as crime and corruption may have entirely different meanings to tribal and clannish peoples."[12]

In these circumstances, those with access to the state are generally motivated to use such access for the benefit of substate actors. This is particularly the case when the society is divided, and groups which were hitherto excluded from state resources suddenly have access. The natural tendency to make up for lost time is accentuated by concern that any new privilege might be temporary. In Iraq, as the insurgency developed and became increasingly costly to combat, debate in the United States intensified, and continuation of the U.S. military presence appeared increasingly tenuous. Although Iraqi expectations changed somewhat as a result of the surge, the Anbar awakening, the decline of al-Qaeda in Iraq (AQI), and the report to Congress by General David Petraeus in 2007, by then the new patterns of patronage were well established. Those in positions of power, particularly in the ministries, sought to exploit their positions for tribal, sectarian, or personal reasons, and were encouraged to do so by the lack of political and military stability and lack of certainty about their ability to maintain these positions. The changes at the top, with Prime Ministers coming and going, added to the incentives for short-term exploitation of public office for private gain.

In Robert Harris's words, political corruption "exploits and operates within any fractures existing in the polity of a state or between the polities of different states."[13] Periods of transition and turbulence accentuate these fractures and create opportunities for rent-seeking—especially as departments and agencies move from one set of rules and procedures to another. Moreover, in Iraq, as elsewhere, institutional changes occurred before institutional safeguards against corruption were fully established and before democratic procedures and mechanisms were put in place. Radical transitions are murky. Corruption thrives in such circumstances, operating as it does in the margins or interstices.[14] Corruption slips

> through the cracks of the state. Where the bureau-political machinery is not mature, coherent, or integrated, or where self-correcting mechanisms such as an independent judiciary or a free press are missing, the interstices are especially visible, enabling corrupt politicians and officials to exploit the resulting conflicts and ambiguities. Where civil society is weak . . . corruption can emerge in low standards of professional conduct and minimal safeguards.[15]

Corruption in Iraq is also inextricably related to oil. In effect, government control over a resource such as oil endows government officials with particularly lucrative opportunities for imposing rents, including those associated with theft and smuggling. Corruption, operating at several levels including the political leadership, political parties, officials in the Oil Ministry, and workers at oil facilities, promotes these activities. Where there are already political divisions, then oil and its smuggling, as discussed above, becomes a source of funding for particular factions and sects. Thus, Iraq's oil industry provides enormous additional incentives for corrupt and criminal behavior.

Compounding the difficulty is that corruption is a dynamic, not static, phenomenon and, as such, can evolve—often into "an emergent normative system" characterized by a vicious circle, with movement cycling back and forth between misadministration and corruption and clientelism and corruption.[16] As Donatella della Porta and Alberto Vannucci state,

"Corrupt exchanges facilitate emergence of new norms, and these norms make corruption more and more attractive. Perverse mechanisms produce and reproduce the resources necessary for corruption. Honest politicians and honest entrepreneurs tend to be expelled from the government and from the public market" as they are an inherent threat to the corrupt system.[17] Not sharing its norms, they arouse suspicion and hostility. Moreover, when there are few limits on violence, honest officials are in danger. Post-Ba'athist Iraq was characterized by an additional vicious cycle in which corruption alternated with violence and intimidation.

In Iraq, the institutions established to fight corruption were attacked both politically and violently. The ability of the Commission on Public Integrity, for example, to investigate government corruption was severely inhibited by the government of Prime Minister al-Maliki which refused to recognize its independence, insisting that the Commission obtain the permission of his office before investigating ministers. In addition, the Commission was not allowed to pass cases involving corrupt officials to the courts until they had the permission of the minister of the department in which these officials worked. While these restrictions severely limited the ability of the Commission to function effectively, the Commission was emasculated further by violence not only against its staff members, but also against their families. In October 2007 Judge Radhi Hamza al-Radhi, the Chairman of the Commission, gave testimony before a U.S. congressional committee in which he observed that the Commission had conducted 3,000 investigations, uncovering departmental corruption that had cost Iraq an estimated $18 billion.[18] He also testified that 31 of the Commission's employees had been assassinated with at least:

> an additional 12 family members. In a number of cases, my staff and their relatives have been kidnapped or detained and tortured prior to being killed. Many of these people were gunned down at close range. This includes my staff member, Mohammed Abd Salif, who was gunned down with his seven-months pregnant wife. In one case of targeted death and torture, the Security Chief on my staff, was repeatedly threatened with death. His father was recently kidnapped and killed because of his son's work at CPI. His body was found hung from a meat hook. One of my staff members who performed clerical duties was protected by my security staff, but his father was kidnapped because his son worked at CPI. This staff member's father was 80 years old. When his dead body was found, a power drill had been used to drill his body with holes.[19]

The toxic mix of corruption and violence thus rendered the Commission's efforts almost futile. Al-Radhi stated that of the 3,000 cases he and his staff had investigated, only 241 had gone to trial.[20] At the end of his testimony, he announced that he was seeking political asylum in the United States.

In sum, corruption in Iraq is both pervasive and endemic. Susan Rose-Ackerman distinguishes "between kleptocracies where corruption is organized at the top of government, and other states where bribery is the province of a large number of low-level officials."[21] This distinction does not apply in Iraq: corruption is both top down and bottom up, coming from within government and from outside. It is both a political and economic condition on the one side, and an instrument of criminal organizations, militias, insurgents, and terrorists and their sympathizers and associates on the other.

Dimensions of Corruption in Iraq.

The various forms of corruption in Iraq are so interwoven that they are devilishly difficult to disentangle and counter. Corruption in Iraq also often leads to or entails violence, which is not always characteristic of corruption elsewhere. Nevertheless, the various manifestations of corruption can be separated, at least analytically.

First is what might be termed direct corruption in which those in positions of public trust exploit their positions for personal enrichment. Sheikh Juburi, who was supposedly protecting oil pipelines but was actually siphoning off pipeline funds for nonexistent workers, provides a particularly blatant example of corruption and profiteering. Others have acted in less obvious ways and therefore elicited less attention. Even so, a large portion of the oil theft and smuggling problem is clearly insider-related, facilitated by the absence of meters to measure and control oil flows, and the lack of effective oversight, the excellent work of the Oil Ministry Inspector-General notwithstanding.

Second is the use of official positions to advance factional agendas. One form of this has been the factions' infiltration of ministries to use their resources to identify targets for sectarian violence and to attack those targets. Indeed, the infiltration of many government departments by Shiite militias and criminal gangs compounded internal corruption while also facilitating the use of violence. This was particularly pronounced in the Ministry of Health where infiltration by JAM not only led to sectarian killings of Sunni patients — and often the doctors who treated them — but also made possible the diversion and sale of large amounts of pharmaceuticals.[22] Along with many other rackets, this was an important funding source for JAM.

Other ministries suffered similar shortcomings. Particularly important in this connection was the Ministry of Interior. As many commentators have observed, the police are central to combating insurgencies.[23] When police forces are part of the problem rather than part of the solution, however, then the whole task becomes much more complicated. In Iraq the Ministry of Interior and the police were infiltrated by members of Jaish-al-Mahdi, with the result that police checkpoints, which should have been a source of enhanced security, became dangerous places for Sunnis who were often kidnapped and killed by those ostensibly responsible for their protection. Although one U.S. report described the Ministry of Interior as "a ministry in name only," the situation was even worse than this suggests. [24] The Ministry of Interior was not only corrupted but also perverted in ways which facilitated levels of violence that, in 2005 and 2006, seemed to be propelling Iraq towards a civil war.

Third is criminal corruption. Critically, corruption is not only a condition characterizing governments and bureaucracies but also an instrument used by criminal organizations to advance their illicit business interests and protect the illicit markets in which they operate. The use of corruption as an instrument, of course, is much easier where direct and factional corruption is endemic. Since corruption is also an "exchange mechanism," those officials who succumb to the bribes and blandishments of organized crime typically offer quid pro quo in return.[25] As Rose-Ackerman points out, "The level of bribes is not the critical variable. One wants to know not just how much was paid, but also what was purchased with the payoff."[26] For example, bribery can buy information, which increases illicit business opportunities and helps criminal organizations to circumvent and neutralize law enforcement. Bribery can also buy protection—from law enforcement, the judiciary, and high-level politicians and bureaucrats—which enhances and perpetuates the ability of criminals to act with impunity. In addition, bribery can buy cooperation, integrating those in public office into criminal networks and making it almost impossible to know where crime ends and corruption begins.

Corruption in Iraq is also closely related to violence: both are instruments of criminal organizations and are typically used by these organizations as part of their risk management strategies. Although corruption and violence are often seen as alternatives, they are most effective when used together in ways which create a compelling mix of incentives for accommodation to the blandishments and disincentives for resistance to them. As suggested above, for those with the responsibility to fight corruption and a commitment to doing so, the risks are enormous. Moreover, even when violence is not used against them, honest anti-corruption officials are subject to character assassination and political harassment.

Consequences of Corruption in Iraq.

Corruption is an indicator that the state does not evoke loyalty and that government is not working well. In turn, corruption worsens and perpetuates inadequate governance, making reform difficult. This is particularly the case where there is symbiosis between organized crime and corruption. The criminals use corruption to protect and advance their illicit activities and expand their profits, while those in the state apparatus seek to maintain the mutually beneficial relationships.

As we have noted, in a lawless environment, efforts to investigate corruption are either rendered impossible or undermined. As a leaked assessment by the U.S. Embassy in Iraq revealed, "Several ministries are so controlled by criminal gangs or militias as to be impossible to operate absent a tactical force protecting the investigator."[27] Another result was a dismal record in the delivery of goods and services by the Iraqi government. Not surprisingly, therefore, the state continued to be seen as lacking in both legitimacy and effectiveness—making militia, tribal, or criminal affiliations even more important for many Iraqis looking for physical and economic protection. This, in turn, further empowered the militias, while simultaneously further weakening the Iraqi state. Not surprisingly, Sunni and Shiite militias have retained a high degree of control over the transportation and distribution of oil, using this control as a funding mechanism for their campaigns of political violence. In short, corruption, organized crime, and insurgent and militia violence become difficult to disentangle analytically, let alone physically disrupt. One American official averred that "corruption funds the insurgency, so there you have a very real threat to the new state."[28]

As well as this direct impact, there are also several indirect but severely debilitating consequences of corruption in Iraq. These have been very succinctly summarized by Stuart Bowen, the U.S. Special Inspector-General for Iraq Reconstruction, who describes corruption in Iraq as "a second insurgency."[29] In his view, corruption:

> directly harms the country's economic viability. In very real terms, corruption stymies the construction and

211

maintenance of Iraq's infrastructure, deprives people of goods and services, reduces confidence in public institutions, and potentially aids insurgent groups reportedly funded by graft derived from oil smuggling or embezzlement.[30]

This assessment was reinforced by a sensitive but unclassified report leaked from the U.S. Embassy in Iraq in 2007. The report surveyed anti-corruption efforts across the spectrum of Iraqi ministries, with its assessments almost entirely bad. According to the report, the problem started from the top. The Prime Minister's Office was openly hostile "to the concept of an independent agency to investigate or prosecute corruption cases as a matter of principle."[31] Moreover, there are few checks and balances in the system to offset this. The courts are "weak, intimidated, subject to political pressure, and clogged with minor cases," while the Commission on Public Integrity is seriously inhibited by "the violent character of the criminal elements within the ministries" which make "investigation of corruption too hazardous for all but a tactically robust police force with the support of the Iraqi government. Currently this support is lacking."[32]

Few departments escaped an utterly scathing assessment. The Ministry of Water Resources, for example, was characterized as "effectively out of the anticorruption fight, with little to no apparent effort in trying to combat fraud."[33] The Ministry of Trade had developed a bad reputation for corruption in its dealings with the food program. In one instance, almost $13 million worth of food disappeared with no indications of where the payments were—although when the Minister was challenged by al-Radhi, the Commissioner for Public Integrity, receipts were provided showing that the money had been paid to the government.[34] Whether this was really the case is uncertain. The assessment of the Ministry of Health concluded that corruption had undermined the "ability to deliver services" and that this in turn had eroded public support for the government.[35] Moreover, the lack of pharmaceuticals was blamed on corruption and the diversion of medicines to the black market – where illicit sales helped to finance the Mahdi Army.[36]

Two other ministries in which JAM also had considerable influence were Transportation and Interior (MOI). The assessment concluded that the Ministry of Transportation was controlled by militias, and as a result suffered from a lack of accountability for aircraft landing fees and for the income from the leasing of its trucking fleet to commercial companies. Moreover, investigation was impossible because of JAM influence.[37] The situation in the MOI was, if anything, even worse. According to the embassy report, groups within the ministry functioned "similarly to a Racketeer Influenced and Corrupt Organization (RICO) in the classic sense. MOI is a 'legal enterprise' which has been co-opted by organized criminals who act through the 'legal enterprise' to commit crimes such as kidnapping, extortion, bribery, etc."[38]

Actually, the situation was even more complicated than the embassy report suggests. A few years earlier, *Oxford Analytica* had alleged that "rather than enforcing the law in an impartial manner," the Ministry of Interior was "riven by political factions" and "myriad competing police and intelligence agencies that pursue various political or sectarian agendas."[39] Little had changed by 2007. This had serious implications for both ordinary Iraqis and the United States. It meant that law enforcement, which is critical to counterinsurgency, has not only been woefully inadequate, but has actually contributed to public insecurity because of the Mahdi

213

Army's co-option of the police to assist with sectarian cleansing. Indeed, Bing West in his useful analysis of the U.S. military in Iraq cites numerous cases in which Iraqi citizens turned to U.S. forces or sometimes even the Iraqi military because they did not trust the police.[40]

Even within the Ministry of Defense (MOD), however, corruption has been pernicious, hindering procurement and thereby slowing the effective deployment of Iraqi military forces. Reports in 2005 revealed that Iraq's military procurement process had been subverted to such an extent that as much as one billion dollars was missing. In a fraud that made the oil for food schemes look almost amateurish, contracts for procurement from Poland and Pakistan were paid up-front to a company based in Baghdad.[41] The weapons supplied were largely obsolete and ineffective. Although this development created a major scandal, it was blamed on a few individuals rather than being treated as a systemic problem. Consequently, the embassy report concluded that corruption investigations in the MOD remained ineffectual.[42]

Pride of place in the corruption stakes in Iraq inevitably goes to the Ministry of Oil. Even though, as discussed in Chapter 3, the Inspector-General for the Oil Ministry produced an excellent analysis of the varieties of oil smuggling, it was one thing to be aware of oil diversion, theft, and smuggling, but quite another to stop it. In this connection, the report noted that:

> there is no incentive to begin accurately accounting for oil production and oil movement to refineries, storage, or export as long as organized criminals move this valuable commodity for the benefit of militias/insurgents, corrupt public officials and foreign buyers. . . . Unfortunately, protection rackets and other violent criminal enterprises

supporting theft, smuggling, and illegal distribution of Iraq's oil products make the correction of the situation difficult.[43]

In November 2006, for example, the head of the Mosul office of the Commission for Public Integrity was dismissed for reportedly accepting bribes from oil smugglers.[44] Once again, those meant to be part of the solution had simply become part of the problem.

The embassy report amounted to a massive indictment of the Iraqi government and its major departments. Yet these same problems were present at the provincial and municipal levels. For example, in the town of Hit, which was freed from insurgent control by the U.S. Marines, corruption was endemic, with the "tangled alliances between local officials, Sunni sheiks, oil smugglers, and remnants of the insurgency movement" proving difficult to break.[45] Although the mayor was believed to be corrupt, a warrant for his arrest was quashed by the governor of Anbar.

The embassy report would have been more effective had it dealt candidly with the fact that Iraq remains a welfare state in which the process of service and commodity distribution is centralized and is therefore inherently vulnerable to corruption and theft. In spite of such gaps, the report revealed very clearly the close linkage between organized crime and corruption, especially the difficulties of anti-corruption agencies when confronted not simply with bureaucratic resistance but also with protective coatings of violence and intimidation.

In some respects, of course, corruption was simply an extension into government of the anomic conditions characterizing the society after the collapse of the Ba'athist regime. In effect, it represented an additional wave of looting, albeit one that was insidiously covert rather than overt, and institutionalized rather than spontaneous. Moreover, although some islands of integrity existed in the ministries, allegations of corruption were often used for short-term political advantage and discrediting political opponents rather than as part of a coherent strategy to deal with what had become a highly corrosive problem.

This situation inevitably spilled over into the lives of ordinary Iraqis. Not only was there a trickle-down effect of corruption, with low-level government employees such as border guards demanding bribes for safe passage and police selling their newly-issued weapons, but also high-level political and administrative corruption undermined respect for laws and norms at all levels of society. The rule of law became extremely problematic in a society in which many of those responsible for establishing or maintaining it were so blatant in their disregard. Not surprisingly, those who were supposed to observe or obey the law displayed a similar attitude. According to a *New York Times* report in December 2007, corruption and theft had become pervasive at all levels of society. Even though it was a high-risk occupation, law enforcement was one of the few growth areas in the economy. As a result, it cost between $400 and $800 to join.[46] Moreover, "nearly everything the government buys or sells can now be found on the black market."[47] Pharmaceuticals stolen from the Ministry of Health, textbooks stolen from the Ministry of Education, computers and office furniture supplied by the United States, are all available for purchase.[48] In part, theft can be understood as a survival strategy. Yet it also suggests that Iraq had not progressed nearly as far from the chaos of 2003 as hoped or anticipated.

Iraq has almost certainly made some improvements since the embassy report surfaced. Progress has been made partly because of the cooperation between many of the Sunni tribes and the United States. The Coalition interventions in Basra and then Sadr City also had a major impact in containing the power of the Sadrists and the Mahdi Army. Even so, efforts to counter organized crime and corruption remain a low priority. The danger is that even though the levels of violence are down, without dealing more effectively with criminal organizations and with pervasive corruption in government, these gains will not be translated into a more viable, legitimate, and effective state which can command the loyalty of all factions, regions, and tribes. In these circumstances, criminal activities will continue to be resorted to by various groups in Iraq. Accordingly, Chapter 7 will examine in some detail the major players in the world of organized crime in Iraq.

ENDNOTES - CHAPTER 6

1. Transparency International, *Corruption Perceptions Index 2007*, available at *www.transparency.org/policy_research/surveys_indices/cpi/2007*.

2. Robert Harris, *Political Corruption: In and Beyond the Nation-State*, London, United Kingdom: Routledge, 2003, p. 6.

3. *Ibid.*, p. 9.

4. Robert Klitgaard, "Three Levels of Fighting Corruption," Address at the Carter Center Conference on Transparency for Growth in the Americas, May 4, 1999, available at *www.cartercenter. org/news/documents/doc1193.html*.

5. This is a major theme in William Reno, *Warlord Politics and African States*, Boulder, CO: Lynne Reinner, 1999.

6. *Ibid.*, p. 3.

7. Susan Rose-Ackerman, *Corruption and Government: Causes, Consequences and Reform*, Cambridge, United Kingdom: Cambridge University Press, 1999, p. 226.

8. Jean-François Bayart, Stephen Ellis, and Beatrice Hibou, *The Criminalization of the State in Africa*, Bloomington: Indiana University Press, 1999.

9. *Ibid.*, pp. 25-26.

10. Sergio Diaz-Briquets and Jorge Perez-Lopez, *Corruption in Cuba: Castro and Beyond*, Austin: University of Texas Press, 2006, p. 25.

11. *Ibid.*

12. David Ronfeldt, *In Search of How Societies Work; Tribes: The First and Forever Form*, Pardee Center Working Paper Series, Santa Monica, CA: RAND, December 2006, p. 40.

13. Harris, p. 199.

14. *Ibid.*, p. 22.

15. *Ibid.*

16. Donatella della Porta and Alberto Vannucci, *Corrupt Exchanges: Actors, Resources, and Mechanisms of Political Corruption*, New York: Aldine De Gruyter, 1999, pp. 249-265.

17. *Ibid.*, pp. 255-256.

18. Testimony of Judge Radhi Hamza al-Radhi, Commissioner, Commission on Public Integrity, Republic of Iraq, *Hearing on Assessing the State of Iraqi Corruption*, House Committee on Oversight and Government Reform, October 4, 2007.

19. *Ibid.*

20. *Ibid.*

21. Rose-Ackerman, p. 114.

22. Aram Roston and Lisa Myers, "'Untouchable' Corruption in Iraq Ministries," *NBC News Investigative Unit*, July 30, 2007, available at *MSNBC.com*.

23. See, for example, Bing West, *The Strongest Tribe: War, Politics, and the Endgame in Iraq*, New York: Random House, August 2008.

24. General James L. Jones, USMC (Ret), Chairman, *Independent Commission on the Security Forces of Iraq*, p. 10, available at *i.a.cnn. net/cnn/2007/imnages/08/05/jonesreportpart1a.pdf*.

25. Porta and Vannucci.

26. Rose-Ackerman, p. 4.

27. See "Draft report: Iraq Government 'not capable' of fighting corruption" at *www.cnn.com/2007/WORLD/meast/09/27/ iraq.draft.report/index.html*.

28. Quoted in Robert F. Worth and James Glanz, "Corrupt Leaders Called Threat to Iraq's Future: Officials Appear to Divert Oil Funds to the Insurgency," *New York Times*, February 5, 2006.

29. Testimony of Stuart W, Bowen, Jr., Special Inspector General for Iraq Reconstruction, "Assessing The State Of Iraqi Corruption," House Committee On Oversight And Government Reform, October 4, 2007.

30. *Ibid*.

31. "Review of Anticorruption Efforts in Iraq, " working draft, U.S. Embassy, Baghdad, Iraq, 2007, p. 65, available at *www.fas.org/ irp/eprint/anticorruption.pdf*.

32. *Ibid*., p. 1.

33. *Ibid*., p. 3.

34. *Ibid.*, p. 20.

35. *Ibid.*, p. 25.

36. *Ibid.*

37. *Ibid.*, pp. 36-38.

38. *Ibid.*, p. 16.

39. "US/UK/IRAQ: Corruption Hurts Effort to Rebuild State," *Oxford Analytica*, April 21, 2006.

40. West.

41. Patrick Cockburn, "What has happened to Iraq's missing $1bn," *The Independent*, September 19, 2005.

42. *Sensitive but Unclassified*, p. 20.

43. *Ibid.*, p. 28.

44. *Ibid.*, p. 73.

45. See "Iraq: High Hopes for Hit Stymied by Corruption," *Los Angeles Times Blog*: Babylon and Beyond, available at *latimesblogs. latimes.com/babylonbeyond/2008/08/hope-was-in-the.html*.

46. Damien Cave, "Non-Stop Theft and Bribery Stagger Iraq," *New York Times*, December 2, 2007.

47. *Ibid.*

48. *Ibid.*

CHAPTER 7

CRIMINALS, INSURGENTS, TERRORISTS, AND MILITIAS

The Players.

Efforts to identify the number, type, size, and structure of criminal organizations in Iraq immediately run up against the lack of effective reporting and policing. The United States and its allies have some information, but even this is incomplete or classified. Anecdotal reporting provides important insights, but it is difficult to draw confident conclusions from these. Nevertheless, it is possible to provide a rudimentary typology of the kinds of groups that appear to be involved in one or another form of criminal activity — keeping in mind that in practice the distinction between some of these groups is often very fuzzy:

> [A] deadly mix of organized criminality and jihadist savagery has increasingly come to blur the distinctions between the acts of violent terrorists and that of common thugs. In some cases, the spoils of crime are used to fund terrorist activity. In others, attacks against Iraqi authorities and community leaders bear closer resemblance to gangland turf wars than any of the various ideological or religious themes propagated by the al-Qaeda driven news cycle.[1]

Even though this chapter seeks to delineate criminal organizations in Iraq, uncertainty is unavoidable. Members of criminal organizations tend to be interested first and foremost in profit, but this is not always an exclusive focus. Indeed, it is possible to identify a range of criminals which includes those whose only concern is profit as well as those who are interested in both personal profit and obtaining money for political causes. As a result, clear distinctions between criminals on the one side, and terrorists, insurgents, and militia members on the other, are not always compelling.

There are several reasons for the fuzziness. First is that individuals often have roles which are multiple, overlapping, and compatible rather than single, distinct, and mutually exclusive. And the greater the proceeds that can be obtained through criminal activities, the less the tensions between personal enrichment and the cause. It becomes easier for multiple roles to coexist. Second, distinctions between political and criminal organizations are sometimes fuzzy because even though motivations may be different, actions are similar. Third, criminals are highly opportunistic. If there are clear advantages (and limited risks) to working in one way or another with politically motivated individuals and groups, then cooperation will occur — sometimes in ways which make it difficult to disentangle motivations. Fourth, both individual and group roles can change over time. Sometimes, basically mercenary criminals become politicized, so that activities initially designed for personal profit become enmeshed in larger political purposes. Sometimes, the movement is in the other direction, with ideological cause and political agenda becoming less important than profit.

Such complications notwithstanding, a typology can be useful, especially one which goes beyond traditional criminal enterprises to include groups which are typically regarded as pursuing political and military agendas rather than profit-making as an end in itself. With this in mind, after drawing together the strands of the preceding chapters, it seems that at least four major kinds of criminal organizations operate in Iraq: traditional criminal enterprises; tribal-based criminal organizations; foreign jihadi groups; and militias which include splinter or rogue factions. The foreign jihadi groups and some of the Sunni tribes were also the main participants in the insurgency, and many commentaries refer simply to insurgent funding. There are two reasons why the analysis here distinguishes between different groups within the insurgency rather than treating it as monolithic. First, the insurgency has changed over time. Initially composed of former regime elements and Ba'athists, it soon extended to include other members of Sunni tribes whose objective was primarily to eject foreign occupiers. As former regime elements became more concerned with the resettling of their families and maintaining them in the style to which they had been accustomed during the Hussein years, the tribes along with the foreign jihadis increasingly drove the insurgency.[2] Consequently, the revenue streams also changed. Indeed, these streams vary over time according to circumstance and opportunity; they are both dynamic and adaptable, making them difficult both to sort out and to block. As one official noted,

> the financing challenge related to Iraq terrorism and insurgency is a complex, formal, and informal multi-dimensional phenomenon involving external money flows and internal revenue generation and distribution networks. These numerous revenue generation and distribution structures are mostly decentralized, with different funding sources and streams overlapping and mutually reinforcing each other. Some networks that finance terrorists and insurgents are self-regenerating, especially networks and revenues sources that are internal to Iraq. Finally, terrorists and insurgents are adaptive. In the past, as we've affected one stream of financing, we've observed terrorists and insurgents transition to other areas in response.[3]

The second reason for deconstructing the insurgency groupings, closely related to the issue of dynamism, is that control of criminal activities and distribution of proceeds became contentious. Although the activities of the tribes and the foreign fighters overlapped and intersected, often promoting cooperation, the issue of control over criminal markets in Iraq—as it has elsewhere—ultimately became a source of serious conflict. It came to drive a major wedge between the tribes and al-Qaeda in Iraq (AQI). Indeed, the ultimate paradox of criminal activities in Iraq is that although criminal activities helped to fund and empower the Sunni insurgent and jihadi groups, they also became a source of tension and conflict among these groups. This coincided with the Coalition's growing sophistication in the development and implementation of a counterinsurgency strategy. As a result, U.S. forces were able to exploit the tensions by co-opting many of the tribes in the struggle to defeat AQI.

Something similar appears to have happened with the Shiite militias, especially Jaish-al-Mahdi (JAM), which strongly opposed the U.S. presence in Iraq. Ironically, while the profits from criminal activities strengthened JAM, some of its activities were so predatory that they alienated its community support base, leading to efforts by the leadership to restrain the criminal activities which purportedly were being carried out by JAM rogue groups. There are indications that U.S. forces encouraged this and cooperated at least tacitly with the Sadrist leadership to eliminate the most violent elements of JAM and thereby help to reestablish Muqtada al-Sadr's control of the Mahdi militia.

Criminal Enterprises.

Traditional criminal organizations, which treat crime as a continuation of business and focus on the monetary proceeds of their activities rather than broader political agendas, became a very important part of post-Hussein Iraq. Despite the dearth of open-source knowledge of the number, size, and composition of these groups, it seems likely that—as in most other countries with high levels of organized crime—a wide variety of criminal organizations are active in Iraq. Some are highly specialized, while others have a broad portfolio of activities. Some are large with a long reach, while others are much smaller and involve little more than a few local thugs banding together and going after vulnerable targets. Clearly, as discussed in Chapter 2, an important component of organized crime in Iraq was the former prisoners released by Saddam Hussein. Many of these criminals were violent, and their presence on the streets contributed significantly to the post-invasion lawlessness. Criminological studies in the United States and elsewhere suggest that bonding among prisoners is often reflected in criminal cooperation after they are released.[4] Indeed, some of the gangs with particularly fearsome reputations were made up of former prisoners. They engaged in a variety of criminal activities, including kidnapping and extortion.

In at least some instances, the leadership of criminal gangs was provided by former regime elements, especially from Saddam Hussein's intelligence agency. These operatives had considerable expertise and knowledge in Iraqi demographics. They almost certainly provided much of the planning and intelligence for criminal activities carried out by the former convicts. The former regime elements also formed groups of their own. During the Hussein era they had a predatory attitude toward the population and probably saw no reason why this should cease, in spite of regime collapse. It seems probable that they were behind much of the upsurge of kidnappings, since they were able to identify lucrative targets. Indeed, in anecdotal accounts from victims and their families, considerable emphasis is placed on the knowledge of the kidnappers concerning the wealth of their targets. Not only was this important in the selection process for abductions, it also limited the bargaining power of the families — since the kidnappers knew how wealthy a particular family was, the ransom payment was set appropriately, and there was limited room for maneuver. In some cases, of course, the former regime elements saw criminal activity as part of the resistance to the occupation; in other instances, it was also simply a way to maintain at least some semblance of their former lifestyle.

Then, too, some members of criminal organizations in Iraq were typically outside the mainstream of the society and others were part of the former elite, some were part of the bureaucracy, the new political elite, or law enforcement agencies. Iraq suffered from the dynamics, uncertainties, and pathologies of a society and economy in abrupt transition. Consequently, the distinction between members of organized crime on the one side and officials in ministries or members of the police force on the other was blurred. The Oil Ministry, in particular, seems to have housed a significant number of criminals. Under Saddam Hussein, smuggling had been state-sponsored, and those who had developed expertise in the smuggling business did not allow their talents to atrophy, especially in a climate characterized by uncertainty, insecurity, and anomie. There are even indications that the situation in Iraq resembled that in Crimea in the mid-1990s, when local government officials were not simply linked to criminal organizations but often led them.[5] In Iraq, insider status was certainly a source of power and influence, facilitating various oil smuggling schemes. Crime and corruption networks seemingly merged in a rich and complex tapestry that could not always be unravelled. Sometimes their motive was profit, sometimes to advance political agendas.

According to Mark Edmond Clark, one important aspect of traditional criminal enterprises in Iraq is that they did not dominate and control the means of violence to the same extent as their counterparts in more stable societies.[6] Although they intimidated and exploited the population, the traditional criminal enterprises were not the biggest and toughest guys on the block. While they provided goods and services for the insurgents and foreign fighters—not least because they had the ability to work across sectarian divisions—traditional criminal enterprises also recognized and respected "the capabilities of the insurgents and foreign fighters" who, driven by strong belief in their cause, "could easily retaliate against them with car bombs or suicide bombers on martyrdom operations."[7] The criminal enterprises, in contrast, were pragmatic, preferring to be "survivors, not martyrs."[8] If this put criminal groups at an unusual disadvantage, however, when the foreign fighters in particular became overly assertive and expansionist in their criminal activities, then some criminal enterprises—particularly those which were tribally-based and a part of the insurgency—began to fight back.

Tribal-Based Smugglers.

The distinction between traditional criminal enterprises and tribally-based groups in Iraq is not hard and fast. Many of Iraq's tribes have a long tradition of smuggling and, if anything, this has expanded since 2003. Rory Stewart in his account of his time as a deputy provincial coordinator of the southern province of Maysan paints a graphic picture of the tribal culture and tribal involvement in criminal activities ranging from carjacking and kidnapping to cannabis smuggling.[9] The dominant tribes in the region, the Beni Lam and the Albu Muhammed, had a major influence throughout the region, even though they were struggling for dominance against the Sadrist militias which were very active in Southern Iraq.

One of the key figures in the Albu Muhammed was Abu Hatim, "Prince of the Marshes," renowned for resisting Saddam Hussein. Abu Rashid, the Coalition-appointed police chief in the provincial capital, Amara, was described by Stewart as "a sheik of the smuggling Nowaffel clan and commander of the militia that supported his kinsman, the Prince of the Marshes."[10] When Abu Rashid was shot and killed on October 24, 2003, some claimed he had been murdered by a rival criminal gang, while others argued that he had been killed by members of his family who wanted the $300,000 he had amassed in the short time he had been police chief.[11] Fingers were also pointed at Iran, while local politicians linked to Iran claimed that Abu Hatim was responsible for the murder, which was designed to discredit them.[12] Whoever was responsible, it was clear that the tribes not only remained a powerful influence, but also that their ability to smuggle commodities through the marshes and across the porous border between Iran and Iraq was an important asset and source of revenue.

Smuggling from and to Maysan paled into insignificance, however, when compared with oil smuggling in Basra. In spite of claims that the political parties were in control and that the Shiite militias imposed taxes on the smuggling operation, tribes and clans appeared to be responsible for much of the smuggling (as discussed in Chapter 3).

Another area where tribal smuggling remains a major activity is along the border with Syria. An illuminating analysis of the tribes in Anbar Province — the main location of the Sunni tribal insurgency — notes that two major tribes in the region are involved in smuggling across the border with Syria, operating in territory which they regard simply as part of their traditional domain.[13]

> The Albu Fahd tribe was known as a tribe of cultivators and sheep herders. Today, members of the Albu Fahd tribe . . . consider the western desert border area near Syria part of their tribal territory and follow their goats, sheep and cattle there to graze. They leave their comfortable homes in al-Ramadi and roam the desert, as far as 250 miles to the west, in the springtime. Smuggling livestock into Syria is also part of a herdsman's life — although no one in the tribe admitted to that — as well as smuggling other things of value.[14]

Similarly, Lin Todd, an authority on the western tribes, writes that another tribe, the Albu Mahals, "are known to use their tribal links that cross into Syria to aid their extensive smuggling operations across the Iraq border with Syria. This is likely the major source of their income."[15]

Foreign Jihadi Groups.

Although most of the insurgents in Iraq have been Iraqis, foreign fighters have provided much of the manning for the resistance and have also provided some of the funding. There were a number of different jihadi groups in Iraq, of course, but the most important has been AQI, along with its umbrella organization known as the Islamic State of Iraq. As Peter Bergen writes, "al Qaeda only established itself in Iraq in October 2004, well after the U.S. invasion, when its leader, Abu Musab al Zarqawi, fused his 'Tawhid and Jihad' group with al-Qaeda by publicly pledging allegiance to Osama bin Laden."[16] Zarqawi had a major impact — bombing the United Nations (UN) headquarters, which led to the UN withdrawal from Iraq; kidnapping and beheading foreigners; and provoking sectarian violence, especially with attacks on Shiite civilians. AQI's February 2006 attack on the Golden Mosque in Samarra tipped Iraq into what virtually became a civil war.

Though AQI's terrorist and insurgent activities are very well-known, its appropriation of organized crime activities as a funding mechanism has received far less attention. Yet, even in open sources, it is possible to find glimpses of this activity, which provide at least some insight into the scope of AQI's criminal fund-raising. Although foreign jihadi groups such as al-Qaeda in Iraq had considerable external funding, they are also engaged in local resource generation through criminal activities.

One of the most important of these was kidnapping. Although AQI under Zarqawi became infamous for its killings of foreign hostages, it seems likely that in some instances, usually in return for significant ransom payments, his group released their victims. On May 1, 2007, U.S. forces in an operation near Taji killed Muharib Abdul Latif al-Jubouri, who was described as a "senior minister of information" for AQI.[17] He had been "involved in both the Jill Carroll and the Tom Fox kidnappings," and had been "responsible for the transportation and movement of Jill Carroll from her various hiding places" as well as "the propaganda and ransom videos from the Jill Carroll kidnapping."[18] According to a U.S. military spokesman, Muharib was "the last one known to have had personal custody of Tom Fox before his death" and was "involved in the kidnapping of two Germans" in January 2006. Between May and September 2006, he worked "as a money and foreign facilitator for AQI in Syria."[19]

Although his death was an important success in the fight against AQI, the group continued kidnapping. Indeed, in November 2007, one detainee who claimed to have managed a $6 million budget for the Mosul branch of the Islamic State of Iraq (an AQI umbrella) and arranged payments for over 500 fighters, stated that most of his budget came "from payments we receive from places like Syria and from kidnappings," which yielded ransom payments as high as $50,000 a person.[20] In part, the ransoms resulted from AQI's ability to obtain good intelligence about wealthy people who were then targeted for kidnapping. An individual captured by the Iraqi army and believed to be responsible for negotiating the release of kidnapping victims was reported to have in his possession checks totaling US$600,000.[21]

Probably an even more lucrative criminal activity for AQI is oil theft and smuggling from the Bayji oil refinery where oil from pipelines is siphoned into trucks and then sold on the black market. This is believed to provide AQI with an estimated $2 million a month.[22] AQI "also sets up quasi-legitimate gas stations and fuel-trucking companies, demands 'protection' payments from legitimate businesses, and hijacks trucks carrying gasoline and kerosene, then resells the fuel."[23] In November 2007 as part of efforts to combat smuggling at the Bayji oil refinery, authorities arrested Saadi Ibrahim, whom they described as "a major oil smuggler" and AQI financier.[24] Reportedly, Ibrahim "was stealing crude oil from the Iraqi-Turkish Export Pipeline in Bayji. He was also supplying Al Qaida. Moreover, he was the Islamic State of Iraq's 'Minister of Oil'. Large maps dealing with oil smuggling were confiscated during his arrest."[25] Although this arrest might have had a detrimental impact on AQI's illicit oil business, there is probably enough redundancy in the AQI network and enough corruption in the refinery to maintain the revenue stream even if it is slightly reduced.

Car theft is another important source of funding for AQI. There is some evidence that it has become one of the most important businesses in Mosul, which is where AQI and its affiliates concentrated after setbacks in Al-Anbar and Baghdad. According to one report,

> in some cases members dressed as police will set up a fake checkpoint, seize late-model cars and either kill or chase off the drivers. They'll then change the license plates and transport the vehicles to be sold in another city — often Kirkuk or Baghdad. AQI sells stolen vehicles through a network of fences.[26]

Such activity is difficult to combat as it is a piecemeal and often seemingly random business.

Much the same is true of extortion. As one observer notes: "AQI in certain parts of Iraq is basically running protection rackets, seizing property and assets, and engaging in criminality."[27] In Diala Province in July 2007, AQI raids on several villages not only killed anyone linked to the Iraq government, but also extorted about $3,000 from a local sheikh almost in passing.[28] Much more has probably been obtained from white collar criminals in Mosul who reportedly have also been targeted by AQI.[29] As one military spokesman notes, "The racketeering operations extended to nearly every type of business in the city, including a Pepsi plant, cement manufacturers, and a cellphone company, which paid the insurgents $200,000 a month."[30]

Theft, fraud, and contraband smuggling also help to fund AQI and its affiliates. One major source of income, for example, was "a real estate scam, in which insurgents stole 26 ledgers that contained the deeds to at least $88 million worth of property and then resold them."[31] Contraband smuggling along the border with Syria also brings in some money. In June 2008, Iraqi Army forces arrested five members of AQI and seized 1,400 cartons of cigarettes valued at around $49,000.[32]

This is not to claim that criminal activities are the only source of funding for AQI. Foreign fighters coming in from Syria often bring cash with them, with volunteers from Saudi Arabia typically bringing around $1,000 per person and those from other countries rather less.[33] As the flow of these fighters has been restricted, AQI has become even more dependent on local criminal activity. Yet there were signs of this dependence as early as 2005, and in November 2006 the *New York Times* published reports of a U.S. Government intelligence estimate on insurgency finances suggesting that groups responsible for many insurgent and terrorist attacks were raising $70 million to $200 million a year from illegal activities.[34] Between $25 million and $100 million of this was estimated to come from oil smuggling.[35] The report concluded that "sources of terrorist and insurgent finance within Iraq—independent of foreign sources—are currently sufficient to sustain the groups' existence and operation. . . ."[36] The analysis received considerable criticism because of the wide range of the estimates and what was felt to be an underestimate of the revenues from oil smuggling.[37] While the argument about oil is persuasive, the other criticisms were somewhat unfair. The revenue from criminal markets or criminal activities is inherently difficult to assess because so much of it is covert. Moreover, the intelligence report on the role of criminality in general was highly cogent. It is important to keep in mind, however, that no group in Iraq has a monopoly on criminal activities. Just as Sunnis had their criminal revenue, so too did the Shiite militias.

Militias.

Probably the most powerful and important group engaged in organized crime in Iraq are the Shiite militias, especially JAM. Whereas the Kurdish Peshmerga forces and the Badr Corps were formed well before the 2003 invasion, JAM emerged out of the chaos that followed the collapse of the regime and became increasingly important as the Sunni insurgency developed. It has been widely regarded as the most dangerous of the militias. This is partly because its membership comes from poor and marginalized Iraqis in the slums of Baghdad and Basra, and it is seen as a challenge by middle class and professional Iraqis. JAM has also generated considerable alarm because of the political agenda of its leader, Muqtada al-Sadr, an agenda which challenges the U.S. occupation, the

Shiite religious establishment, and the government of Prime Minister Al-Maliki. JAM can be understood only as one component—albeit a major one—of the broader Sadrist movement. As one report stated, the Sadrists reflect "an authentic social movement" which gives voice to the "frustrations, aspirations, and demands of a sizeable portion of the population that has no other genuine representative."[38] In other words, Muqtada has a high degree of legitimacy with many Iraqis even as he is reviled and ridiculed by many others.

Although JAM is nominally under the control of Muqtada al-Sadr, it has become factionalized, and many of its members (who are typically young and poor) have engaged in a wide range of criminal activities. Muqtada himself encouraged this when he issued a fatwa in May 2003, saying that "looters could hold on to what they had appropriated so long as they made a donation (khums) of one-fifth of its value to their local Sadrist office."[39] While this gesture offered short-term benefits for an organization which was not particularly well-endowed with resources, it further alienated mainstream Shiites, especially those with property, and encouraged additional criminal activities. The absence of payment for militia members made crime particularly attractive for them. Also, it was convenient, at least initially, for Muqtada al-Sadr.

Four criminal activities have provided Mahdi army members with important revenue streams: extortion and protection; black market sales of petroleum; seizures of cars and houses (inextricably linked with sectarian cleansing if not done completely under its guise); and involvement in oil smuggling in Basra.

Where groups such as JAM have territorial control, they almost invariably engage in protection rackets. Businesses and merchants pay for what is nominally called protection but which in practice amounts to extortion. One Iraqi, for example, admitted to a western journalist that he paid the local Mahdi army the equivalent of $13 a month for protection—and although this was a small amount, with a large volume of such payments extortion became a significant revenue source.[40] Those who pay are immune to violence or kidnapping; those who do not pay become targets. With the insurgency and the increased sectarian violence, however, the protection was very real. As an officer in the U.S. military who regularly dealt with JAM acknowledged, "People count on the militias. . . . It's like the mob—they keep people safe."[41]

In this connection, reports from Baghdad in late 2007 suggested that the Mahdi army had obtained control over Jamila market, "the most important wholesale center in Baghdad, the receiving point for millions of dollars of market-bound goods into the capital."[42] Until summer or early fall 2007, Sunni truck drivers from Anbar moving goods from Jordan and Syria to Baghdad had transferred their loads to local haulers outside the city to avoid the Mahdi army at Jamila.[43] After that, however, the long-haul truckers completed the trip to the Jamila market themselves, a development that created rumors about an agreement among the wholesale merchants, truckers, and the Mahdi army.[44] If so, then the Mahdi army had obtained another lucrative source of revenue:

> With the high volume of goods arriving at Jamila market on a daily basis, bound for Baghdad's millions of consumers, any arrangement allowing a militia to take a cut of the action in exchange for non-interference with shipping operations could pay very well indeed.[45]

In addition, the Mahdi army controlled black market sales at many gasoline stations and also dominated "the Shia trade in propane-gas canisters, which Iraqis use for cooking."[46] Yet there is an irony here: "Sometimes the militiamen sell the propane at a premium, earning healthy profits; at other times they sell it at well below market rates, earning gratitude from the poor and unemployed."[47] *IraqSlogger*, which provides some of the best reporting from Iraq, noted that in certain Mahdi-controlled areas, black market prices of food and fuel were less than elsewhere. It speculated that since the Mahdi army "ran its own distribution operations in the neighborhoods where it holds power, providing lower-priced staples to poorer Iraqis," downward pressure was thereby exerted on prices. The other possibility was that "consolidated militia control" had a "perversely stabilizing effect on economic activities, avoiding the security uncertainties that drive prices higher in more restive areas such as Ghazaliya and Mansour."

As "death squads" in Baghdad became particularly active in kidnapping people for torture and murder, car theft became a bonus and even a form of funding for the atrocities themselves. This was all the more important because many members of the Mahdi army were not paid. As a result any "spoils" they could obtain were more than a bonus and helped cement their loyalty to the Sadrist cause. Stolen cars were easily sold on the black market with no questions asked about their origin and ownership. Something similar appears to have occurred with houses: when Sunnis were evicted from Shiite-dominated areas, their houses were often taken over by Mahdi army members who subsequently rented or sold them. In effect, as the International Crisis Group puts it, JAM began "dealing in violence."[48] Not only did the militia sell "its services to merchants and businesspeople seeking protection, but assassinating Sunnis also became highly lucrative."[49]

The fourth revenue stream came from taxes imposed on oil smuggling in Basra. This brought the Mahdi army into a sporadic but often intense conflict with two other Shiite militias, one belonging to the Fadhila political party, and the Supreme Council of the Islamic Revolution in Iraq (SCIRI)/the Supreme Islamic Iraq Council (SIIC)/the Islamic Supreme Council of Iraq's (ISCI) Badr organization.[50] All three militias demanded a cut from the oil smuggling proceeds carried out by several tribes, while Fadhila also appeared to be directly involved in some of the smuggling. The conflict was further complicated by militia infiltration of the police and government agencies, so that militia violence in Basra occasionally involved different police units fighting against one another.

It is likely that at least some of the proceeds of JAM's criminal activity subsidized the provision of services to the poor and marginalized, especially in Sadr City.

> In Baghdad the Sadrists gained additional legitimacy and influence from 2006 through the first half of 2007 wherever violence was most intense. In a city virtually abandoned by the state, Sadrist offices in several neighborhoods became the last and only resort for Shiite residents in need of help.[51]

In early 2008 a nongovernmental organization (NGO) called *Refugees International* even claimed that the Sadrists were engaged in service provision similar to Hezbollah.[52] In fact, aid and services for the poor are simply a continuation by Muqtada al-Sadr of the charity work of his father, reflecting the populist dimension of the movement. The Sadrists provide shelter, food, and other staples to displaced and poor Iraqis.[53] They also house families in vacant homes (vacant as a result of ethnic cleansing) and provide heating fuel and cooking fuel.

Though service provision adds to the legitimacy of al-Sadr and his movement, it has been offset by widespread criminality. How much responsibility al-Sadr had for this after his initial fatwa remains uncertain. His movement:

> had always had a loose structure and its fighters were largely unpaid. Units often had their origin in locally raised vigilante groups that were never amenable to discipline from the center. And as the sectarian war got bloodier, local commanders became more independent and more powerful.[54]

Indeed, most accounts agree that Muqtada al-Sadr has very limited control over his followers. To some extent the JAM name was appropriated by groups of his followers heavily involved in criminal activities and political assassinations. The dual nature of JAM was most obvious in the Ministry of Health and Ministry of Interior. Although control over the Ministry of Health was imposed to give the movement greater control over—and greater credit for—service provision in Iraq, JAM also exhibited a vicious sectarianism as noted earlier. The sectarian killings became even more pronounced as JAM members infiltrated the Ministry of Interior and police in 2006 and 2007. It became clear that they were using the ministry as a base from which to kidnap and kill Sunnis.

Criminal activities by JAM militia also increased as "bands of young gunmen used the Mahdi army's name as a cover for extortion, black marketeering, and other crimes."[55] Indeed, Mahdi army violence and the resulting profits created a self-perpetuating spiral that ultimately became counterproductive. As the peak of the sectarian violence passed, many of those who had seen JAM as their best protection against Sunni insurgents came to regard it as a mixed blessing at best and highly pernicious at worst. As one report in October 2007 states, "In a number of Shiite neighborhoods across Baghdad, residents are beginning to turn away from the Mahdi army, the Shiite militia they once saw as their only protector against Sunni militants. Now they resent it as a band of street thugs without ideology."[56] According to one Shiite, "We thought they were soldiers defending the Shiites. . . . But now we see they are youngster-killers, no more than that. People want to get rid of them."[57]

Al-Sadr has periodically tried to reestablish central control and to punish or expel those who engage in gratuitous violence or are unduly exploitative of the Shiite population. This process began in 2004 when he established courts to examine the behavior of militia members and to discipline them. This had limited impact, however, and there are reports from late 2006 that he was trying to eliminate rogue commanders by giving their names to U.S. and Iraqi forces in order to "clean house."[58] Reportedly this led to death threats against al-Sadr.[59] The situation became even more urgent in September 2007 after the violence at Karbala between rival Shiite groups. In the aftermath, al-Sadr imposed a "freeze" on violence while also trying to reassert control over JAM by clamping down on rogue elements involved in such predatory behavior that they were undermining Shiite support for the movement.

There were several distinct elements to this effort to restore control. One was the establishment of new procedures under which existing militiamen as well as new applicants had to prove they had no criminal records and provide "written statements from three known community members vouching for their good character."[60] In effect, this device sought to strengthen discipline and accountability. A second component of the strategy was to eliminate the worst offenders: "To restore order, Sadr and his aides formed a review committee and set up a 'Golden Division' to mete out punishment to rogue fighters."[61] A Sadr loyalist acknowledged that members of this unit "conduct spot checks, and . . . deal harshly with troublemakers."[62] In one instance, 25-year-old Saif Awad, who was known as "the Assassin" and was heavily involved in kidnapping and extortion in the Hurriya neighborhood of Baghdad, was killed by three men on motorcycles. He was in one of his two new cars at the time.[63] In fact, such killings were not uncommon, and there was deliberate targeting of those "whose thuggish tactics have disgusted ordinary Iraqis."[64] Although there were formal denials of such reports, these were unpersuasive, as it was clear that the targets were intended as examples of what would happen to those who went too far in their criminal activities. The third element of the strategy was to increase communication between Sadr loyalists seeking to purge the movement and U.S. forces which had the capability to hunt down the rogue elements.[65]

In effect, the JAM leadership was trying to impose internal self-discipline to avoid the tarnishing of the organization's name. As after the 2004 crisis, "Muqtada's objective was to improve his movement's reputation. . . . Seeking to distance himself from abuses, he blamed excessive violence on rogue elements and overzealous militants, claiming to be a moderate leader urging calm."[66] In March 2008, however, the Prime Minister launched a military offensive in Basra which was justified as an attempt to reestablish control in a city marked by violence and criminality. A more cynical view is that it was part of the continued struggle for control of Basra and its resources among Fadhila, the Badr Corps, and JAM, with the key difference that much of the Badr Corps was now integrated into the Iraqi army. Although the offensive initially appeared to be something of a debacle for the government — with many deserting rather than fighting fellow Shiites — in retrospect, it significantly weakened JAM. So too did the subsequent campaign against JAM in Sadr City. In both cases, U.S. forces played an important role in strikes against JAM, although they continued to describe their actions as being directed against criminal and rogue elements. Significantly, al-Sadr did not respond by formally renouncing the "freeze" on violence.

The setbacks in Basra and Sadr City provided an opportunity for Muqtada al-Sadr to move unequivocally and directly into the political mainstream. This was recognized by one U.S. officer who acknowledged that there are "all sorts of different flavors of JAM" including those who can be integrated into the political process, irreconcilable elements which are "as bad as AQI," and "criminal elements that use JAM as their cover."[67] The dilemma that Muqtada al-Sadr continues to face is that the more he follows a political track and seeks to constrain criminal and military activities by JAM, the more frustrated and unhappy are the extremists in his movement — not least because of the concomitant reduction of revenue flows. Arguably, though, these elements have been weakened by both the internal and external pressures. Moreover, JAM has already passed the peak of its criminal profit-making as the opportunity for criminal activities in Iraq has contracted as the state inches toward pacification. This is not to suggest that factions and groups within JAM will give up their criminal activities. More likely, they will continue to pursue them but with greater prudence and restraint. If Muqtada al-Sadr does become more integrated into the mainstream political process, the real question is whether he will leave the criminal elements behind or tolerate renewed opportunities for the linkage between the political and the criminal in Iraq.

Relationships.

As suggested above, AQI members have been heavily engaged in criminal activities as a source of funding. AQI has also been heavily dependent on human smuggling organizations and their brokers to bring new members into Iraq. Yet, the process has not been entirely smooth. It appears that while some of the necessary networks are supportive of, if not affiliated with, the insurgency in Iraq, others are simply criminal businessmen who are not scrupulous about whom they smuggle, only about whether it is profitable. Since many such "coordinators, smugglers, and other middlemen" are criminals concerned more about cash than cause, AQI has not been entirely comfortable with them.[68] Although AQI has been concerned that its fees to these smuggling networks are excessive, it has continued to pay them because the flow of fighters depends on the smugglers' cooperation.

Though the relationship with the Syrian smuggling network has been characterized by a lack of trust, it has been a model of harmony when compared to that between AQI and the Sunni tribes. The dramatic change in the relationship between tribal organized crime and AQI has been well-documented by Austin Long.[69] In his view, AQI's attempt to obtain control of "revenue sources—such as banditry and smuggling— that had long been the province of the tribes" was the key factor in creating dissension.[70] As he puts it, the tribes actually began to fight with AQI in early 2005 "before most of the [AQI] violence towards civilians and tribesmen in Anbar occurred. The primary motive was not moral; it was self-interested."[71] The first tribe to break with AQI was the "Albu Mahal tribe around the city of Qaim," which resented AQI's challenge to its "lucrative smuggling operations."[72] Supported by members of the Albu Nimr tribe, the Albu Mahal formed the Hamza Battalion and sought help from the Marines.[73] For a variety of reasons, U.S. assistance was too little, too late. Although AQI seemed to have emerged victorious, in November 2005 a U.S. offensive against AQI in and around Qaim was coordinated with the Albu Mahal.[74] "Cooperation improved still further after the operation, when Marines and Iraqi army personnel stayed behind to support the Albu Mahal in providing security."[75]

Members of the Dulaimi tribal confederation also fought AQI near Ramadi in August 2005, but "tribal leaders were targeted by al-Qaeda in a coercive campaign of murder and intimidation which sapped many tribes of the will to fight."[76] Indeed, AQI used a mix of money and coercion to divide clans and families and thus weaken tribal cohesion. Some of those who could not be bought were simply killed. Yet, this in turn helped to create a cycle of mistrust and hostility, and as a result, clashes escalated—a process which led to the Anbar Awakening and the defection of Sunni tribes from AQI. The tribes clearly felt betrayed by AQI, with anger and resentment becoming almost palpable. As a result, what had been scattered opposition to AQI coalesced into what was in effect a blood feud. Though some of the original divisions had been sparked by mere economic disputes, they developed into a primeval hatred — reinforced by the U.S. willingness to provide financial support for the Sunni tribes.

A key figure in this process was Sheikh Abdul-Sattar Abu Risha, who became the leader of the Anbar Salvation Council before being killed by AQI. In the words of Joy Price and Leila Fadel, "Abu Risha was a controversial figure. He was a sub-tribal sheik who made his living off smuggling and was a known bandit." [77] Reportedly, he was involved in oil smuggling; and a high-ranking U.S. military officer in Anbar even acknowledged that he "made his living running a band of thieves who kidnapped and stopped and robbed people on the road between Baghdad and Jordan. That's how he made his fortune."[78] When AQI had muscled in on these activities in 2005, Abu Risha tried to mobilize Sunni tribal support but failed. As a result, he turned for help to "the strongest tribe" — U.S. military forces in Iraq. Eventually Abu Risha became the "counterinsurgency coordinator" for the province and provided both manpower and intelligence for the fight against AQI.[79] In return, the United States ignored his "extra-legal revenue generation" and arranged a meeting with President Bush.[80]

More senior leaders among the tribes were not entirely happy with Abu Risha's role and condemned him as little more than a thief. His effectiveness, however, made him a priority target for AQI, and he was killed in a bomb explosion on September 13, 2007. Ironically, he was betrayed by his security chief, Captain Karim al-Barghouthi:

> [Al-Barghouthi was] in debt to some people in the car smuggling racket in Mosul who were affiliated with AQI. The men in the car smuggling racket had a deal with AQI: the terror group would allow them to operate, guaranteeing their security, and in return they would

pass information to AQI about who was in debt to them. The men in the smuggling racket passed on information about al-Barghouti's debt, and AQI told them to put pressure on him to repay the debt immediately — something he was unable to do. This put al-Barghouti in a no-win situation. He couldn't go to the authorities because doing so would have exposed his corruption and illegal activities. Then AQI approached him to offer a way out: they would repay his debt. [81]

In exchange, they demanded that he facilitate access to Abu Risha by an assassin. Ironically, criminal activities similar to those that had led to the defection of Abu Risha from AQI were also the source of his demise.

Implications.

Many groups have contributed to the continuing disorder in Iraq, much of it driven by creed, greed, or a mix of the two. Compounding the disorder has been a vicious cycle in which the lack of law, order, security, and social control generated opportunities and incentives for the development of alternative power centers. These power centers continued to generate considerable resources, in turn giving rise to vested interests with a stake in ensuring that law, order, security, and social control were not established. The U.S. inability to provide security was in large part a result of self-funding mechanisms that nourished the asymmetric conflict against Coalition military forces and the internecine warfare of the Iraqi groups, factions, and tribes.

One result of the U.S. military ascent to its status as the "strongest tribe" was that it became a de facto adjudicator and enforcer in criminal disputes dressed up as political differences. In effect, it sided with one set of violent armed groups engaged in criminal activities against other groups which were judged to be even more dangerous. The tribes were losing the turf wars to AQI until the United States came to the rescue. Similarly, Muqtada al-Sadr was losing his battle for control of JAM until U.S. military forces targeted those elements of his militia which were creating the greatest discord.

Whether there has accordingly been real progress in reducing organized crime in Iraq is uncertain. In 2007 and 2008 there were many signs of progress, though resource generation opportunities for political and military opponents of the regime remained widely available. Nevertheless, as the Iraqi government has become stronger and taken on greater responsibility, some of the more blatant forms of organized crime have diminished. The free-for-all which sprang into existence in the immediate aftermath of regime collapse has given way to more subdued expressions of criminal activities. Yet, it seems unlikely that these activities have been terminated. As U.S. forces in Iraq draw down, organized crime will assert itself, likely becoming a lingering problem for the Iraqi government.

ENDNOTES - CHAPTER 7

1. *American Citizen-Soldier: Buck Sargent's Warrior Politics,* *www.bucksargent.net/2006/05/csi-iraq.html.*

2. Interview with official.

3. Defense Intelligence Testimony, available at *www.dod.mil/* *dodgc/olc/docs/Test05-07-28Temple.doc.*

4. See Francis A. J. Ianni, *Black Mafia: Ethnic Succession in Organized Crime,* London, United Kingdom: New English Library, 1975.

5. Phil Williams and John Picarelli, "Organized crime in Ukraine: Challenge and Response," *Trends in Organized Crime*, Vol. 6, No.3-4, March 2001, pp. 100-142.

6. Mark Edmond Clark, "Observations on Local Insurgents and Foreign Fighters in Iraq: An Interview with Mark Edmond Clark," Mark Edmond Clark Interviewed by Columbia International Affairs Online, May 2005.

7. *Ibid.*

8. *Ibid.*

9. Rory Stewart, *The Prince of the Marshes*, Orlando, FL: Harvest, 2007.

10. *Ibid.*, p. 80.

11. *Ibid.*, p. 137.

12. *Ibid.*, p. 138.

13. Lin Todd, *Iraq Tribal Study – Al-Anbar Governorate: The Albu Fahd Tribe, The Albu Mahal Tribe, and the Albu Issa Tribe*, Study Conducted Under Contract with the Department of Defense, June 18, 2006.

14. *Ibid.*, p. 4-17.

15. *Ibid.*, p. 4-31.

16. Peter Bergen, Statement of Peter Bergen, Senior Fellow, New America Foundation, Committee on House Select Intelligence, April 9, 2008.

17. John Banusiewicz, "Coalition's 'Operation Rat Trap' Targets al Qaeda in Iraq," Armed Forces press Service, *www.defenselink.mil/news/newsarticle.aspx?id=33043*. For some questions about al-Jubouri's involvement in the Jill Carroll case, see Dan Murphy, "A Jill Carroll Captor Killed, Says US Military," *Christian Science Monitor*, May 4, 2007, p. 6.

18. *Ibid.*

19. *Ibid.*

20. Amit R. Paley, "Iraqis Joining Insurgency Less for Cause Than Cash," *Washington Post* Foreign Service, November 20, 2007, p. A01.

21. *Ibid.*

22. Lennox Samuels, "Al Qaeda Nostra," *Newsweek Web Exclusive*, May 21, 2008, available at *www.newsweek.com/id/138085.*

23. *Ibid.*

24. "Oil Smuggler And Al Qaida Supplier Arrested In Bayji," *Al Mashriq Newspaper*, November 22, 2007.

25. *Ibid.*

26. Samuels.

27. Paul Cruickshank, quoted in David Axe, "Financial Squeeze for Al Qaeda in Iraq," *wired.com*, January 24, 2008, available at Danger Room from *wired_com.mht.*

28. Sam Dagher, "Risky U.S. Alliances in Iraq," *Christian Science Monitor*, July 17, 2007, available at *www.csmonitor.com/2007/0717/p01s01-wome.html.*

29. Paley.

30. Twitty quoted in Paley.

31. Lieutenant Colonel Eric Welsh, commander of the battalion responsible for Mosul, quoted in Paley.

32. "ISF Detain Nine Suspected AQI Members Throughout Northern Iraq," Multi National Corps-Iraq, Public Affairs Office, Camp Victory, Release No. 20080810-06, August 10, 2008.

33. Joseph Felter, "Al-Qa`ida's Foreign Fighters in Iraq: A First Look at the Sinjar Records," *Bombers, Bank Accounts, and Bleedout: Al Qa'ida's Road in and Out of Iraq*, West Point, NY: Combating Terrorism Center, July 2008.

34. John F. Burns and Kirk Semple, "Iraq Insurgency Has Funds to Sustain Itself, U.S. Finds," *New York Times*, November 26, 2006, Section 1; Column 5; Foreign Desk; *The Struggle for Iraq*, p. 1.

35. *Ibid.*

36. *Ibid.*

37. *Ibid.*

38. International Crisis Group (ICG), *Iraq's Muqtada Al-Sadr: Spoiler or Stabilizer?* Middle East Report, No. 55, July 11, 2006, p. 1.

39. Patrick Cockburn, *Muqtada: Muqtada al-Sadr, the Shia Revival, and the Struggle for Iraq*, New York: Scribner, 2008, p. 130.

40. Jeffrey Bartholet, "How Al-Sadr May Control U.S. Fate in Iraq," *Newsweek*, December 4, 2006.

41. *Ibid.*

42. "Anbari Trucks, Mahdi Guns, & High-Volume-Trade," *IraqSlogger*, October 2, 2007.

43. *Ibid.*

44. *Ibid.*

45. *Ibid.*

46. Bartholet.

47. *Ibid.*

48. ICG, *Iraq's Civil War: The Sadrists and the Surge*, Middle East Report No. 72, February 7, 2008, p. 6.

49. *Ibid.*

50. Reidar Visser, quoted in Ben Lando, "Shia Parties Battle for Control of oil-Rich Basra Region," UPI, August 18, 2007.

51. ICG, *Sadrists and the Surge*, p. 7.

52. See Michael Gordon, "In Sadr city, Basic Services Are Faltering," *New York Times*, April 22, 2008.

53. Dean Yates, "Cleric Sadr Key Player in Helping Poor Iraqis-Report," *Reuters*, April 15, 2008.

54. Cockburn, p. 184.

55. "Al-Sadr Restructuring His Mahdi Army Militia," Fox News, September 10, 2007, available at *www.foxnews.com*.

56. Sabrina Tavernise, "Relations Sour between Shiites and Iraq Militia," *New York Times*, October 12, 2007.

57. *Ibid.*

58. Babak Rahimi, "Muqtada al-Sadr Steps Into the Power Vacuum," *Terrorism Focus*, Vol. 4, Issue 19, June 19, 2007.

59. *Ibid.*

60. "Al-Sadr Restructuring His Mahdi Army Militia."

61. Babak Dehghanpisheh, "The Great Muqtada Makeover," *Newsweek*, January 28, 2008.

62. *Ibid.*

63. *Ibid.*

64. *Ibid.*

65. *Ibid.*

66. See ICG, *Iraq's Muqtada Al-Sadr: Spoiler or Stabilizer?* p. 13.

67. Department of Defense Bloggers Roundtable with Colonel Martin N. Stanton, Chief of Reconciliation and Engagement, Multinational Corps-Iraq via Teleconference, *Federal News Service,* November 2, 2007.

68. *Bombers, Bank Accounts, and Bleedout,* p. 61.

69. Austin Long, "The Anbar Awakening," *Survival,* Vol. 50, No. 2, April 2008, pp. 67-94, especially p. 77.

70. *Ibid.,* p. 77.

71. *Ibid.*

72. *Ibid.,* p. 78.

73. *Ibid.*

74. *Ibid.,* p. 78-79.

75. *Ibid.,* p. 79.

76. *Ibid.*

77. Jay Price and Leila Fadel, "Key U.S. Iraqi Ally Killed in His Own Compound," *McClatchy Newspapers,* September 13, 2007.

78. Joshua Partlow and John Ward Anderson, "Tribal Coalition in Anbar Said to Be Crumbling: U.S.-Backed Group Has Fought Al-Qaeda in Iraq," *Washington Post Foreign Service,* June 11, 2007, p. A11.

79. Long, p. 80.

80. *Ibid.*

81. Daveed Gartenstein-Ross, "The Anatomy of a Betrayal Counterterrorism Blog" available at *counterterrorismblog.org/2007/09/the_anatomy_of_a_betrayal.php.*

CHAPTER 8

CONCLUSIONS

Given the scope and impact of organized crime in Iraq, the lack of attention devoted to it is almost as striking as the lack of planning for the aftermath of the military campaign itself. This monograph is an attempt to help mend the deficiency. Chapter 8 seeks to do three things: (1) provide a summary assessment of the nature and impact of organized crime in Iraq; (2) set forth initiatives that could be taken in Iraq to combat organized crime more effectively; and (3) elucidate the broader considerations and lessons for future U.S. military interventions.

The Nature of Organized Crime in Iraq.

There is no perfect prism through which to view organized crime. The analysis here has focused on criminal organizations (often network-based) and illicit markets; but even these do not capture all the dimensions and dynamics of organized crime in Iraq. Consequently, it is important to identify other facets of organized crime which could inform the development of comprehensive strategies to combat organized crime, insurgency, and violence, while recognizing the inherent limits of enforcement efforts and the need for changes in both governance and incentive structures.

Organized crime in Iraq can be understood first as a complex adaptive system exhibiting emergent behavior and characterized by high levels of persistence and resilience. It is driven by need, greed, and creed, which are difficult to disentangle. As a mixture of organizations and activities, organized crime cannot be decapitated by one broad stroke, and is highly resistant to displacement. It has roots in a tribal culture where smuggling is the norm and national boundaries are respected only by the map-makers. Other roots can be found in corruption and criminalization stemming from a dictatorial regime which had monopoly control and no oversight, and circumvented international sanctions. Yet others can be found in the massive dislocation following the toppling of the regime which resulted in what was, in effect, a governance vacuum with an attendant mix of anomie and anarchy.

Second, organized crime is a means of "primitive capital accumulation."[1] Regime change in Iraq meant that elites which had hitherto been in a privileged position were replaced by another group previously excluded from power. This had a dual impact on organized crime and corruption: for the new elites, obtaining a share of long-denied spoils became a priority, and the state became simply a mechanism for "rent-seeking" and personal and private accumulation. For the displaced elite, criminal activities allowed the retention of at least some wealth and power.

Third, organized crime is closely linked to alternative (that is, nonstate) forms of governance, whether these provide security when the state fails to do so and/or services when the state marginalizes or neglects certain populations. In Iraq, these alternative forms of governance include the Sunni tribes with their tradition of patrimonialism, and the Sadrist movement which is based on both sectarianism and nationalism combined with a sense of religious duty and a tradition of social obligation and activism. The Sadrists and the Jaish-al-Mahdi (JAM) militia have been simultaneously protective and predatory, and both supportive and exploitative of their young, marginalized, and disenfranchised supporters. They have looked after displaced Shiites, even providing homes (often taken from expelled Sunnis). Alternative forms of governance, however, pose an inherent challenge to the government. This is why some observers, including the U.S. Ambassador in Iraq, and some relief organizations have compared JAM to Hezbollah and Hamas. As noted above, service provision is a form of warfare through welfare — especially when legal revenues are insufficient to provide services. Systematic criminal activities become critical in generating the necessary revenues for both service provision and the struggle against the state.

Fourth, organized crime is a safety valve and safety net. In a society and economy characterized by massive economic and social dislocation and extremely high levels of unemployment, criminal activities, the insurgency, and militia activities (including sectarian cleansing) have been sources of employment and money. This is not to suggest that organized crime is benign; it is simply to acknowledge that it benefits more people than is usually acknowledged. From this perspective, the Anbar Awakening and the creation of a U.S.-funded Sunni militia were important not only because of the fight against al-Qaeda but also because of the economic opportunities. Indeed, acknowledgments by U.S. military officers that it was hard to find Sunni tribal leaders who were not involved in smuggling revealed that — unlike AQI — the United States had learned not to interfere with activities that were economically necessary for ordinary tribesmen and lucrative for the tribal leaders.

Fifth, for all its benefits, organized crime is predatory and parasitic. Organized crime is largely about money whether as an end in itself or as a means to other ends, and those involved do not care how they obtain this money. The predatory nature of organized crime in Iraq was evident in the kidnapping business. Victims of kidnapping for profit ranged from businessmen, doctors, and bankers, to the children of ordinary Iraq families. In some case, the targets have been small businessmen whose entrepreneurial activities, so critical to the future of Iraq, were inhibited or disrupted by their abduction. Ransom payments robbed these businesses of start-up capital or profits and, in some instances, led to their closure.

Sixth, organized crime sustains conflict and can also precipitate conflict. As suggested earlier, organized crime in Iraq has something of a hybrid quality, with criminal activities providing a major funding source for insurgents, jihadi groups, and militias, enabling all of them to accumulate substantial war-chests to pursue their campaigns of political violence. Yet criminal activities have also been a source of tension and conflict among the organizations. Though organized crime has given some Iraqis a safety net and provided some opportunities for the United States to play one faction against the other, its overall consequences have been profoundly negative.

Since 2003 criminal enterprises and activities and corruption have derailed or hindered U.S. efforts to restore political, economic, and military stability in Iraq. Organized crime helped to finance insurgency, terrorism, and sectarianism; hindered the emergence of a viable central government; and rendered the complex economic problems associated with economic reconstruction even more intractable. In the immediate months and years after the invasion, insecurity became pervasive. Kidnapping and extortion as well as sexual violence (which for cultural reasons was significantly under-reported) were compounded by a lack of trust in the police and the low U.S. priority on policing the kidnapping of ordinary Iraqis. The impact was far-reaching. As Anthony Cordesman notes,

> the crime problem . . . affects Iraqi confidence in the government and its popular legitimacy. Far more Iraqis face day-to-day threats from criminals than from terrorists and insurgents. . . . If Iraqis are to trust their new government, if insurgents are to be deprived of recruits and proxies, and if Iraq is to move towards economic development and recovery, the crime problem must be solved.[2]

Organized crime also added to the economic woes facing ordinary Iraqis by undermining reconstruction and development. The problems in supplying electrical power contributed to disillusionment with the United States, which seemed unable to turn the lights back on. Given the scale and scope of the deficiencies in the system, such judgments were unfair. Nevertheless, they added to the frustrations of Iraqis and "to the image of ineffective governance" by both the Coalition and the nascent Iraqi government.[3]

Iraq's centralized distribution system was also subject to diversion and interruption by criminals (and terrorists and insurgents) as well as corrupt officials, making the system less efficient and reliable. Extortion from contractors involved in construction projects also had a debilitating impact, increasing the costs of most projects and offering opportunities for diversion of funds to insurgent groups.

Organized crime also had an impact on the NGO community and its capacity for assisting with economic development and social problems. The kidnapping of aid workers and their transfer from criminal groups to terrorists who murdered them led many NGOs to leave Iraq. For those that remained, security became the overwhelming concern, limiting their reach and effectiveness. Kidnapping also made partnerships between military forces and NGOs much more problematic.

Though some NGOs continued to operate even in an extremely inhospitable environment, many international businesses lacked this level of commitment. Organized crime, insurgents, and militias, for several years at least, contributed significantly to deterring potential investors, thereby perpetuating the unemployment problem. The major exception to this trend was in the Kurdish-controlled region, where violence was much lower and investment more attractive. In the rest of Iraq, foreign direct investment was very low. This, in turn, perpetuated and worsened the violence as organized crime and the insurgency became major sources of employment and income.

Organized crime in Iraq also contributed to poor governance, which in turn created another vicious circle. Criminal organizations sought to perpetuate a permissive environment creating more opportunities for crime and high levels of immunity to punishment. This contributed to the corruption and continued weakness of Iraqi political and judicial institutions and government agencies. The infiltration of government departments and agencies by organized crime made the state apparatus far less effective, thereby ensuring that levels of disaffection with—and alienation from—the Iraqi state remained high, while legitimacy remained low.

What, then, can be done about organized crime in Iraq? A pessimistic answer to this question would suggest not much. After all, the very conditions that allowed the blossoming of organized crime in post-Hussein Iraq make it difficult to counter. Nevertheless, it is possible to outline a broad program that would reduce the criminalization of Iraqi political and economic life, in tandem with the rebuilding of the state, the re-creation of infrastructure, the revitalization of the economy, and the creation of legitimate employment opportunities. Unless combating organized crime is integrated into this broader program for Iraq, the program stands little chance of success. Moreover, unless the Iraq government incorporates an effective strategy to combat organized crime, the prospects for long-term state stability will remain poor. The next section offers several recommendations, most of which are rendered more urgent and important by the ongoing U.S. drawdown of its military presence in Iraq.

Combating Organized Crime in Iraq.

Since 2003 the U.S. military has treated organized crime in Iraq, implicitly if not explicitly, as a secondary problem, separate from the main fault lines in the society. At the command level, it was therefore treated primarily as a law enforcement issue as opposed to military, and consequently as an Iraqi government responsibility. In fact, however, organized crime in Iraq was inextricably connected with state weakness, the emergence of multiple, competing power centers, the dearth of economic opportunities, and the collapse of norms and standards of behavior—all of which were central to the challenges facing the U.S. military. Profit-oriented criminal groups created their own forms of intimidation and exploitation, easily crossing from the criminal economy to the conflict economy. At the same time, the appropriation of organized crime methodologies by key Iraqi power centers increased the resilience of insurgents, terrorists, and militias.

As the United States draws down its forces in Iraq, it could usefully focus more seriously on organized crime. One element in this focus is the need for closer cooperation between military units and law enforcement agencies. As Paul Kan has convincingly urged, having "gumshoes at the generals' table" would add a new and useful dimension to both planning and operational activities.[4] At the same time, the military emphasis on "lessons-learned" and after-action reports could be usefully adopted by law enforcement agencies.[5]

Unfortunately, cross-fertilization between the two is limited. The initiatives taken by the Department of Justice, such as the Major Crimes Task Force and the Law and Order Task Force, although important and helpful, were almost an afterthought. They have had a positive impact, especially in training Iraqi police, but the resources devoted to them have remained modest — 200 employee and contract personnel working with Iraqis, and a total of 300 personnel working under the Rule of Law Coordinator at the U.S. Embassy in Iraq.[6] These elements comprise only a small part of the total effort, one that seems more of an add-on rather than a key component of a holistic and fully-integrated strategy designed to suppress the most egregious activities of organized crime such as kidnapping and extortion. This does not mean that the United States should clamp down on the smuggling activities of Sunni tribes. To do so would simply repeat the mistake of al-Qaeda in its efforts to take over such activities. The focus instead must be on those criminal activities that contribute to the insecurity of the citizenry. As U.S. forces draw down, this goal must receive the highest priority until the final transition to Iraqi responsibility for security and order.

None of this is to deny the role U.S. military forces have played in targeting those who were victimizing ordinary Iraqis through extortion, home evictions, car thefts, and kidnappings. In 2007 and 2008, in particular, the emphasis on establishing a more secure environment blurred the line between military operations and combating organized crime. In addition, units of the 82nd Airborne were on the front line in the fight against corruption at the Bayji oil refinery, assisting the Iraqis in implementing new security and loading measures. These reduced opportunities for theft and diversion of refined fuel, leading to an increase in the licit flows of petroleum products from Bayji. Such initiatives, though, have been ad hoc and directed from the bottom up rather than from the top down. They need to be integrated as a core mission in a holistic strategy designed to establish stability and facilitate state building.

In a similar vein, intelligence collection and analysis have to be broadened to include targets beyond those groups directly attacking U.S. forces. Financiers, facilitators, and criminal groups working with insurgents also need to be on the target list. Unfortunately, even though military intelligence has an increasingly sophisticated understanding of Iraqi culture, tribal traditions and relationships, and social and political networks, the integration of criminal intelligence into traditional military intelligence has been limited. Among the difficulties are (1) the military's lack of interest in the law enforcement mission, especially complex investigations; (2) the military's reluctance to offend local power brokers who are part of organized crime; and (3) the military's firm dichotomy between intelligence and military operations on the one side and reconstruction and rule of law operations on the other.[7] In addition, military intelligence collectors and analysts are not trained for the specific requirements of criminal intelligence. They are even less suited for criminal investigations, which remain crucial in learning the nature and extent of criminal networks involved in the larger crime problem. On the other side of the equation, civilian law enforcement agencies are reluctant to embed their own analysts and agents with military units for the long term.

These barriers are not insurmountable, but given the projected drawdown of military forces in Iraq, efforts to overcome them are unlikely to be given priority, this despite the likelihood that the insurgency and AQI are kept alive primarily through criminal activities. Given this situation, criminal intelligence has become more important than ever. In this connection, there is a largely untapped source of information in the NGO world that could be used much more extensively if fused with military and law enforcement intelligence. Although NGOs are generally reluctant to deal with military or intelligence issues (and vice versa) — arrangements based on reciprocity could and should be worked out. Even if this process starts with narrow and restricted exchanges of information, it could provide a basis for trust-building and eventually more extensive collaboration.

Within the formal institutional structures in Iraq, more focused intelligence resources and the development of greater analytic capabilities in criminal intelligence would make it possible not only to delineate the detailed topography of criminal activities in Iraq, but also to prepare a valid strategic net assessment of organized crime. These steps would facilitate the effective reallocation of priorities, the creation of appropriate measures of effectiveness, and more effective targeting. A valid net assessment would provide a basis for a three-pronged strategy seeking to constrict the opportunity space for organized crime; reduce the incentives for corrupt, violent, or other criminal behavior; and develop a selective targeting campaign against the most dangerous criminal organizations and crime corruption networks.

An important component of such a targeting strategy would be an effort to destroy mutual trust, which Kan has described as "the true center of gravity for criminal organizations."[8] This can be done in a variety of ways, including the spread of misinformation to discredit key figures and the disruption of criminal activities in ways which point to insider betrayal. The phased withdrawal of U.S. forces makes such an approach more rather than less important—fighting smarter becomes particularly important when forces are reduced. In the final analysis, however, the government of Iraq rather than the United States will have to take the lead in combating organized crime.

To be effective, a net assessment and a selective targeting strategy need to include regional and transnational dimensions. This is an area where both the United States and the international community could augment the Iraqi effort. Analysts from the Drug Enforcement Administration (DEA), the Central Intelligence Agency's Crime and Narcotics Center, and even state and local law enforcement could provide support for Iraqi efforts. Enhanced cooperation with international law enforcement agencies such as Interpol, Europol, the World Customs Organization, and the UN Office of Drugs and Crime (UNODC) would also be invaluable in identifying and disrupting regional and transnational criminal linkages.

Another major priority should be targeting of corruption and increasing accountability and transparency. This would reduce opportunities for state-led criminal activity. Mechanisms and structures for combating corruption already exist, but are often circumvented by bureaucrats and politicians and undermined by violence. Consequently, it is essential to protect Inspectors General (IGs) as well as members of the Commission on Public Integrity. An interesting parallel here is that of judges in Colombia who were spared the choice between silver and lead by the creation of a system protecting their anonymity. By providing escorts and protective details for IGs and Commission members during the drawdown period, the U.S. military would demonstrate continued seriousness about good governance. Such measures, however, would need to be reinforced by diplomatic and political pressure on the Prime Minister to lift the immunity of Ministers. Ministers in turn should be pressed to stop protecting corrupt departmental officials.

An important concomitant of anti-corruption efforts is the restriction of opportunities for the theft, diversion, and smuggling of oil and petroleum. Investigations of such activities are inherently complex because of the difficulties in differentiating them from legitimate commerce. Nevertheless, some progress has been made. Enhancing physical security of petroleum infrastructure needs to be accompanied by the installation of gauges and meters throughout the oil sector.[9] The continued absence of these devices throughout much of Iraq's oil infrastructure (despite the lucrative contracts provided to U.S. companies to install meters) is a serious weakness. Gauges and meters are not a panacea, but would provide an additional layer of safeguards against theft.

Opportunities for theft, diversion, and smuggling of oil and oil products obviously need to be restricted, but at the same time disincentives to commit those crimes should be strenthened. The removal of subsidies — which at the urging of the International Monetary Fund (IMF) have been significantly reduced — is essential. So too is a regional dialogue with Iraq's neighbors. Harmonizing domestic fuel prices would minimize opportunities for arbitrage and incentives for smuggling.

More generally, reducing opportunities for criminal activities requires more effective policing than currently exists. Although considerable improvements have occurred at the local level where police recruits are part of the community, even these forces are "often outmatched in leadership, training, tactics, equipment, and weapons by the terrorists, criminals, and the militias they must combat."[10] At the national level, "the Iraqi Police Service is fragile, . . . underequipped, and compromised by militia and insurgent infiltration."[11] Consequently, continuing robust training should be accompanied by selection of particularly promising and carefully vetted officers for more specialized work in intelligence and in community-led law enforcement. Building on pockets of integrity and efficiency to improve law enforcement would shrink the opportunities and create disincentives for criminal activity.

Such efforts need to be accompanied by the creation of alternative incentive structures in the licit economy. Security and economics in Iraq are synergistic — with the key being to replace negative synergies (unemployment, leading to crime and insurgency) with positive synergies (long-term legal employment, thereby reducing incentives for criminal and violent career paths that have hitherto been the main game in town). Carefully conceived incentives would build on progress made in 2007 and 2008 in establishing security and order; would help to neutralize the forces of disorder; and would enhance the authority, legitimacy, and effectiveness of the Iraqi state. Indeed, efforts to combat organized crime have to be integrated into a broader program reducing the criminalization of Iraqi political and economic life, while rebuilding the state and revitalizing the Iraqi economy. Conversely, unless the attempt to rebuild Iraq incorporates an effective strategy to combat organized crime, long-term stability will remain elusive.

The longer-term issue is one of legitimization. The U.S. embrace of the Anbar Awakening in which former enemies became allies and former insurgents worked side by side with U.S. forces showed how this could be done as a short-term measure. It also showed how criminal activities can be largely overlooked when it is prudent to do so. The longer-term issue, however, is how to turn criminals who have amassed significant funds into legitimate entrepreneurs. In some cases, this is simply a matter of going ahead and playing the hand already dealt. As Peter Andreas has shown in relation to the siege of Sarajevo, war typically brings about a redistribution of wealth, creating a new set of financial power brokers and businessmen who obtain much of their wealth through dubious means but gradually come to be seen as legitimate.[12] There is something to be said for encouraging this process so long as the normal rules of economic competition supersede old habits of violence and intimidation.

The Lessons from Iraq.

Experience in Iraq has revealed not only the way in which organized crime can undermine efforts to promote security but also the importance of criminal activity as a funding mechanism for a variety of violent nonstate armed groups. Indeed, the rise of criminal organizations is part of a much broader global phenomenon in which violent nonstate armed groups are challenging the Westphalian state. Militias and warlords often come into existence to provide security or even welfare services because the state has failed to do so. Acting as a proxy for the state, their existence and their activities further undermine state legitimacy. Iraq, like the Balkans and Afghanistan, revealed the vulnerability of conflict and post-conflict situations to organized crime. From this perspective, the rule of law does not *follow* stabilization. Rule of law is instead integral from the outset and is critical to reestablishing security, which is the first and foremost responsibility of the state. If the state or the occupying power is unable to make adequate provision for personal security, then nonstate actors will step into the vacuum.

At the same time, it is important for the occupation or the government to distinguish among informal economic activities which are technically illegal but relatively benign coping strategies, those which are purely criminal and predatory, and those which are linked directly to the conflict economy and to insurgent or militia resource generation. Although the informal, criminal, and conflict economies are enmeshed, efforts have to be made to sort them out and deal with each separately. To do this, it is necessary to accept and perhaps even encourage informal, possibly questionable economic activity, which is an important survival mechanism, while selectively targeting the criminal economy, and comprehensively targeting the conflict economy. Key to this discriminating approach is the disruption of recruitment of those in the informal economy by criminal and insurgent groups. Priority needs to be given to the immediate establishment of work programs for unemployed youths and young men who otherwise gravitate towards criminal and insurgent organizations which offer them employment opportunities and a sense of self-worth they otherwise lack.

It is also essential to view security, the rule of law, and economic development as being mutually reinforcing, producing a result greater than the sum of their individual values. As Mills and McNamee argue:

> [T]he overall . . . post-conflict peace building challenge is . . . to sustain a virtuous cycle in which economic recovery and political stability are mutually reinforcing. Indeed, economic recovery has a number of political jobs to do: in the short run, it needs to placate or neutralize political opposition (from insurgents and militia to legislators); build support for government in both the rural and urban areas and the capital; and in the short run and beyond, signal a return of confidence and change for the better.[13]

Considerable emphasis should be placed on the provision of services. When government is unable to meet demands for services (whether security or garbage removal), their place will be filled by criminal organizations and violent political actors. Enhancing the capacity for such government services as health, education, and alleviation of poverty is critical to establishing state legitimacy.

Another priority in development aid should be an enhanced capability to combat organized crime. Insofar as development assistance is part of a comprehensive strategy for post-conflict situations, explicit efforts should be made to change the incentives for spoilers in the postwar environment. Organized crime is typically a very important spoiler. In this connection, Ballentine and Nitzschke suggest both legitimization and exploitation of the shadow economy. In their view,

> peace missions and donor agencies engaged in post-conflict peace building and reconstruction need to address shadow economies and economic criminalization with "carrots and sticks." An often-overlooked fact of war economies is that warlords sometimes provide basic services that the state is unable or unwilling to offer. Post-conflict reconstruction programs need to thus provide incentives for shadow entrepreneurs to join the legal economy. In addition, the state's capacities to provide basic services, security, and employment need to be strengthened in order to free civilians and conflict dependents from the often predatory control of warlords and mafia structures. . . . To address the challenges posed by the entrenched interests of conflict entrepreneurs, improved law enforcement, police training, and judicial reform are required.[14]

The close relationship between corruption and organized crime needs to be attacked from both ends. Going after criminal organizations is particularly difficult when they have patrons or protectors in government. The protectors can provide warnings, derail investigations, and offer additional opportunities for gain. In turn, criminal organizations give corrupt officials access to a capacity for violence which enables them to protect their corrupt activities. In other words, there is a symbiosis of interests, which acts as a force multiplier for both corrupt officials and criminal organizations.

One response to this symbiosis is the introduction of measures to strengthen transparency. An important initiative in development assistance should thus be efforts to strengthen the capacity for independent investigative journalism. Newspapers and journalists need to be given greater protection by government or occupation forces. In Iraq, for example, journalists have been major targets, making the country the most hazardous in the world for those who would report the news. While it is impossible to protect all journalists all the time, investigating the killings of journalists should receive a much higher priority, including police efforts to identify and apprehend the perpetrators. Effective democracy requires a free press capable of investigating crime, corruption, and malfeasance of any kind.

NGOs and research institutions can also assist in the battle against crime and corruption. There is a tendency by the military to regard NGOs as adversaries, sometimes with justification. At best, NGOs are seen as part of the security problem since they work independently of the military and are reluctant to affiliate with the military; at worst they operate at cross-purposes with the military, either deliberately or inadvertently. Yet, efforts should be made to develop closer relationships with NGOs since, like it or not, they will be a fixture on the battlefields of the future. Moreover, they offer alternative perspectives and often have information that is not readily available to military intelligence. Women's NGOs, for example, have periodically tracked the illegal trade in women and girls. Although this pursuit has been largely from a victim perspective, it has provided important insights into a criminal activity that has largely been ignored. In other words, in situations such as Iraq and Afghanistan, it is important to see intelligence in very broad terms, to look at all available sources, and to go beyond in-house information, analysis, and assessment.

None of the foregoing points means that efforts to combat organized crime should automatically have priority. In some cases, for example, interference with criminal activities would be counterproductive, destroying an important safety net in the society. But in the final analysis, efforts to manage post-conflict situations which ignore the role and impact of organized crime are dangerously incomplete and likely to fail.

ENDNOTES - CHAPTER 8

1. On this point, I am grateful to Dr. Michael Pugh.

2. Anthony S. Cordesman, *Iraq's Evolving Insurgency and the Risk of Civil War* (working draft), Washington, DC: Center for Strategic and International Studies, June 22, 2006, p. 182.

3. *Ibid.*, p. 184.

4. Paul Kan, "The Blurring Distinction Between War and Crime in the 21st Century: Breaking the Target Selection Paradigm in a Globalizing World," *Defense intelligence Journal*, Vol. 13, Nos. 1 and 2, 2005, pp. 39-45, especially p. 43.

5. I am grateful to Dr. Paul Kan for this observation.

6. *Fact Sheet: Department of Justice Initiatives in Iraq*, February 13, 2008, available at *www.usdoj.gov/opa/pr/2008/February/iraq-factsheet021308.pdf.*

7. Marc Hess provided very useful comments on some of the difficulties of integrating law enforcement intelligence into military intelligence.

8. Kan, p. 43.

9. Yochi J. Dreazen, "US, Iraq Launch Campaign to Cut Oil Smuggling," *Wall Street Journal,* March 15, 2007.

10. General James L. Jones (Ret.), Chairman, Independent Commission on the Security Forces of Iraq, p. 9, available at *i.a.cnn.net/cnn/2007/imnages/08/05/jonesreportpart1a.pdf.*

11. *Ibid.,* p. 10.

12. See Peter Andreas, *Blue Helmets Black Markets: The Business of Survival in the Siege of Sarajevo,* Ithaca, NY: Cornell University Press, 2008.

13. Greg Mills and Terence McNamee, "New Thinking on a 'New Deal' for Post-Conflict Countries?" *Smallwarsjournal.com,* available at *smallwarsjournal.com/blog/2007/11/print/new-thinking-on-a-new-deal-for-1/.*

14. Karen Ballentine and Heiko Nitzschke, *The Political Economy of Civil War and Conflict Transformation,* Berlin, Germany: Berghof Research Center, p. 19, available at *www.berghof-handbook. net/uploads/download/dialogue3_ballentine_nitzschke.pdf.*

ABOUT THE AUTHOR

PHIL WILLIAMS is currently Visiting Research Professor, Strategic Studies Institute, U.S. Army War College, and Professor of International Security in the Graduate School of Public and International Affairs at the University of Pittsburgh. From 1992 to 2001, Dr. Williams was the Director of the University's Matthew B. Ridgway Center for International Security Studies. His research has focused primarily on transnational organized crime, and he was founding editor of the journal, *Transnational Organized Crime* (now *Global Crime*). He has published on alliances among criminal organizations, global and national efforts to combat money laundering, and trends in cyber crime. Dr. Williams has been a consultant to both the United Nations and various U.S. Government agencies. He has edited or coauthored books on the Carter, Reagan, and Bush Presidencies, and written *Russian Organized Crime, Illegal Immigration and Commercial Sex: The New Slave Trade*, and *Combating Transnational Crime*. He has published book chapters on the financing of terrorism, the relationship between organized crime and terrorism, trafficking in women, complexity theory and intelligence analysis, and intelligence and nuclear proliferation. He has also conducted research on how to attack terrorist networks. At the Strategic Studies Institute, Dr. Williams worked on monographs on organized crime in Iraq and the Madrid bombings. Dr. Williams is a National Intelligence Council Associate and works closely with the Office for Warning.